Laws and Legislation Series

CONTEMPORARY PERSPECTIVES ON LEGAL REGULATION OF SEXUAL BEHAVIOR: PSYCHOLEGAL RESEARCH AND ANALYSIS

LAWS AND LEGISLATION SERIES

State Secrets Protection Act
Lara H. Nellington (Editor)
2009 ISBN: 978-1-60692-711-3

Revisiting and Evaluating the Congressional Review Act
Katherine R. Williamson (Editor)
2009 ISBN: 978-1-60692-687-1

Clean Diamond Trade Act
James T. Williams (Editor)
2009. ISBN: 978-1-60741-111-6

Federal Torts Reform, Claims and Liability
Ben V. Colligan (Editor)
2009. ISBN: 978-1-60692-989-6

Restoring the Rule of Law
Patricia V. Barkley (Editor)
2009. ISBN: 978-1-60692-970-4

Statutory Interpretation: General Principles and Recent Trends
Y. J Kim
2009. ISBN: 978-1-60692-997-1

Contemporary Perspectives on Legal Regulation of Sexual Behavior: Psycholegal Research and Analysis
Monica K. Miller (Editor)
2009. ISBN: 978-1-60741-161-1

Laws and Legislation Series

CONTEMPORARY PERSPECTIVES ON LEGAL REGULATION OF SEXUAL BEHAVIOR: PSYCHOLEGAL RESEARCH AND ANALYSIS

MONICA K. MILLER
EDITOR

Nova Science Publishers, Inc.
New York

For permission to use material from this book please contact us:
Telephone 631-231-7269; Fax 631-231-8175
Web Site: http://www.novapublishers.com

LIBRARY OF CONGRESS CATALOGING-IN-PUBLICATION DATA

Library of Congress Cataloging-in-Publication Data

Contemporary perspectives on legal regulation of sexual behavior: psycho-legal research and analysis / [edited by] Monica K. Miller.
p. cm.
ISBN 978-1-60741-161-1 (hardcover)
1. Sex and law--United States. I. Miller, Monica K.
KF9325.C66 2009
345.73'0253--dc22

2009003881

Published by Nova Science Publishers, Inc. ✝ New York

CONTENTS

PREFACE

Throughout history, the law has regulated sexual behaviors. Some regulations become outdated and are no longer enforced. For instance, many states have cohabitation laws that are rarely or never enforced. Other regulations have been adopted more recently, as culture and technology have advanced. For example, laws regulating internet pornography are relatively recent. Often, these regulations are controversial and prompt analysis and research. This book is a compilation of such discussions.

My interest in this area began in 2005, as I was reading the news. Army General Kevin Byrnes was removed from his command because he committed adultery. Another news item discussed the Interstate Abortion Act, which proposed to make it illegal to transport a minor across state lines in order to receive an abortion. These stories, along with others, got me thinking about the ways in which the law has been used to regulate sexual behaviors and their outcomes. This curiosity led me to apply for a fellowship from the American Association of University Women. This organization provided me with a summer fellowship which started it all. Although the projects they funded are published in many sources around the academic community, this book is also a testament to what fellowship funds can do. As a result of the summer I spent on fellowship, I developed a course to teach these topics to a new generation of scholars. Their perspectives are diverse and certainly add to the continuing dialogue on these important topics. As a result of this class, many scholars embarked on a journey to investigate these topics. This project is not possible with out all the chapter contributors. Thanks for all your hard work, many revisions, and overall dedication to producing a quality product. I think we've succeeded!

The purpose of this book is to present a variety of original research and legal analyses concerning regulations of sexual behavior. Research in psychology and social justice is particularly applicable to the study of legal regulations of sexual behavior. As such, this edited volume will take a 'psycho-legal' approach by addressing such issues using both psychological and legal principles. This book will contain original research articles, psycho-legal analyses, and psycho-legal briefs. All will involve current issues relating to the legal regulation of sexual behavior and its outcomes. Some themes include access to sex (e.g., prostitution) or sexual materials (e.g., obscenity), teen sexual behavior, the legal implications of the media's portrayal of sexual behavior, the outcomes of sexual behavior (e.g., abortion), psychological factors that predict support for laws that regulate sexual behavior and outcomes, and ways in which the legal system can improve the lives of those it serves. It is the goal of this book to present original perspectives and prompt discussion within legal and social science communities.

As with any project, there are special people who provide the moral support that makes it possible. I'd like to give a special thanks to Kevin, for your superhuman love, patience, and willingness to eat frozen dinners. I would not be where I am today without you; nor would I want to be anywhere else.

Monica K. Miller

PART I: ORIGINAL RESEARCH ARTICLES

Part I of this book presents four original research articles that investigate how various players impact the legal regulation of sexual behavior and its outcomes. The first chapter investigates the factors that influence whether legislators vote for certain laws regulating sexual behavior or its outcome. The second chapter looks at the role jurors play in the legal system; specifically, jurors in obscenity cases have the role of deciding whether the defendant has broken the law by violating 'community standards.' The third chapter investigates the role of media in regulation of sexual behaviors. If the media perpetuates rape myths and victim blame, victims may hesitate to report the crime, police may be hesitant to investigate, and jurors may be less willing to convict a defendant. Finally, the fourth chapter investigates how under-enforcement makes it difficult to know what sexual behaviors are acceptable. In the context of statutory rape, young men and women may read conflicting media reports—some reporting mild or no penalties for such couples and some reporting much more serious penalties. These four research reports, taken together, present a picture of how a variety of players can impact how sexual behavior is regulated, enforced, and prosecuted.

In: Contemporary Perspectives on Legal Regulation... ISBN 978-1-60741-161-1
Editor: Monica K. Miller

Chapter 1

A STUDY OF PREDICTORS OF LEGISLATIVE SUPPORT OF THE CHILD INTERSTATE ABORTION NOTIFICATION ACT

Sarah DeArman and Monica K. Miller
University of Nevada, Reno, Nevada, USA

ABSTRACT

State statutes regarding minors' ability to obtain an abortion range in restrictiveness; some have no regulation, while others require consent from both parents. This variability could encourage minors in restrictive states to travel to less restrictive states to obtain abortions. The Child Interstate Abortion Notification Act is a federal bill introduced in order to reduce the number of minors who cross state lines to obtain abortions by creating criminal and civil penalties for doctors and individuals who transport minors. A comparative analysis revealed which states are most affected by this legislation; some are at risk for having their minors leave their state while others are at risk of having minors enter their state for abortions. Legislators' support for the bill was predicted by the restrictiveness of the law in their state, their state's risk for minors leaving the state, and the legislator's gender and political party.

Some states have no restrictions on minors' ability to have an abortion, while other states have laws that are quite strict (e.g., requiring both parents to give permission for the abortion). This variation increases the likelihood that some minors will leave their states to obtain abortions in other states. The Child Interstate Abortion Notification Act is a federal bill intended to reduce the number of minors who cross state lines to obtain abortions.[1] The Act imposes both criminal and civil penalties for individuals who transport minors across state borders to have an abortion. Additionally, doctors can be fined if they fail to notify minors'

---

1 The Act has since been renamed the "Child Custody Protection Act;" however because it was called the "Interstate Abortion Notification Act" at the time of the legislative voting that is the heart of this analysis, this title is preserved.

parents in writing, according to the minors' home state abortion laws, twenty-four hours before performing the abortion.

The first purpose of this article is to determine which states would be most affected by this Act. A comparative analysis will illustrate the variation in state laws and determine the level of restrictiveness of each law. Mapping the restrictiveness of each state law will identify the states that are most at risk of having their minors cross the border to another state. It will also reveal which states are most at risk of having minors from other states enter into their state to have an abortion.

The second purpose of this article is to determine what factors are related to legislative support for the Act. It is predicted that legislators who support the Act will be Republicans, will be from states with restrictive abortion laws, and will be from states that are at high risk for either minors entering or leaving their state for abortions.

This article will first describe the history of abortion laws and the Child Interstate Abortion Notification Act. Next, the positions of the Act's supporters and opponents will be explained. Each state's abortion law will be assessed and given a restrictiveness score. States will then be assigned risk levels based on their restrictiveness score, their proximity to other states, and the size of their state. Analyses will determine what factors are related to support for the Act.

A Brief History of Abortion Laws

Abortion was made illegal by many states in the 1800s (National Abortion Federation, 2006). Many states repealed their abortion laws in the late 1960s and early 1970s because of advances in technology that made abortion a considerably safer procedure for women. In *Roe v. Wade* (1973), abortion was legalized nationwide. Nevertheless, some states imposed restrictions on the right to receive an abortion, some of which were challenged in court. In *Planned Parenthood v. Danforth* (1976), the Supreme Court decided that a provision in a Missouri statute was unconstitutional. The statute gave a minor's parents the sole authority to decide whether she could obtain an abortion. The Court sanctioned a judicial bypass process to overcome this "absolute" deciding authority. A judicial bypass is a judicial order that allows a minor to have an abortion without notifying her parent. Any state that wishes to restrict a minor's right to an abortion must include a bypass provision.

In 1992, the court in *Planned Parenthood of Southeastern Pennsylvania v. Casey* recognized and reaffirmed the right of the state to impose restrictions on abortions, as long as the restriction is not an "undue burden." Parental consent and notification laws pass this "undue burden" test when a bypass is included. States have adopted a variety of statutes because they can impose some restrictions on abortions. Some laws are very strict, which could encourage minors to go to neighboring states that have more lenient laws. Federal legislators who were concerned about minors who cross state lines to obtain abortions proposed a bill to prevent this phenomenon.

History of the Child Interstate Abortion Notification Act

The Child Interstate Abortion Notification Act prohibits individuals from transporting minors across state lines for abortions. There are exceptions; for instance, if the abortion is necessary to save the minor's life, if the parent is taking the child across the border, or if the parental notification/consent was given before the minor was taken across state lines. In addition to criminal penalties, parents are allowed to take civil legal action against the person who transported their daughter. The Act also forbids doctors from performing abortions on minor patients from out of state unless they follow the requirements of the minor's home state. A fine and prison term may be imposed on a doctor who fails to meet this requirement (Library of Congress, 2006a).

The Child Interstate Abortion Notification Act was introduced in the House of Representatives and passed on April 27, 2005 (Library of Congress, 2006b). The Senate passed its own version of the bill, called the Child Custody Protection Act, on July 25, 2006 (Library of Congress, 2006a). The House of Representatives amended the Senate bill to include many of the same provisions from the Child Interstate Abortion Notification Act, and this version passed on September 26, 2006 (Library of Congress, 2006b). A few months later, the bill was brought back to the Senate; however, it failed to pass before the legislative session ended on September 29, 2006. The bill did not see any activity in 2007 and has essentially stalled. Nevertheless, President George W. Bush has expressed his support for the bill stating, "I appreciate the Senate's efforts to preserve the integrity of state law and protect our nation's families" (Colb, 2006 p.1). President Bush has implied that if an agreeable version of the bill passes, he will sign the Act into law. Even if this particular bill never passes, it is informative to discover the effects that similar future bills may have. Similarly, it is interesting from a research perspective, to discover factors that predict support for this (and possibly similar) bills. These are the purposes of this article.

Pro Choice groups generally oppose the Act. They believe that it will leave pregnant minors without a choice in the decision whether to abort their pregnancies (Center for Reproductive Rights, 2006). These groups believe that this law imposes the same restrictions on all minors without attention to their specific situation. They believe this Act will impose an "undue burden" on a minor's decision to abort and therefore, contradicts the constitutionally guaranteed right to choose (Center for Reproductive Rights, 2006). In contrast, Pro Life groups generally support the Act. They emphasize that the law will not affect state laws; it will only prevent minors from crossing state lines in order to avoid their own state's abortion restrictions (NRLC, 2006). Thus, the Act helps states enforce their state abortion laws.

Several public opinion polls have been conducted over the past few of years to measure the public's opinion about the Act and related issues. One poll conducted by Fox News revealed that seventy-eight percent of the 900 registered voters surveyed supported requiring a minor to notify her parents in order to have an abortion (Fox News, 2005); this coincides with a CBS News Poll in which eighty percent of the 632 adults surveyed favored parental notification (CBS 2005). The public also generally supports restrictions on taking minors across state borders to obtain abortions. The Polling Company recently found that eighty-two percent of 1,000 adult respondents disapproved of (and fifteen percent supported) the transportation of minors across state lines for an abortion without parental knowledge (The Polling Company, 2005).

Although the general public seemingly supports the Act, not every state will be equally affected by the Act. High-restriction states that are near low-restriction states are likely to be most affected by this Act; minors in high-restriction states could cross the border to receive an abortion. Similarly, low-restriction states located near high-restriction states are at risk of receiving these minors. Thus, it is necessary to analyze the restrictiveness of each state law to determine how much each state will be affected.

MINOR ABORTION REGULATIONS

Current abortion regulations vary greatly among the states. One major difference among laws is the type of parental notification or consent the law requires. The concept of consent is a general principle of the medical profession. In order for any medical procedure to take place, a physician is generally required to obtain the informed consent of the patient. Specifically, the patient must be informed of what the procedure entails and the risks that are involved (Ehrlich, 2003). Patients must agree to have the procedure before a doctor can proceed. Minors, however, are legally not able to give consent because of their age.

The common assumption is that parents are more mature and are capable of making decisions that are in the minor's best interest (Ehrlich, 2003). Thus, some states have adopted laws requiring either parental consent or parental notification. Statutes also vary as to the age at which the minor can consent for herself. This section details these various restrictions.

Age Restrictions

Regulations differ in how the age of a minor is defined. Some laws define a minor as an individual under eighteen years old (e.g., Florida; Fla. Stat. Ann. §390.01114), while other states define a minor as an individual under sixteen years old (e.g., Connecticut; Conn. Gen. Stat. Ann. §19A-601). The regulation regarding age affects the restrictiveness of the particular law by defining the age at which the minor can consent for herself.

Consent Restrictions

The purpose of consent restrictions is to require a minor to receive permission from a specified adult in order to have an abortion. Some states require that specified adult to be a parent (e.g., Alabama; Ala. Code §26-21-2), while other states allow a family member to give consent (e.g., Wisconsin; Wis. Stat. Ann. §46.24, 48.375). Some states require consent from both parents or legal guardians (e.g., North Dakota; N.D. Cent. Code §14-02.1-03.1), while other states only require consent from one (e.g., Arizona; Ariz. Rev. Stat. Ann. §36-2152). Still other states allow the doctor performing the abortion to give consent for the minor (e.g., Connecticut; Conn. Gen. Stat. Ann. §19A-601). Consent requirements generally require that the adult specified give actual permission before the abortion can be performed.

Notice Restrictions

The other type of restriction is the requirement of notice. These restrictions require a minor to tell a specified adult(s) that she is going to have an abortion. Adults in this type of regulation have no say in the minor's decision; they only have to be notified that the minor has chosen to have an abortion.

Similar to consent restrictions, some states require minors to notify both parents that they are going to have an abortion (e.g., Minnesota; Minn. Stat. Ann. §645.452, 144.343), while other states require minors to inform only one parent (e.g., Montana; Mont. Code Ann. §50-20-202). Some states allow a minor to notify a family member/relative instead of a parent (e.g., Delaware; Del. Code Ann. Tit. 24 §1780). Some state laws will be more affected by the act than others because state laws vary in their restrictiveness. The following analysis is designed to compare the laws of each state.

Analysis of States' Abortion Laws and Risks

The first purpose of this article is to determine which states would be most affected by the Child Interstate Abortion Notification Act. Specifically, this analysis will determine which states are at risk of having their minors travel to another state for an abortion. The analysis will also reveal which states are at risk for having minors enter their state to obtain an abortion. The minor abortion laws from each state were collected[2] and their restrictiveness was analyzed. By mapping the states according to restrictiveness, it is possible to determine each state's risk level. This will allow us to determine whether these risk levels (among other factors) affect legislators' votes, which is the second purpose of the article.

Scoring States' Restrictions on Minor Abortion

Each law was assigned a particular score to reflect its restrictiveness. Scores were based on the law's consent or notification requirements, as described above. Scores range from 0 (least restrictive) to 17 (most restrictive). The restrictiveness scores were then mapped to demonstrate which states are most at risk for minors entering or leaving their state to obtain an abortion.

The first step was to determine how many "points" each restriction was worth. Although some assumptions were made, we believe that this is a defensible system. Ultimately, the level of restriction may be an individualized perception. That is, one minor may not perceive a one-parent *consent* to be restrictive at all because she has one supportive parent. That same minor may feel that a two parent *notification* is much more restrictive because the second parent is not supportive. Even though the minor in the second example only has to notify both

2 The laws that are applicable for this analysis are the ones that were in effect at the time legislators' were voting on the Interstate Abortion Act. Although some states' laws have since changed, this is irrelevant to the current analysis. A change in a state's law that occurs AFTER the legislator votes is unlikely to affect the legislator's vote (unless the legislator somehow knew that his or her state was considering a change in its abortion law). Because this article assumes that the law that was in place at the time of the legislator's vote is the one that will influence the legislator's vote, these are the laws that are analyzed here.

parents, and does not have to get actual permission, she could perceive the notification restriction as a bigger restriction than the consent restriction. Thus, we assigned points based on our belief about how *most* minors would perceive each law. Table 1 lists the points given for each restriction.

Table 1: Points awarded for various restrictions

Points	Type of restriction
15	Two parent consent
10	One parent consent
8	Two parent notice
8	One family member (e.g., parent or other family member) consent
5	One parent notification
3	One family member (e.g., parent/other family member) notification
1	Abortion provider consent
0	No law or inactive/invalid law
2	Minor defined as under 18
1	Minor defined as under 17

State laws with the most restrictive requirements, which require the *consent* of two parents, were given 15 points. This represents the highest level of restriction. The second highest level of restriction, one parent *consent*, was given 10 points.

Statutes requiring the *notification* of both parents and statutes requiring the *consent* of a family member were both considered as mid-level restrictions. In the first type, a minor has to *notify* two parents, which is likely less restrictive than getting consent from one or both parents (because the parent cannot prevent the abortion under a notification statue). In the second type of restriction, the minor has to obtain *consent* from a family member. It is likely a lighter burden to find some family member who will consent rather than being restricted to consent from one or both parents. Even though the type of restriction represented by these types of statutes may be different, both were given 8 points because each places a mid-level restriction on the minor. Simply put, both types of regulations represent less restriction than the high-level restrictions, but more restriction than the low-level restrictions.

Low-level restrictions included one parent notification laws (which were awarded 5 points) and one family member notification laws (which were awarded 3 points). Laws that require only the abortion doctor's consent are only minimally restrictive on the minor. Thus, such laws were awarded 1 point.

Another factor that contributes to the point system is the age at which a minor is defined. Most states define a minor as an individual under 18 years old. As this is the most restrictive age category, two points were added. Only 1 point was added for a definition of a minor as under seventeen years of age because this is less restrictive than statutes requiring the minor to be eighteen. Finally, a definition of a minor as being under sixteen years old is the least restrictive age limit and no points were added to the restrictiveness score of these states.

Finally, if the state does not have an active or valid law, then there is assumed to be no restriction on a minor's ability to receive an abortion. Such states were given scores of 0.

Thus, restrictiveness scores range from 0 (no restrictions) to 17 (i.e., states that require consent of two parents and define a minor as someone under eighteen).

Determining States' Risk Levels

Table 2 lists each state's restrictiveness score. These scores are not enough, however, to determine a state's risk of having its minors leave, or having minors from other states enter, to obtain abortions. There are many other factors that affect this phenomenon. Each state varies as to the number of states that surround it; the restrictiveness of these surrounding states can have a significant impact on minors crossing state lines. For instance, a state with a low restrictiveness score that is surrounded by states with higher scores is at risk of having minors enter to obtain abortions. The number of surrounding states can also affect a state's risk, such that a low-restriction state that is near one high-restriction state is at less risk than if the low-restriction state was near two or three high-restriction states. Size also matters; two states with similar restrictiveness scores could be at different risk levels based on the state's size. For example, Rhode Island and Oklahoma both have moderately high restrictiveness scores of 12 and both are next to one state with a lower restrictiveness score. Oklahoma was given a lower risk level than Rhode Island, however, because Oklahoma's large size makes travel less likely. Theoretically, it is harder to travel across a large state; thus, some larger states were given lower risk levels based on their size.[3] As such, risk levels were based on the state's own restrictiveness score, the number of neighboring states, the scores of neighboring states, and geographical ease of travel.[4]

Restrictiveness scores were mapped to determine which states were most at risk for minors leaving the state or entering the state for abortions. States were then assigned a risk level of 1 (low risk), to 4 (high risk) for minors leaving the state for abortions (Figure 1). States were also assigned a risk level of 1 (low risk) to 3 (high risk) for minors entering the state to obtain abortions (Figure 2). There are only three risk levels for minors entering the state (as opposed to the four risk levels for minors leaving the state) because there was not enough variety among states' relative risk to justify a fourth level of risk. Although there was some subjectivity in determining risk levels, the two researchers first designed an analysis plan and then assigned risk levels accordingly. Researchers agreed on 96 percent of all risk level assignments. These differences were discussed until an agreement was reached.

---

3 It is important to note, however that some minors would have the means (e.g., air travel) to fly to states such as Alaska and Hawaii, or to other countries such as Mexico. While these are possibilities, it would be physically easier for the minor to go to a neighboring state (as compared to flying to Hawaii, for example), and presumably only a small number of minors would have that option. Further, the Act does not apply to other countries; thus consideration of other countries' laws is beyond this analysis.

4 Admittedly, these are not the only factors that could influence a minor's decision to travel across the state. Uncountable factors, such as population density, the state's age demographics, urban/rural population distribution, rates of unplanned pregnancy, the number and location of clinics within the state, and other abortion laws that affect all women in that state, could also affect a minor's decisions; however these factors

Table 2: Restrictiveness scores and risk levels

State	Restrictiveness Score	Leaving Risk Level	Entering Risk Level
Alabama	10		11
Alaska	9	1	1
Arizona	10	3	1
Arkansas	10	1	1
California	10	3	1
Colorado	n/a (0)	1	3
Connecticut	1	1	3
Delaware	n/a (0)	1	3
Florida	7	1	2
Georgia	7	1	2
Hawaii	0	1	1
Idaho	12	4	1
Illinois	n/a (0)	1	3
Indiana	10	3	1
Iowa	5	2	2
Kansas	7	2	2
Kentucky	12	4	1
Louisiana	12	1	1
Maine	3	1	3
Maryland	2	1	3
Massachusetts	12	4	1
Michigan	12	1	1
Minnesota	10	3	1
Mississippi	17	1	1
Missouri	12	3	1
Montana	7	1	2
Nebraska	7	2	2
Nevada	7	2	2
N. Hampshire	7	3	2
New Jersey	7	3	2
New Mexico	12	3	1
New York	0	1	3
N. Carolina	12	1	1
North Dakota	17	1	1
Ohio	12	3	1
Oklahoma	12	2	1
Oregon	0	1	3
Pennsylvania	12	4	1
Rhode Island	12		3
S. Carolina	9	1	1
South Dakota	7	1	2
Tennessee	12	1	1
Texas	12	1	1

are beyond the scope of this analysis, which is primarily to determine whether a state's laws put them at risk for minors leaving or entering the state to receive an abortion.

State	Restrictiveness Score	Leaving Risk Level	Entering Risk Level
Utah	12	3	1
Vermont	0	1	3
Virginia	12	4	1
Washington	0	1	3
West Virginia	3	1	3
Wisconsin	n/a (0)	1	3
Wyoming	12	3	1

Note: N/A means the state has an ineffective statute.

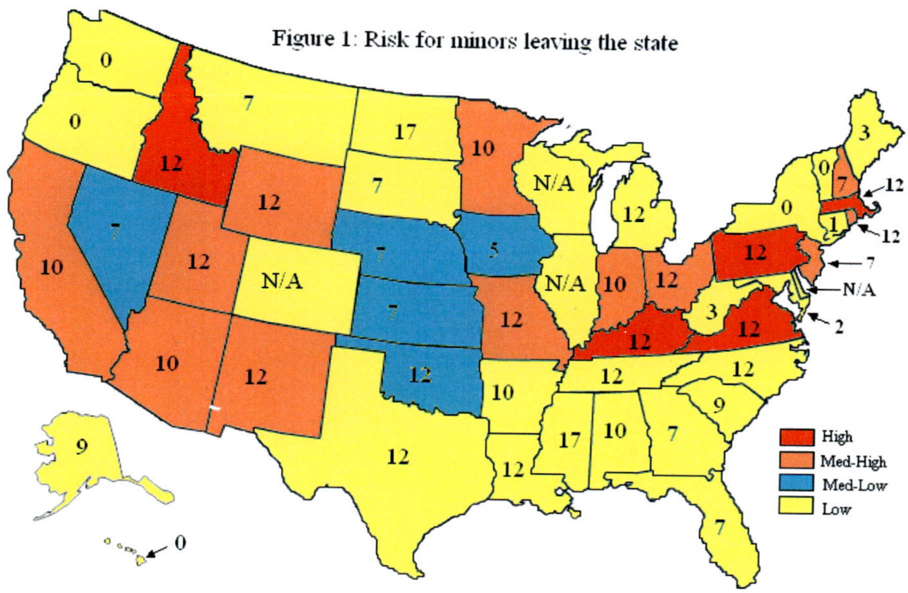

Figure 1: Risk for minors leaving the state

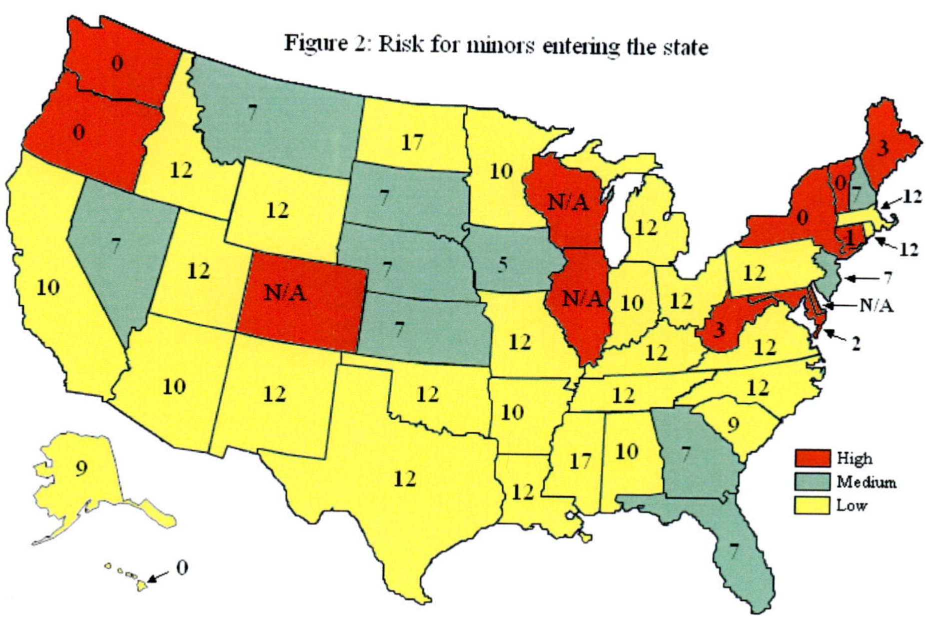

Figure 2: Risk for minors entering the state

States at Risk for its Minors Leaving

A four-point risk scale was developed to assess each state's risk level for having minors leave the state to obtain abortions. See Figure 1.

Figure 1 demonstrates that Idaho, Kentucky, Virginia, Massachusetts, and Pennsylvania were the states at the highest risk (level 4). These states had a restrictiveness score of 10 or more and were surrounded by at least *two* other states with easier access to abortions (i.e., a score of 3 or less).

The medium-high risk category (level 3) included states that had either a score of 10 or above and were next to *one* state with a score of 3 or less (e.g., Rhode Island, Ohio, Indiana) or a score of 7to 9 and were next to at least *two* states with scores of 3 or less (e.g., New Hampshire, New Jersey).

States in the medium-low risk (level 2) had a score of 7 and were next to one state with a score of 3 or less (e.g., Kansas, Nebraska) or had a score of 5 and were next to at least two states with a score of 3 or less (e.g., Iowa). Oklahoma has a relatively high score of 12 and is close to one state (Colorado) with a score of 3 or less. Thus, it would qualify as a medium-high state, but because if its large size, and the fact that only a tiny portion of the panhandle actually borders Colorado, Oklahoma was ranked at a medium-low risk for leaving.

Among the low risk states (level 1) are Texas, Louisiana, Alabama, and Mississippi. Even though these states have high restrictiveness scores, they are at lower risk because they are completely surrounded by states with highly restrictive laws, leaving minors without another nearby option. It is unlikely that a minor in these states could drive to another state to get an abortion. Other low risk states included those that had a restrictiveness score of 0, 1 or 2 (e.g., Hawaii, Colorado, Delaware). It is assumed that few minors will be leaving those states when abortion is relatively easy to access in their own state. Other states have lower scores however they border no states with lower scores. For instance, Florida has a score of 7 but borders states with scores of 7 and 10, making it unlikely that minors will leave Florida. Alaska was included in the low risk category because of the distance between this state and the rest of the U.S.

States at Risk for Minors Entering the State.

A three-point risk scale was developed to assess each state's risk level for having minors entering the state. See Figure 2.

Figure 2 indicates states such as Oregon, Colorado, Wisconsin, Illinois, West Virginia and Vermont are at the highest risk. These states have little or no restrictions (a score of 3 or less) on abortions and are near at least one state with higher restrictions (a score of 10 or more). Thus, they are at highest risk of having minors from other states enter their state to obtain an abortion.

The states considered medium risk (level 2) were assigned to this category because they had scores of 5 or 7 and were surrounded by one or more states with scores of 10 or more. Even though these states (e.g., New Hampshire, Montana, Georgia) are somewhat restrictive, they are near states that are even more restrictive. It is possible that minors will turn to these less restrictive states when seeking an abortion, rather than complying with their states' comparatively more restrictive abortion measures.

Finally, states with a score of 9 or above (e.g., Pennsylvania, Rhode Island, Wyoming, North Carolina) were placed in the low risk category (level 1). It is unlikely that minors will enter a highly restrictive state for an abortion. Hawaii and Alaska were placed in the low risk category because they are so far away from other states that the risk of minors entering either state to have an abortion is very minimal.

As this analysis indicates, there is great variance among state abortion laws. As such, minors in states with highly restrictive laws may travel to states with less restrictive laws in order to obtain abortions. This is the fear of the legislators who support the Act. This analysis indicates that some states are at risk of having minors enter to obtain abortions, while others are at high risk of having their minors leave their state to obtain abortions. Each state is in a unique position and will be impacted by the Act differentially. The possibility that legislators consider the situation that their state is in when voting on the Act is considered next.

FACTORS THAT INFLUENCE LEGISLATORS' VOTES

There are many different factors that can influence the way a legislator will vote on a particular bill. These factors include the legislators' race, gender, religion, party affiliation, and the needs and desires of their constituents (Regens, 1993). These factors work together to form the legislators' value system and help determine how they will vote on a particular bill (Regens, 1993). Legislators often make decisions by considering more than one of these factors. For instance, a female legislator may want to vote a certain way because she feels it is best for women in general, but may also want to vote the other way because of her constituency's community sentiment.

Gender, race and party affiliation all can affect legislative voting in general; there is also evidence that these factors can affect voting on abortion issues. Female legislators are more likely to vote pro-abortion than male legislators (Gohmann, 1994; Regens, 1993). Religion affects legislative voting; for instance, legislators who consider themselves to be religious may have a more structured belief system than legislators that do not adhere to formalized religious beliefs (Fastnow, 1999). When considering abortion, many denominations and formalized religions take an official stance on the issue and count on their members to hold the same beliefs (Fastnow, 1999). Religious legislators may therefore be influenced to vote in a way that reflects these beliefs. Similarly, race affects legislator voting behavior on abortion issues. Black legislators may be less supportive of abortion issues than non-black legislators (Regens, 1993). It is theorized that this is due to the mentality that abortion is a measure that is used to suppress population growth among black communities (Regens, 1993). Party affiliation also influences the voting behavior of legislators. Republicans tend to vote more conservatively, while democrats tend to vote more liberally on many issues, including abortion (Jaenicke, 1998). Republicans are usually opposed to abortion rights, while democrats usually support or try to protect abortion rights (Jaenicke, 1998). The party a legislator identifies with is a strong predictor of their roll call vote (Page, 2001). Legislators will vote in line with their party's position for the majority of issues.

In addition to these personal factors, legislators are influenced by other factors, such as the desires and needs of their constituents or the districts they serve (Snyder, 2003). House and Senate members are generally understanding and responsive to their constituents' interests when casting a vote on a particular bill (Lopez, 2004). Further, legislators' votes are impacted, when voting on abortion issues, by their constituents' expected demand for abortion services in their district (Gohmann, 1994). In other words, legislators are affected by their constituents' views on abortion and whether or not it is a service that people in that district want to make available. Upcoming re-elections also influence a legislators' need to represent and align their views with their constituents (Snyder, 2003). Legislators with upcoming re-election bids may vote a particular way in order to gain support from their constituents and to overcome any opposition they may encounter (Snyder, 2003). Re-election goals may also drive legislators representing a diverse district to take another approach and abstain from voting or taking positions that may be offensive to their constituents (Jones, 2003). Just as legislators are influenced by their own race, they are also influenced by the race of their constituents or district. African American legislators representing black districts are more likely to vote in favor of legislation supporting black interests than other legislators (Grose, 2005).

Although many different factors may influence whether or not a legislator will vote for a bill, the purpose of this article is to specifically look at how legislators' state abortion laws and the risk of minors leaving or entering their state will affect their vote on the Child Interstate Abortion Notification Act. As described above, the political party and the constituency legislators serve are among the most important factors in predicting a legislators' vote on abortion issues.

Analysis of Factors Influencing Legislators' Votes

The second purpose of this article is to determine whether a number of variables (e.g., the states' risk for minors leaving the state) affect legislative voting. All senators and representatives were categorized as "supporters" or "opponents" based on their vote in the initial House and Senate voting. Legislators' that abstained were not included. The sample included 191 opponents and 335 supporters.

Four hypotheses are offered. Hypotheses one predicts that Republican legislators and male legislators will be more likely to be supporters, while Democrats and females will be more likely to be opponents. This is because the parties typically favor these positions on bills regarding abortion. Hypothesis two predicts that opponents will be from states with lower restrictiveness scores than supporters. Legislators supposedly are the voice of their constituents. If so, legislators from states with high restrictiveness scores (i.e., strict abortion laws) should also favor this restriction on abortion. Hypothesis three expects that opponents will be more at risk for minors entering the state than supporters. It would be logical that states want to protect their doctors. Thus, states that are at high risk for their doctors being persecuted may object to the bill. Hypothesis four predicts that opponents will be less at risk for their minors leaving the state. Legislators who fear their minors will leave the state will support the bill; legislators who have little fear of their minors leaving the state will not be as supportive.

TESTS OF HYPOTHESES

As predicted by hypothesis one, party affiliation was strongly related to legislators' votes. Chi Square analyses revealed that 15 Republicans opposed the bill, while 266 Republicans supported the bill. In contrast, 174 Democrats opposed and 69 supported it. Two Independents opposed the bill. This effect was highly significant ($\chi^2(2) = 251.0$, $p < .001$). Similarly, gender was strongly related to vote. Chi Square analysis indicated that 27 females supported and 52 females opposed the law. Meanwhile, 308 males supported the law and 139 males opposed the law. This was highly significant ($\chi^2(2) = 41.4$, $p < .001$).

Hypothesis two was also supported; opponents of the Act are from states that have lower restrictiveness scores ($M = 6.08$) than supporters ($M = 9.18$; $t\ (524) = 7.64$, $p < .001$). In support of hypothesis three, risk level for minors entering the state also was related to legislators' voting. Risk level was assigned using a 3-point scale. Opponents were at greater risk ($M = 1.94$) than supporters ($M = 1.43$; $t\ (524) = 6.89$, $p < .001$). In contrast, hypothesis four was not supported. Supporters and opponents did not differ based on risk level for minors leaving the state ($t\ (524) = .91$, $p > .05$).

DISCUSSION

The Child Interstate Abortion Notification Act is intended to prevent minors from crossing state borders to obtain abortions. Some states are at risk for minors entering their state to obtain abortions because states differ greatly in their laws' restrictiveness. Some states are at risk of minors leaving their state to obtain abortions. The states that fell into either high risk level are the states whose interests are most at stake. The states that fell into either medium risk categories also have an interest in this legislation, while this legislation will have little or no impact on the states in both low risk levels.

Each state's abortion law was analyzed, given a restrictiveness score (0-17), and mapped to show which states will be most affected by the Act. Each state was given a risk level for both their risk of having minors leave their state to have an abortion and risk for having minors from neighbor states enter their state to receive an abortion. Both of these categories come with their own problems and policy issues.

States that are at high risk for minors leaving their states must figure out what they can do to keep their minors inside state lines. On the other hand, states that are at high risk for minors entering their states must figure out how to prevent pregnant minors from crossing into their states for abortions. Regulating abortion clinics and keeping track of the age of the patients is a burden these states may have to meet if they are to protect their doctors and enforce the Act. Although the burdens and interests are different, both types of states will need more money and resources in order to carry out this legislation.

The second purpose of this article was to identify how the Act's supporters and opponents differ. Party affiliation was strongly related to vote; Republicans voted for it, while Democrats voted against it. Females were more likely to oppose the law, while males were more likely to support the law. Opponents were also from states that had lower restrictiveness scores, which is logical because legislators who are from states that have adopted strict abortion laws also vote for the Act, which further restricts abortions. Meanwhile, legislators from states with more lenient abortion laws (or no law) tended to vote against the Act. This means that legislators are listening to their constituents' wishes (or at least voting consistent with their states' laws).

In addition, opponents were from states that are at higher risk for having minors enter their states. This finding also makes sense because states that are at risk of their doctors being prosecuted do not want the Act, while states that are at little risk vote for the Act. These states will bear much burden, as their doctors will be required to follow the administrative procedures outlined in the Act or face criminal and civil penalties.

Finally, counter to the prediction, there was no effect for the risk of minors leaving the state. This is an unexpected effect, as the risk for a state's minors leaving the state would seemingly be a strong influence on a legislator's vote. This could possibly be a result of the coding scheme chosen. Many states (e.g., Texas) have strict abortion laws, yet are at very low risk of their minors leaving the state because the nearby states are also very restrictive. Other states received lower risk levels because their large size makes travel less likely. Had location and state size not been included in the analysis, perhaps results would have been different. This would explain why the state's restrictiveness score would be related to legislators' votes, but risk level is not. Restrictiveness scores were highly related to legislative vote. It is likely that this effect is so strong that actual risk level is not considered. Legislators strongly wish to vote in a way that reflects their state's own law, yet they may not consider their state's actual risk. The state's law reflects the state's wishes; this is a factor that is easy to assess. In opposition, actual risk is a more subjective factor that is less likely to assess, making it less likely to affect votes. In sum, there are several identifiable factors related to legislators' votes.

This study has a number of limitations that deserve to be mentioned. First, this study does not take into account the level of enforcement of the abortion laws. A state may have a very restrictive law, but if it is not enforced, then minors will be able to obtain abortions and are less likely to cross the border. It is beyond the scope of this article, however, to discuss the amount of enforcement these regulations currently receive. For the purposes of this article, actual enforcement was not considered; it was assumed that states enforce their laws.

Second, this analysis does not account for the possibility of air travel. While the analysis considers the feasibility of travel from one state to another (e.g., Alaska is considered at low risk because of the long distance between Alaska and other states), it does not consider that a minor could fly to another state. It is somewhat uncommon, presumably, that a large number of minors would be able to fly. Nevertheless, it is a limitation of this analysis.

Third, the study does not account for states' proximity to Canada or Mexico. It is possible that minors in some states (e.g., Texas) could go to Mexico to receive an abortion. While the Act is concerned with preventing minors from leaving a state to obtain an abortion, foreign countries are not bound by the Act. Thus, this factor is not considered in the coding scheme or analysis.

Finally, risk levels are somewhat subjective. Although some guidelines were created (e.g., a restrictiveness score of at least 10 was needed to be scored as a high risk for minors leaving the state), other aspects of the coding were more subjective. For instance, some states' scores were adjusted according to the size of the state. There was no exact size required for such adjustment; instead, researchers discussed and agreed on each risk level assignment. Restrictiveness scores are somewhat less subjective, as there is a strict coding scheme (e.g., Table 1 specifies how many points each type of restriction is worth). Nevertheless, the actual points given were somewhat subjective. For instance, the decision to assign 10 points to a one parent consent law was made only because 10 was less than the number (15) assigned to more restrictive two parent consent laws, and more than the number (5) given to less restrictive one parent notification laws. Though there was some subjectivity in the scoring, the actual numbers given are less important then the degree of restrictiveness that the numbers represent.

Conclusions

States have a variety of minor abortion laws. Varying restrictiveness can lead minors in highly restrictive states to cross the border into less restrictive states in order to obtain abortions. The Child Interstate Abortion Notification Act is the federal government's attempt to prevent minors from crossing state lines to obtain abortions. States identified as being at high risk for either minors entering the state or minors leaving the state have the most interest in this act. High risk states have enforcement, tracking, and monitoring issues that must be met financially and administratively if this act passes. Simply put, states must find a way to regulate the number of pregnant minors crossing state lines to effectively meet this legislation's demands.

The second part of the article analyzed the differences between supporters and opponents in order to determine what factors affect legislators' votes. Not surprisingly, legislative voting is not random; several factors affect voting. Specifically, legislators vote according to their party affiliation and their own states' laws. They also vote to protect their doctors.

In sum, state legislatures, criminal justice systems, abortion clinics, minors and parents all have a stake in this Act. This analysis determined which states will be most impacted by this Act, and which factors determined legislators' support for the Act. Future research should be conducted to determine the actual impact (e.g., costs of enforcing criminal aspects of the Act) on each individual state. Such research will help address the problem of minors crossing state borders to obtain abortions in other states. Legislators have identified this as an important social, criminal and civil legal issue; as such it deserves further research.

References

CBS News Poll (July 13-14, 2005). Retrieved April 22, 2008 from www.cbsnews.com/htdocs/CBSNews_polls/scotus.pdf

Center for Reproductive Rights (2006). The teen endangerment act: Harming young women who seek abortions. Retrieved April 22, 2008, from http://reproductiverights.org/pub_fac_ccpa.html

Colb, S. F. (2006). Criminalizing interstate abortion travel: Congress targets people who assist minors in trouble. Retrieved April 22, 2008 from http://writ.news.findlaw.com/colb/20060809.html

Ehrlich, J. S. (2003). Grounded in the reality of their lives: Listening to teens who make the abortion decision without involving their parents. *Berkeley Women's Law Journal, 18,* 61-180

Fastnow, C., Grant, J. T., & Rudolph, T. J. (1999). Holy Roll Calls: Religious tradition and voting behavior in the U.S. House. *Social Science Quarterly, 80.*

Fox News/Opinion Dynamics Poll (April 25-26, 2005). Retrieved April 22, 2008 from www.foxnews.com/projects/pdf/poll_040606.pdf

Gohmann, S. F. & Ohsfeldt, R. L. (1994). Voting in the U.S. House on abortion funding issues: The rôle of constituents' and legislators' ideology, before and after the Webster decision. *American Journal of Economics and Sociology, 53*, 455-474.

Grose, C. R. (2005). Disentangling constituency and legislator effects in legislative representation: Black legislators or black districts? *Social Science Quarterly, 86*, 427-443.

Jaenicke, D. W. (1998). Abortion and partisanship in the 104th U.S. Congress. *Politics, 18*, 1-9.

Jones, D. R. (2003). Position taking and position avoidance in the U.S. Senate. *The Journal of Politics, 65*, 851-863.

Library of Congress (2006a). Child Custody Protection Act (S. 403) – All Actions. Retrieved April 22, 2008, from http://thomas.loc.gov/cgi-bin/bdquery/z?d109:sn00403:@@@x

Library of Congress (2006b). Child Interstate Abortion Notification Act (H.R.748). Retrieved April 22, 2008, from http://thomas.loc.gov/cgi-bin/bdquery/z?d109:hr00748:x

Lopez, E. J. & Sutter, D. (2004). Ignorance in congressional voting? Evidence from policy reversal on the endangered species act. *Social Science Quarterly, 85*, 891-912.

National Abortion Federation (2006a). History of abortion. Retrieved April 22, 2008, from http://www.prochoice.org/about_abortion/history_abortion.html

National Abortion Federation (2006b). Teenage endangerment act repackaged: A menacing maze for young women, their families, and their doctors. Retrieved October 10, 2006, from http://www.prochoice.org/policy/national/teen_endangerment.html

National Right to Life Committee, Inc. (2006a). Letter to members of the U.S. Senate regarding the "Child Custody Protection Act" (S. 403). Retrieved October 2, 2006, from http://www.nrlc.org/Federal/CCPS/CCPASenateLetter092806.html

National Right to Life Committee, Inc. (2006b). Parental involvement statutes. Retrieved April 22, 2008, from http://www.nrlc.org/federal/ccpa/ParentalLawsFS.pdf

Page, B. I., Shapiro, R. Y., Gronke, P. W., & Rosenberg, R. M. (2001). Constituency, party, and representation in congress. *Public Opinion Quarterly, 48*, 741-756.

Planned Parenthood v. Danforth, 428 U.S. 52 (1976).

Planned Parenthood of Southeastern Pennsylvania v. Casey, 505 U.S. 833 (1992).

Regens, J. L. & Lockerbie, B. (1993). Making choices about choice: House support for abortion funding. *Social Science Research 22*, 24-32

Roe v. Wade, 410 U.S. 113 (1973).

Snyder, Jr., J. M. & Ting, M. M. (2003). Roll calls, party labels, and elections. *Political Analysis, 11*, 419-444.

The Polling Company (2005). National Right to Life Committee. Retrieved April 22, 2008 from www.nrlc.org/federal/ccpa/parentalinvolvementpolls.html

Tomel, A. (1999). Parental involvement laws and minor and non-minor teen abortion and birth rates. *Journal of Family and Economic Issues, 20*, 149-162.

In: Contemporary Perspectives on Legal Regulation... ISBN 978-1-60741-161-1
Editor: Monica K. Miller

Chapter 2

OBSCENITY IS A FOUR LETTER WORD. OR IS IT? AN EXPLORATORY INVESTIGATION INTO COMMUNITY STANDARDS OF OBSCENITY

Alicia Summers and Monica K. Miller
University of Nevada, Reno, Nevada, USA

ABSTRACT

The legal definition of obscenity was established in *Miller v. California* (1973) and relies primarily on the ability of a jury to determine contemporary community standards. This definition assumes that a community standard exists and that jurors are capable of determining this standard. The current study utilizes a convenience sample of community and student participants to provide an initial exploration of community standards in order to determine if a standard exists and the capability of jurors in determining this standard. Results indicate that the there is quite a bit of variability surrounding obscenity definitions and examples. This information, combined with significant demographic differences, suggests that a community standard may not exist. Further, results indicate that individuals demonstrate the cognitive bias pluralistic ignorance, as individuals' *personal* standards of obscenity are significantly different than their perceptions of *community* standards, which may mean jurors are incapable of accurately determining community standards.

"The problem with obscenity is no one really knows what it is," a former federal prosecutor was quoted as saying in regards to a current obscenity case (Deutsch, 2008). Obscenity, although seemingly a straightforward term, is wrought with complexity and confusion, especially in the legal sense. Of particular concern are the assumptions surrounding the legal concept of "community standard." In order to convict someone of an obscenity crime, the jury must determine that the material in question meets the community standards of obscenity. This definition includes two significant assumptions. First, there is an assumption that a community standard exists. That is, that there is an objective consensus (i.e., standard) among the community as to what material is considered obscene. Second, there is an assumption that jurors are capable of understanding and applying this community standard at trial.

The legal definition and criteria for determining obscenity were established in *Miller v. California* in 1973 and have not been updated to present. The fact that the legal criterion for a crime has not been modified in 35 years is not in itself problematic; it is the legal definition itself that is in question. The legal definition has many subjective terms that are not properly defined by the legal system, including the term community standard. According to the definition, jurors are required to determine the community's standards of what qualifies as obscene. Yet, research in the area has yet to determine if jurors are good judges of community standards. Legally, judges have come to opposing decisions regarding the ability of jurors to determine community standards; some judges allow expert testimony to inform the debate (*Saliba v. State,* 1985), noting that jurors need the help of expert testimony to determine community standards, while other judges have ruled that no experts are needed because the evidence can speak for itself (*Hamling v. United States,* 1974).

Some research supports the notion that jurors may not be good judges of the community's standards. Various demographic variables impact decisions regarding what is considered obscene (Scott, 1991); thus, jurors may be biased in their perceptions of community standards. Further, jurors may be susceptible to cognitive biases, such as pluralistic ignorance, which may influence their decisions.

This article presents an exploratory study that assesses the assumptions that the courts make concerning obscenity laws and prosecutions. First, the obscenity law and the courts that hear such cases assume that there *is* a community sentiment. Second, there is also an assumption that jurors *know* the community's sentiment. In the current article, we will examine the variability of perceived community standards to determine if a community standard exists, identify demographic variables that may predict standards of obscenity, and examine the ability of potential jurors to determine community standards. Based on research findings, recommendations will be made for legal actors as to how this information can be used in legal cases (i.e., jury selection), and suggestions are made for improving the legal system (e.g., providing experts to testify as to the community's standards).

LEGAL DEBATE REGARDING COMMUNITY STANDARDS OF OBSCENITY

The legal definition and method of determining obscenity was established in *Miller v. California* (1973). Whether an object (called a 'work' in the *Miller* definition) is obscene depends primarily on three factors. First, whether an average person applying community standards would find that the work appeals to a prurient interest (i.e., an unhealthy, morbid or degrading interest) in sex. Second, whether an average person, applying community standards would find that the work depicts sexual conduct in a patently offensive manner. The final prong is whether the work, taken as a whole, lacks any artistic, literary, political or scientific value. This three prong test remains the national standard for establishing if material is obscene. States, however, can add to this definition by providing examples, written into their laws, as to what is considered obscene.

Critics have taken the position that this definition is problematic because many of the concepts used in the law lack clear definitions, including the definition of community standards (Summers & Miller, 2007). Although the *Miller* (1973) court was vague in its definitions, it did note that a community standard is not a national standard. Cases following *Miller* have also helped clarify the definition of community. The court in *Hamling v. United States* (1974) noted that community standard is not a statewide standard, but instead is the area from which the defendant resides. Additionally, in *Pinkus v. U.S.* (1978), the court found that children are not part of the community in the community standards criteria. The community standards that should be applied are that of an adult (not national) community. Community was not further clarified, indicating that it could be a city, town, or jurisdiction.

Because the definition of community has never been clearly articulated, there is concern as to whether jurors are capable of determining community standards. In an early obscenity case (pre-*Miller*), oral arguments revealed disagreement regarding this question (*Jacobellis v. Ohio*, 1964). While some judges believe that jurors are capable of making their own decisions regarding community standards (*Hamling v. United States,* 1974), others believe that expert testimony is necessary to inform the jury of what community standards exist (Holley, 1996). The court has ruled that the defense has the right to enter expert evidence in obscenity cases (*Smith v. California*, 1959), even noting that public opinion polls are uniquely suited to determining community standards (*Saliba v. State,* 1985). Allowing expert testimony and saying that it is uniquely suited to inform the courts indicates that some courts have recognized the jury's need for outside assistance in understanding community standards.

All of these rulings are based on the assumption that a consensus or community standard exists. Yet, not all researchers believe this. In *People v. Nelson* (1980), an expert testified that there were no community standards in the community regarding obscenity. However, this testimony was disqualified by the judge who agreed with the prosecutor that the testimony invaded the province of the jury. This implies the judge felt that the testimony was opinion and not sufficient evidence that community standards do not exist (*People v. Nelson,* 1980). This ruling and testimony indicate a clear lack of consensus regarding community standards and the ability of the jury to understand them. Social psychological research further adds to this debate.

RESEARCH REGARDING COMMUNITY STANDARDS OF OBSCENITY

Research specifically focused on determining community standards of obscenity is relatively uncommon, but some social psychological research in the area has found important results, which may help inform the legal debate. Early research conducted following the *Miller* case discovered that the size of the community is important in determining community standards, with urban areas being less conservative in their view than rural areas (Glassman, 1978). Research has also discovered that viewing obscene material does not significantly change opinions on obscenity, but does change opinions about what qualifies as "prurient interest." Specifically, individuals who watched potentially obscene material were less likely to consider it as a prurient interest after viewing, as compared to before viewing (Linz, Donnerstein, Land, McCall, Scott, Shafer et al., 1991). Gender and age differences in perceptions of community standards of obscenity have also been documented, although the researcher noted that demographic variables are not great predictors of community standards (Scott, 1991). Further studies have found that younger individuals and males were more likely than their counterparts to volunteer to participate in a study in which obscene materials would be viewed (Linz et al., 1991). This may indicate that these groups hold more liberal views toward obscene behavior. That is, males and younger individuals might hold more liberal views towards obscenity, as they volunteered to participate in studies with obscene material more often than females and older individuals.

Research on community standards in general has also found important results. One finding is that community standards change over time; they may change from lenient to harsh to lenient again over the years (Finkel, Burke, & Chavez, 2000). This might be particularly problematic when state statutes provide examples of obscene material, especially as perceptions of obscenity may change as times change. For example, a state may have a law on the books that selling sex toys is obscene. However, over time the community may become more liberal and sex toys may not longer viewed as obscene, yet they are still listed as obscene in the state law. This could result in prosecutions that may be perceived as unfair. Additionally, community standards research has determined that contextual variables, such as age of the defendant or severity of crime, influence sentiments (Finkel et al., 2000). These studies indicate that perception of community standards may be complex and involve multiple variables, which may be why legal decisions regarding obscenity cases have yet to reach consensus.

The previous issues bring to light some of the complexities of understanding community standards of obscenity and the potential need for experts. The understanding of community standards is further complicated by potential cognitive biases of the jurors. One such bias that may play a role is pluralistic ignorance.

Pluralistic Ignorance

Pluralistic ignorance is a cognitive bias in which individuals believe that their attitudes and behaviors differ from the expressed social norm (Allport, 1924). Recent research indicates that pluralistic ignorance is widespread and occurs in many diverse domains (Bowen, & Bourgeois, 2001; Lambert, Kahn, & Apple, 2003; Segrist, Corcoran, Jordan-Flemming, & Rose, 2007). Individuals may believe their attitudes are more conservative or more liberal than current public norms. For example, individuals believed that their attitudes toward gays and lesbians were significantly more favorable than the attitudes of their friends or others students (Bowen & Bourgeois). Other areas of research have shown differing perceptions in relation to drinking behaviors (Segrist et al.) and attitudes toward sexual behavior (Lambert et al.). These studies indicate that individuals may not be the best judge of others' attitudes, because they feel their attitudes are different from the expressed norm. Therefore, pluralistic ignorance might influence whether individuals are capable of accurately gauging community standards related to obscenity.

Study Overview

The current study tests two assumptions regarding the obscenity standard established in *Miller*. First, the study will determine if a community standard of obscenity exists. Second, the study will test the assumption that jurors are capable of understanding these community standards. Previous research indicates that community standards are complex. They may change over time (Finkel et al., 2000) and may be influenced by demographic variables such as town size (Glassman, 1978), gender and age (Scott, 1991). These studies indicate that community standards of obscenity may be quite variable and that a true 'community standard' may not exist. Even if it does exist, legal rulings indicate that jurors may not be capable of understanding what the community standard is and may need experts to provide research and testify about the community standards (see for example *Saliba v. State,* 1985). Social cognitive research supports this hypothesis, as there are many potential biases, such as pluralistic ignorance, which may impact individuals' perceptions. To test these assumptions, two primary research questions will be addressed: 1) Is there a community standard of obscenity? 2) Are jurors capable of understanding this community standard?

Hypotheses

Three hypotheses are posed to address the two research questions. Hypotheses one and two are designed to address research question 1, while hypothesis three is designed to address research question two.

Hypothesis 1. There will be a great deal of variability in what participants consider to be obscene. Variability indicates a lack of consensus, meaning there is no community standard.

Hypothesis 1a. There will be a great deal of variability in qualitative responses regarding the definition and examples of obscenity.

Hypothesis 1b. There will be a great deal of variability (defined as standard deviations greater than two) in quantitative ratings of obscenity, but only for moderately obscene items. Items which are considered not at all obscene or highly obscene will have less variability. This will occur because items which are considered not at all obscene or highly obscene should be agreed upon by the majority of respondents, thus decreasing variability.

Hypothesis 2. There will be demographic differences in perceptions of community standards. If demographic variables influence perceptions of obscenity, then the perception of what the community standard is will change depending on the makeup of the jury and thus, a universal set community standard does not exist.

Hypothesis 2a. Males will have less conservative views of obscenity (i.e., rate materials as less obscene) than females, supporting earlier research (Scott, 1991).

Hypothesis 2b. Older individuals will have more conservative views of obscenity (i.e., rate materials as more obscene) than younger individuals, supporting prior research (Scott, 1991).

Hypothesis 2c. Individuals from rural communities will have more conservative views of obscenity (i.e., rate materials as more obscene) than individuals from urban communities, supporting prior work (Glassman, 1978).

Hypothesis 3. Participants will demonstrate the cognitive bias pluralistic ignorance in their responses concerning community standards of obscenity. Specifically, individuals will indicate that their perceptions of what is considered obscene are different from what the community considers to be obscene.

METHOD

Participants

Participants included a convenience sample of 47 community members and 54 students from a mid-size western university. There were 28 males and 73 females. Participants were from rural (40.6%), suburban (39.6%), urban, (15.8%), and metropolitan (4%) areas. Seventy-four percent indicated they were eligible for jury duty, and 22% said they were not. Additionally, 37% said they had been called for jury duty, while 63% had not. Participants ranged in age from 18 to 76 (M = 29.7; Mdn = 24). The ethnic breakdown included 83.8% White/Caucasian, 5.1% Black/African American, 3% Asian, 1% Native American, and 7% Hispanic/Latino.[1]

Materials

In order to answer the research questions posed above, an instrument was designed to gain a better qualitative and quantitative understanding of views on obscenity as well as measure differences in individual opinions compared to perceived community standards. The survey included demographic variables, asked participants to define obscenity and to provide examples of what they consider to be obscene. Individuals were given the legal definition of obscenity and were asked to rate how obscene they personally felt that 24 items were, on a scale from 1 (*not at all obscene*) to 8 (*highly obscene*). Next, participants were asked to rate the degree of obscenity of the same items based on their perception of community standards (i.e., they were asked: How would your community rate the item?). The survey included items that were expected to be seen as not obscene (e.g., art books with nudity), items that were expected to be seen as moderately obscene (e.g., magazines that portray group sex), and items that were expected to be seen as highly obscene (e.g., magazines that portray sex with animals). Items were selected based on examples in the research and examples in recent obscenity cases.

Procedure

Community participants were recruited via email through a snowball sampling procedure. Student participants were recruited from criminal justice and introductory psychology courses. All participants were given a description of the study and asked to participate. Those interested were sent a link to the survey website via an email. All participants were emailed

1 Because there were few members of minority ethnic groups in this study, analyses were not conducted on this variable.

the same introduction, same email link, and sent to the same survey site to maintain consistency.

Study Design

The study was a survey design with both qualitative and quantitative components, utilizing a mixed methods design (i.e., both within and between subjects). For the qualitative part, participants were asked open ended questions (e.g., "How would you define obscenity?") and responses were analyzed to identify patterns. Participants were asked to rate the how obscene a list of items were, based on their opinion; then they answered the same questions based on their perception of community standards of obscenity (within subjects design). Gender and age were also used for comparisons (between subjects).

RESULTS

The first step in analyzing the data was to examine the qualitative responses for themes. This allows researchers to examine the variability of definitions and examples of obscenity. The second step includes analysis of quantitative data.[2]

Variability of Responses

To test the assumption that a community standard exists, both variability of responses across participants and demographic differences between participants were examined. A high degree of variability indicates a lack of consensus as to what is considered obscene, and as such indicates that a community standard may not exist. To examine variability of responses, both qualitative and quantitative analyses were utilized. First, responses to the questions asking participants to define and provide examples of obscenity were qualitatively analyzed to identify any patterns and degree of variability.

Definitions of Obscenity

Participants were asked to define obscenity and responses were coded into themes. There was not one single definition of obscenity that emerged from the data. In fact, the most common definitional theme occurred only 19% of the time. This theme was that respondents defined obscenity as vulgar language or gestures. In fact 20 of 101 respondents cited use of language in their definition. As obscene language is rarely the subject of obscenity cases, this suggests a layperson's definition of obscenity is quite different from what prosecutors and lawmakers consider obscene (or at least worthy of prosecution). Other themes, which occurred even less frequently, included context (e.g., sex in public) and subjectivity (e.g., it

2 There were few significant differences between community members and students. As such, the data is collapsed between the two groups and results are reported in aggregate.

depends on the individual). The lack of consensus indicates there may be not be one clear definition of obscenity.

Examples of Obscenity

Patterns for the question asking for specific *examples* of obscenity were similar to the responses to the question asking for the *definition* of obscenity. There was also a great deal of variability among responses when participants were asked to give examples of obscenity. The most common response was use of vulgar or obscene language, which was given by 40% of participants, reaching almost a majority consensus. Examples which included a contextual element were provided in 35% of responses. Specifically, contextual variables included different types of behavior in public or at an inappropriate place, such as cussing in church, sex in public and obscene language in front of one's mother. Despite the high number of these examples, neither reached a clear majority. Thus, there was quite a bit of variability in participants' examples of obscenity.

Variability of Obscenity Ratings

The final measure of variability was the variability of responses to ratings of potentially obscene items. An examination of the variability (i.e., standard deviations) of mean obscenity scores for the 24 items revealed that most ratings varied quite a bit. Of the 24 items, 21 of the items garnered ratings with a range of one to eight, indicating some individuals found the item not at all obscene while others rated it as highly obscene. The items with the least variability (i.e., lowest standard deviation) were websites with sexual stories about children (SD = .85) and magazines with pictures of people having sex with animals (SD = .95). Items with the most variability were magazines with nude pictures of men (SD = 2.31) and websites with sexual stories about adults (SD = 2.28). This variability indicates that a community standard may not exist. When items were sorted from the lowest means (i.e., least obscene) to the highest means (i.e., most obscene), the expected pattern of variability emerged in which the moderately obscene items had the most variability while the least or most obscene items had less variability (see Figure 1). This may show that items considered average or moderately obscene are the hardest to categorize as obscene or not obscene. This may also indicate that a ceiling effect occurred, as the lack of variability in extremes may be due to range restrictions. The average variability across all items was 1.88 (with a range of .47 to 2.26). Since the range was only seven points, standard deviations above 2.0 indicate quite a bit of variability of responses.

Demographic Differences

Multiple demographic factors were examined including hometown size, gender, and age. Hometown size was categorized as rural, suburban, urban or metropolitan. Increasing populations marked the difference between each category (i.e., rural is the smallest and metropolitan is the largest). Demographic differences can illustrate how perceptions of the community standard may change based on the makeup of a jury. These differences also indicate that community sentiment is difficult to determine because there are a lot of factors that influence it, thus creating more variability and less consensus.

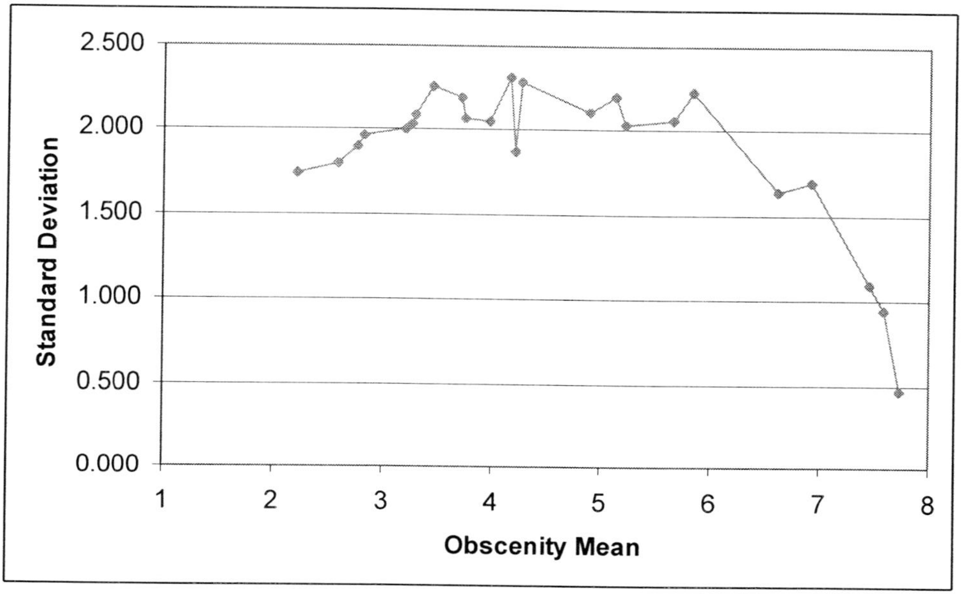

Figure 1. Patterns of Standard Deviation as Obscenity Means Increase.

Hometown Size

Despite prior research indicating that town size has an impact on obscenity ratings, (Glassman, 1978) only one difference emerged between town size and individual ratings of obscenity. Hometown size made a difference regarding how obscene individuals rated magazines with nude pictures of men, F (3, 97) = 3.41, $p < .05$. Post hoc analysis revealed that only the urban (M = 3.13, SD =2.09) and suburban (M = 4.86, SD = 2.26) groups significantly differed from each other. This pattern supports earlier research indicating more liberal ideas in larger communities (Glassman, 1978). No differences were found for hometown size on variables measuring participants' perceptions of their community's standards.

Gender

Males and females also differed in their perceptions of obscenity. For individual ratings, two items differed by gender. Females found magazines that portray group sex, t (98) = 4.99, $p < .05$, as more obscene than did males. On the other hand, males found websites with sexual stories about children, t (99) = 6.08, $p < .05$, to be more obscene than females. For perceptions of community standards of obscenity, three gender differences were found: Magazines that portray sex with animals, t (95) = 10.46, $p < .05$, movies that portray sex with corpses, $t(96) = 4.81, p < .05$, and movies with explicit homosexual scenes, $t(95) = 5.03, p < .05$. For each of these, males felt that community standards were more conservative (i.e., they thought that these objects were obscene based on community standards) than did females. Means are presented in Table 1.

Table 1. Mean Obscenity Ratings for Males Compared to Females

Variable	Mean Obscenity Rating	
	Males	Females
Individual Differences		
Magazines that portray group sex	4.89	5.86
Websites with sexual stories about children	7.90	7.60
Perceptions of Community Standards		
Magazines that portray sex with animals	7.89	7.52
Movies that portray sex with corpses	7.68	7.46
Movies with explicit homosexual scenes	7.50	6.90

Note: All scores reported are significantly different at $p < .05$.

A mixed model design was used to examine gender differences between subjects' individual ratings of obscenity of magazines with nude pictures of males compared to magazines with nude pictures of females. There was a significant interaction between obscenity ratings comparing nude pictures of males and ratings of nude pictures of females and gender, $F(1, 96) = 8.44, p < .01$. Post hoc analysis revealed that there was a significant difference in ratings of obscenity for magazines with nude pictures of males ($M = 4.39$, $SD = .438$) as compared to ratings of magazines with nude pictures of females ($M = 3.21$, $SD = .418$) for males, $F(1, 96) = 15.73, p < .001$. Simply put, males believed magazines that portray nude pictures of men were more obscene than magazines that portray nude pictures of females. However, there was no significant difference in these ratings for females $F < 1$.

Age

Despite prior research (Scott, 1991) indicating that older individuals hold more conservative views toward obscenity, age was only significantly correlated with obscenity ratings of sexually graphic language, $r = .21, p < .05$. Older individuals rated sexually graphic language as more obscene than younger individuals.

Capability of Understanding Community Standards

In order to test whether participants demonstrate a pluralistic ignorance bias, a within subjects analysis was used to compare *individual* ratings of obscenity with the corresponding perception of *community* standards of obscenity. To do this, all 24 individual ratings of obscenity were averaged to create an average individual obscenity score. Then, all 24 perceptions of community standards ratings of obscenity were averaged. These two averages were compared for differences. Overall, there was a significant difference between individual ratings of obscenity (M = 4.59, SD = 1.38) and perceptions of community standards of obscenity (M = 5.50, SD = 1.38), t (97) = -5.95, p < .001. That is, participants' ratings of obscenity were less conservative than their perceptions of community standards, demonstrating a pluralistic ignorance bias. A mixed model design was also utilized to examine gender differences in pluralistic ignorance. A significant interaction occurred between comparisons of individual and community standards of obscenity and gender F (1, 96) = 4.67, p < .05 (See Figure 2). Females' individual ratings of obscenity (M = 4.7) were closer to their community perception of obscenity (M = 5.4), while males' individual ratings of obscenity (M = 4.4) were much more liberal than their perception of community standards (M = 5.8). These analyses indicate that individuals, especially males, believe that the community is more conservative than they are personally.

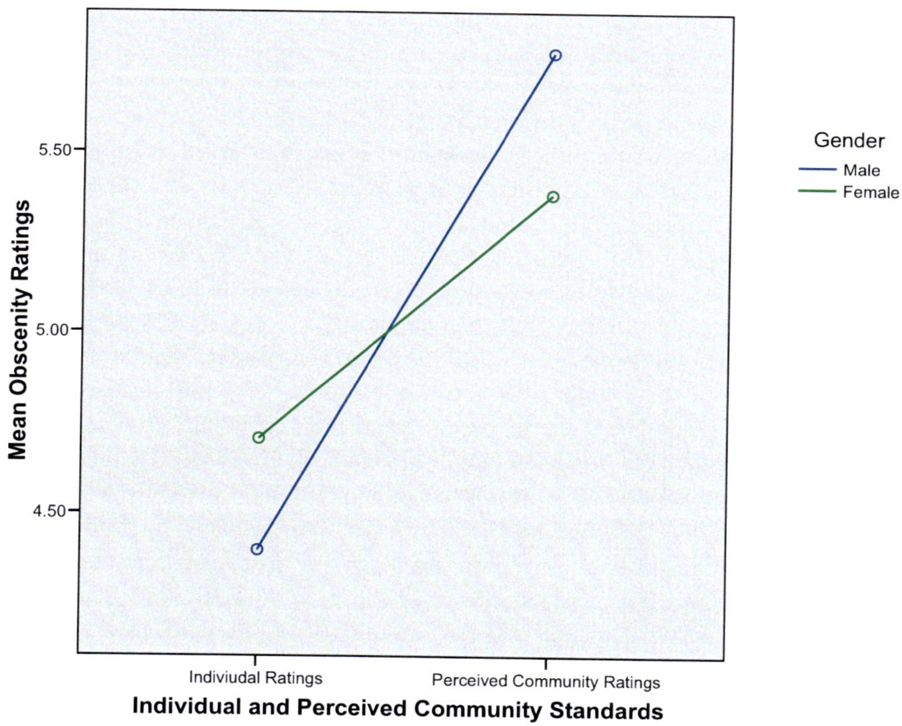

Figure 2. Gender Comparisons of Individual and Community Perceptions of Obscenity

Discussion

Results of both the qualitative and quantitative analysis reveal that there is a great deal of variability in responses as to what individuals perceive as obscene. As one participant noted, "what might be obscene to one person might be art to another." The amount of variability of responses is an indication that one set consensus (or one set standard) does not exist.

Therefore, it is difficult to say that there is a community standard of obscenity if no consensus is reached, and variability among community members is so high.

Demographic differences somewhat support this conclusion, as males and females had different perceptions on several items. Although prior research indicated that age (Scott, 1991) and town size (Glassman, 1978) were related to perceptions of obscenity, the current study only found one significant difference (out of 24 variables) for each demographic. This may be because earlier studies included a broader range of community sizes and age. Replication would be necessary with a larger sample to determine if these differences still exist.

The current research did, however, discover several key gender differences, supporting earlier research that has identified demographic differences in perception of obscenity (Scott, 1991). One particularly interesting gender difference is that males find nude pictures of women *less* obscene than nude pictures of males, an attitude that females do not share. This might be because of the patriarchal society that dominates in the United States. Women have long been objectified in the media and it is thus more acceptable, at least to males. However, the fact that women do not make this distinction could show a trend toward more feminist thoughts of equality. These gender differences also support the lack of a clearly delineated community standard. If males are more lenient than females (at least for some material), then perceived community standard would vary depending on the gender makeup of a jury, again indicating a lack of a set community standard. The majority of gender differences occurred for highly obscene items. This may be because males view their community as more conservative than it really is. Males were more likely to demonstrate a pluralistic ignorance bias than females. Simply put, men think the community is more conservative than they are personally; females do not demonstrate this difference to such a great degree.

The current study also revealed that jurors may not be the best judge of community standards. Results indicated that participants' personal ratings of obscenity were more conservative than their perceptions of community standards of obscenity, demonstrating the cognitive bias pluralistic ignorance as demonstrated in previous research (e.g., Lambert et al., 2003). Even though individuals are part of their community, they believe their views are different from the community at large. In the case of obscenity, individual ratings of obscenity are more liberal than those they perceive the community to hold. This signifies that individuals may not be aware of the 'actual' community standards (which might not even exist, as the first part of this study indicates). Therefore, in a legal case, jurors may perceive the community to be more conservative than it is in reality. This misperception of community standards might cause a jury to convict an individual of an obscenity crime, even though jurors do not personally feel he is guilty.

Implications for the Legal System

The previous findings not only demonstrate that assumptions regarding community standards (i.e., that they exist and jurors can determine them) are erroneous, but also illustrate several ways in which legal actors can influence the outcome of obscenity cases by selecting an appropriate jury or testifying as to facts related to perceptions. This study has several important implications for legal actors, such as lawyers and trial consultants. First and foremost, research in the area of community standards and obscenity suggests a need for expert testimony in court. Lawyers or consultants can hire researchers to poll local community members to determine if the material in questions should be considered obscene. Presenting this information to the jury can help jurors to better understand the actual community standards instead of their perception of community standards. This would relieve the jury from making this complex decision by relying on their beliefs about community sentiment, which can be erroneous.

Second, by identifying gender, age, and community size differences, lawyers and trial consultants can attempt to hand pick a jury that will be more lenient or harsher on obscenity laws as needed. Males considered some items less obscene than did females, suggesting that the defense should prefer male jurors and the prosecution should prefer females. However, important distinctions can be made which can provide more specific guidance for jury selection. The understanding that males consider nude images of males as more obscene than nude images of females indicates that the context of the material plays a large part in who would be a good candidate to sit on the jury. For example, if the material in question is a magazine portraying group sex, then the defense will want males on the jury, while the prosecutor will want females. However, for other items, gender would not matter.

Although age and hometown size largely were not related to perceptions of obscenity, the two analyses that reached significance showed trends that support earlier work (Glassman, 1978; Scott, 1991). Individuals, who are older or from small towns, are more conservative. These demographic differences can provide a foundation for jury selection, or at least provide knowledge of how individuals on a jury might view the obscene material.

Further, legal actors can use the understanding that the majority of examples of obscenity given by participants provide some sort of context (i.e., sex in public). In cases where it is applicable, prosecutors can remind the jury that the material in question was 'in public,' which should increase perceptions that the material in question meets the definition of obscenity. In different cases, the defense attorney could remind the jury that the material was 'in private' which should decrease perceptions that the material meets the definition of obscenity.

Finally, by understanding that individuals demonstrate pluralistic ignorance, researchers can advise lawyers as to the most effective way to frame arguments. To convince jurors to rely on their own standards (and be more lenient), defense lawyers might tell jurors that their attitudes make up the community, and are not different from community standards. Reliance on personal perceptions of obscenity should lead jurors to adopt a more lenient view of obscenity. On the other hand, prosecutors may persuade the jury to think more conservatively by applying the opposite argument. They may tell jurors that it is not their opinion that matters but that of the community. Reliance on perceptions of the community's standard for obscenity should lead jurors to adopt a more conservative view of obscenity. This knowledge can be valuable in influencing the outcome of obscenity cases.

Limitations

The study is meant to be an exploratory analysis, and thus lacks the methodological rigor of a more advanced study. As such, it has several limitations. One potential concern was the small number of ethnic minorities in the study. Because the number was so small, analysis could not be conducted comparing ethnicity. In order to gain a better understanding of ethnic differences in perceptions of obscenity, researchers should recruit a more ethnically diverse sample. On the other hand, the small number of ethnic minorities may be representative of a typical jury, depending on the community in question.

A second concern is that results are not from a random selection of community members and may thus not generalize. However, the study is meant to be exploratory and provide researchers with an initial assessment of the obscenity laws and concerns mentioned above.

A third limitation is that the study itself is not an actual mock jury study. If it were, different results might have been found. Further, the researchers did not examine the impact of group decision making, which may have changed the outcome. Group dynamics could influence juror perceptions by allowing discussion of opinions of obscenity, which may have created more conservative or more lenient opinions. This in turn would affect jury verdicts.

The final concern is that the research instrument has never been used before and thus has not been tested for reliability and validity. As prior research (Finkel, 1995) indicates that even small wording changes can influence results, the phrasing of the survey itself may have influenced results. Further, the research design was not counterbalanced. For instance, all participants rated their personal perceptions first and their perceptions of the community's standards second. Future research should vary which condition (i.e., personal perception or community perception) comes first. This would prevent any priming effect that may have occurred due to the order of questions.

Conclusions

In sum, the current research tested the assumptions of the obscenity law and found the standard lacking. Both the assumption that community standards exist and the assumption that jurors are capable of understanding community standards are flawed. Individual perceptions of obscenity do not match perceptions of community standards of obscenity, an important fact when considering the legal definition relies primarily on 'community standards.' Jurors may not be able to accurately understand community standards. In fact, a community standard may not even exist. The variability and demographic differences found indicate that there is no one standard. Further research should again test the assumptions that community standards of obscenity exist and that jurors are capable of determining these standards. If community standards do not exist or jurors are not capable of determining them, then policy makers need to take a serious look at the obscenity standard and consider revising it for the 21st century.

References

Allport, F. H. (1924). *Social psychology*. Boston: Houghton Mifflin.

Bowen, A. M., & Bourgeois, M. J. (2001). Attitudes toward lesbian, gay, and bisexual college students: The contribution of pluralistic ignorance, dynamic social impact, and contact theories. *Journal of American College Health, 50*(2), 91-96.

Duetsch, L. (June 10, 2008). LA obscenity case nauseates some potential jurors. *Associated Press*. Retrieved online July 5, 2008 from http://my.earthlink.net/article/nat?guid= 20080610/484dfc40_3ca6_1552620080610-447618930.

Finkel, N. J. (1995). *Commonsense Justice: Juror's Notions of the Law.* Cambridge, Massachusetts: Harvard University Press.

Finkel, N. J., Burke, J. E., & Chavez, L. J. (2000). Commonsense judgments of infanticide: Murder, manslaughter, madness, or miscellaneous? *Psychology, Public Policy, and Law, 6*(4), 1113-1137.

Glassman, M. B. (1978). Community standards of patent offensiveness: public opinion data and obscenity law. *Public Opinion Quarterly, 42*(2), 161-170.

Hamling v. United States, 418 U.S. 87, 94 S. Ct. 2887 (1974).

Holley, P. (1996). Obscenity and child pornography: sociology in defense of sexually oriented materials. In P. J. Jenkins & S. Kroll-Smith (Ed.) (pp. 194-210). *Witnessing for Sociology: Sociology in Court.* Westport, Connecticut: Praeger.

Jacobellis v. Ohio, 378 U.S. 184, 84 S. Ct. 1676, 12 L Ed.2d 793 (1964).

Kaplan v. California, 413 U.S. 115, 93 S. Ct. 2680 (1973).

Lambert, T. A., Kahn, A. S., & Apple, K. J. (2003). Pluralistic ignorance and hooking up. *The Journal of Sex Research, 40*(2), 129-133.

Linz, D., Donnerstein, E., Land, K. C., McCall, P. L., Scott, J., Shafer, B. J., Klein, L. J., & Lance, L. (1991). Estimating community standards: the use of social science evidence in an obscenity prosecution. *Public Opinion Quarterly, 55,* 80-112.

Miller v. California, 413 U.S. 15, 93 S. Ct. 2607 (1973).

People v. Nelson, 88 Ill.App.3d 196 (1980).

Saliba v. State, 475 N.E.2d 1181 (1985).

Scott, J. E. (1991). What is obscene? Social science and the contemporary community standard test of obscenity. *International Journal of Law and Psychiatry, 14*(1-2), 29-45.

Segrist, D. J., Corcoran, K.J., Jordan-Flemming, M. K., & Rose, P. (2007). Yeah, I drink...but not as much as other guys: The majority fallacy among male adolescents. *North American Journal of Psychology, 9*(2), 307-320.

Smith v. U.S. 431 U.S. 291 (1977).

Summers, A., & Miller, M. K. (2007). How social science can right 35 years worth of obscenity wrongs. Manuscript under review.

In: Contemporary Perspectives on Legal Regulation... ISBN 978-1-60741-161-1
Editor: Monica K. Miller

Chapter 3

A Content Analysis of Media Portrayals of Rape: Rape Myth Acceptance, Just World Beliefs, and Victim Blame

Sarah D. Merz and Monica K. Miller
University of Nevada, Reno, Nevada, USA

Abstract

The media has potential to impact consumers' attitudes, cultural norms, and legal responses to crime. For example, media reports of crime victims can outwardly suggest or subtly imply that the victim deserved the outcome. This is especially true in rape cases, because media reports sometimes suggest that the victim's behavior (e.g., being out late at night, walking alone) led to the rape. Such media reports affect readers' assignments of blame; it may also affect a victim's willingness to report a crime, a prosecutor's willingness to prosecute the accused rapist, and a jury's willingness to convict the accused rapist. A content analysis of newspaper articles reveals the most common myths reported in printed media. These include whether the attack occurred late at night, if her attacker was a friend or acquaintance, and if a newspaper article implies a victim was alone at the time of the attack. Implications for cultural norms and influence on the legal system are discussed.

Through the stories they choose to report, journalists communicate to their readers what topics are important and "newsworthy." They also communicate more subtle messages through the words they use within these stories. For instance, the words used can make the subject of the article look clumsy by stating that he "bumped" a woman, who fell and was injured; alternately, the words used can make him look villainous by stating that he "pushed" her. The choice of "bumped" or "pushed" significantly change the perception the reader has of this man. Thus, journalism has a powerful influence on readers' perceptions.

This is true of news articles that report crime, and may especially be true of stories reporting alleged rapes. Knowingly or unknowingly, journalists may encourage victim blame through choices in the details they choose to report. For instance, a reader may come to believe that the victim is at least partially at fault for her attack because the article reported that she was out alone late at night, had been drinking, or knew her assailant. If individuals are prone to such "rape myths" in general, the news article could perpetuate these myths. After reading many stories containing rape myths, readers come to believe myths and blame the victims for doing things that "cause" the rape (e.g., drinking alcohol or being out late at night). This is not to say that journalists intentionally blame the victim or perpetuate victim blame. They may be unaware of the effects of the words they use, and they may be simply following the "typical" protocol for such stories. The media has norms of what to print; including, for example stories reporting crime usually include the time and circumstances of the attack. However, occasionally these norms can lead to rape myth acceptance and victim blame. In the above example, a news article reporting that a woman was walking home alone at 2 a.m. may lead readers to blame the woman for being out alone so late at night.

This is concerning in and of itself, but it is even more concerning because such myths have far reaching ramifications for victims and the criminal justice system. When rape myths are prevalent, victims may be reluctant to report being raped, knowing that they will be blamed. Those in the justice system may also blame the victim, which could affect their behavior. Police may investigate alleged rapes less vigorously, prosecutors may be less likely to bring charges in rape cases, and juries may be less likely to convict the alleged rapist. Thus, it is important to understand whether rape myths are perpetuated in the media.

The current study is a content analysis of media articles from 1977 to 2007. The intent is to determine how often the victim is described in the article (i.e., was there any information given about the victim), and whether this prevalence has changed over the years. Next, the research will identify the most common rape myths found in the sample of articles, and whether the prevalence of rape myths changed over the years. Finally, this study will determine how often articles encourage just world beliefs (i.e., describe a victim's "negative character" or "her behavior after the crime"), and identify the most common just world themes among these articles.

The results will indicate whether the media should consider revising the way they report rape crimes; specifically, journalists may adopt policies which omit certain details which might encourage victim blame and rape myth acceptance.

Media Effects on the Public and Jurors

The media can affect public attitudes toward crime and punishment. Redman and Taylor (2000) note that media portrayals of child spanking can influence whether the public perceives spanking to be a legitimate parental practice. Media can affect jurors attitudes and beliefs in general (Greene, 1990) and can even affect jurors' attitudes toward specific defendants, as represented in decades of pretrial publicity research (Steblay, Besirevic, Fulero, & Jimenez-Lorente, 1999). Thus, it is important to understand how the media communicates information about rapes in order to understand how they might affect public and juror sentiment.

Rape Myth Acceptance

Rape myths foster trivialization and justification of men's sexual aggression against women (Bohner, Siebler, & Schmelcher, 2006). The common theme in these myths is that rape victims are deserving of the violent act that was committed against them; for instance one rape myth is indicated by agreement with the statement "If a girl engages in necking or petting and she lets things get out of hand, it is her own fault if her partner forces sex on her" (Burt, 1980). Additionally, these myths suggest the innocence of rapists; this is indicated by agreement with statements such as "Any healthy woman can successfully resist a rapist is she really wants to." Rape myths also minimize the violence that is often characteristic of rape; this belief leads to agreement with statements such as "Many women have an unconscious wish to be raped." Such myths are widely held in our society (Burt & Albin, 1982; Gilmartin-Zena, 1994) and can lead to dangerous outcomes. Rape attitudes are strongly correlated with acceptance of interpersonal violence, distrust of the opposite sex, and sex role stereotyping (Burt, 1980). Acceptance of interpersonal violence includes legitimizing force and coercion as ways to gain compliance in intimate and sexual relationships. Therefore, damaging effects of accepting rape myths and interpersonal violence include denying the perceived injury to rape victims, as well as blaming them for their own victimization (Burt, 1980). Additionally, studies have shown that rape myth acceptance is associated with higher levels of victim condemnation and defendant acquittals (Burt & Albin, 1981; Kramer, 1994).

The current research will determine whether a variety of common rape myths are portrayed in newspaper articles describing sexual assaults, and whether these have changed over time.

Belief in a Just World

People often believe that individuals get what they deserve. In other words, bad things happen to bad people, and good things happen to good people (Lerner, 1965). This "belief in a just world" proves problematic when individuals blame victims of crime. Victim blame may occur because a strong belief in a just world often includes the denial of observed injustices (Furnham & Procter, 1989). People may either believe that the victim's suffering is not taking place (or is highly exaggerated), or believe the victim is blameworthy. For example, many Germans living under the Nazi regime have denied the Holocaust's occurrence, or concluded that those murdered were impure and deserving of their fate (Hallie, 1971). This example illustrates the extent to which people will rationalize violent injustices. In these cases, a belief in a just world prompts individuals to cognitively "right social wrongs" (Rubin & Peplau, 1975). Instead of conceptualizing injustices as random occurrences, the belief in a just world leads people to blame the unfortunate and suffering. For example, Lerner and Simmons (1966) found that if an observer is unable to stop another's suffering, this observer often chooses to devalue and reject the victim.

Those who believe in a just world might be more likely to blame victims of crimes, such as rape. Rape is a particularly violent crime, and victims often experience serious physical and emotional suffering (Burgess & Holmstrom, 1974). Upon hearing about a victim's suffering, individuals who believe in a just world may be more likely to blame the victim than those who do not adhere to such a philosophy. They may seek out the victim's faults or mistakes, which make her look like a "bad" person who deserves to experience bad things. This is comforting, because it makes the rape look less random and allows perceivers to believe that they will never be victimized because they are "good" people. Although this form of self preservation may be useful in calming one's fears, it also can have detrimental effects. For example, the belief in a just world can result in a guilty defendant's acquittal.

Rape myth acceptance may encourage just world beliefs and victim blame. For example, believing a rape victim's behavior encouraged her attack places blame on the victim, and may further promote the belief that she deserved to be victimized. In fact, studies have shown that attending to victim characteristics, rather than the descriptions of the attacker, can increase the likelihood of blaming victims of rape (Branscombe, Owen, Carstka & Coleman, 1996; Tendayi Viki & Abrams, 2002; Workman & Freeburg, 1999). The current study will investigate the extent to which newspaper articles promote just world beliefs, for instance by portraying the victim in a negative light (e.g., by pointing out that she was a prostitute or an alcoholic). By providing negative character information, the media may encourage readers to presume that the victim was a bad person, and that explains why something bad happened to her. This study will determine the frequency that newspaper articles report details of rapes and the victims that could encourage rape myth acceptance and just world beliefs, which in turn could lead to victim blame.

Overview of Study

By analyzing newspaper articles which report alleged rapes, this study measured the frequency that articles provide details that could promote rape myths, just world beliefs and victim blame. This qualitative and quantitative analysis identified various rape myths included in these articles, as well as their frequency in four decades.

Method

Researchers searched Lexis Nexis using the keywords, "rape*," and "sexual* assault*."[1] It would be unfeasible to analyze every article from 30 years, so a small sample was taken from each decade. In order to obtain a sample from different decades, we included articles published in 1977, 1987, 1997, and 2007. These years were chosen because researchers wanted to examine possible trends over time, for instance, to determine whether rape myths were more common in one time period than another. Therefore, a span of thirty years was chosen, with each particular year representing that respective decade.

Researchers began searching for appropriate articles in January of each of these years, searching until 40 appropriate articles were found. The same was done for July of each year chosen. If 40 articles were not available in January, articles from February were also chosen, and if 40 articles were not available in July, articles from August were also included. Researchers chose summer and winter months so different times of the year would be represented. It is possible that some rape myths would not be as frequent during certain

1 Asterisks are 'wild cards' which tell the search engine to find any word beginning with those letters. So the search term "rape*" would find articles which use the terms "rape" and "raped."

seasons; for instance women might be less likely to be out late at night in the winter in very cold climates. To avoid any effects due to differences in behavior that might be related to the season, researchers took samples from both winter and summer.

For the analysis, researchers chose articles that focused on a particular crime of rape. Articles were considered appropriate if they described sexual crimes against a female victim with at least minimal details about the crime. For example, "A woman was walking home when a man raped her..." would constitute "minimal detail" about the crime. Articles that did not contain minimal detail about the crime were left out because they were not considered to be "articles about rape crimes." For instance, an article that simply stated "John Doe was accused of rape" was not considered to be an article about the crime because it was only mentioned in that one sentence. Articles with male victims were not included because little is known about how individuals think about male victims. While much research has investigated rape myths and just world beliefs about rape, these have focused on female victims. It is possible, even likely, that male victims provoke different kinds of rape myths and other beliefs. Because these remain unstudied, the few articles describing male victims were omitted from the study.

The coding process was designed to determine whether articles just contained descriptions of the attack, or if they gave details regarding the female victim that implicitly or explicitly promote rape myths and the belief in a just world. Thus, it was necessary to create a codebook which would allow us to measure whether each article contained "variables" related to rape myths and just world beliefs.

To create a codebook, researchers read through the past journal articles that discussed factors that suggest rape myth acceptance (RMA) (Burt, 1980) and belief in a just world (BJW) (Lerner, 1965; Lerner & Simmons, 1966). These items were selected for the codebook (see Table 1). Coders practiced coding articles using the codebook, and added several new variables as a result of the practice. Specifically, when a researcher read an article that included a possible RMA or BJW factor that was not in the codebook, the researchers would discuss whether it should be included. If they agreed that the factor was an indicator of RMA or BJW, it was added to the codebook. Several open ended items were included, in case an article included an element that suggested RMA or BJW that had not been included in the codebook.

Four coders participated. One was a male undergraduate student in his 20s, one a female graduate student in her 20s, and two females (one professor and one undergraduate student) both over 30. All were Caucasian. The coding process began with all coders coding the same 15 articles. After the reliability check determined that the coders were coding very similarly, the remaining articles were only coded by one coder. Each coder coded approximately the same number of articles from each decade. A database was established to enter in responses for each item in the code book. The four coders' data were combined into a complete database, which was used for analysis.

Table 1. Rape Article Variables

Variable name	Operational definition	How measured	Frequency	Rational For Variable Inclusion
Year	Year of article publication	1977, 1987, 1997, or 2007		To determine possible trends over time
Info about victim	If the article gives any detail(s) about the victim	0=no information 1=at least minimal information	223/261 (85.4%)	To examine if reporters protect victims by not giving information about them
Alcohol or drugs	If the article describes if the victim used alcohol or drugs	0=no 1=yes	29/261 (11.2%)	Aspect of RM that women who get drunk and have intercourse are "fair game"
Party, bar or club	If the article stated the victim was at a bar, party, or club	0=no 1=yes	28/261 (10.7%)	Infers that drinking or inappropriate behavior that "asks for rape" according to RM
Night	If attack occurred at night 10pm to 6am, or terms such as "at night" or "early morning hours". Excludes terms such as "evening"	0=no 1=yes 99=can't tell	87/261 (33.5%)	Aspect of RM that women put themselves in situations where they are likely to be attacked
Went with attacker	If victim voluntarily went with attacker	0=no 1=yes	34/261 (13%)	Aspect of the RM that hitchhikers who get raped get what is deserved
Abducted	If victim was abducted by attacker	0=no 1=yes	51/261 (19.5%)	Opposite of the RM that women who willingly accompany their attacker are deserving
Danced	If victim danced with attacker	0=no 1=yes	2/261 (.8%)	Infers a RM that victims allowed things to "get out of hand"
Flirted/Talked	If victim flirted/talked with attacker	0=no 1=yes	14/261 (5.4%)	Infers a RM that victims allowed things to "get out of hand"
Clothing	Article gave description of victim's clothing	0=no 1=yes	7/261 (2.7%)	Aspect of RM that women who wear provocative clothing are asking to be raped

Table 1. Continued

Variable name	Operational definition	How measured	Frequency	Rational For Variable Inclusion
Previous sexual relations	If victim had previous sexual relations with attacker	0=no 1=yes	15/261 (5.8%)	Infers BJW that it couldn't have been a true rape if victim was familiar with attacker
Friend/Acquaintance	If victim was an acquaintance or friend of attacker	0=no 1=yes	50/261 (19.2%)	Infers BJW that it couldn't have been a true rape if victim was familiar with attacker
Negative Character	Article describes victim's negative character	Written in by coder	Common Themes: Accepted ride/Hitchhiked , Previous drug/alcohol abuse	Aspect of RM that majority of victims have bad reputations; Also infers BJW that victims get what they deserve
Behavior after rape	Victim's behavior after the rape infers that it was not rape	Written in by coder	Common Themes: Didn't report immediately, Couldn't Identify Attacker at first	Aspect of RM that women often falsely accuse men of rape
Alone	If article explicitly states the victim was alone	0=no 1=yes	19/261 (7.3%)	Aspect of RM that women put themselves in situations where they are likely to be attacked;
Implied alone	If article implies that the victim was alone	0=no 1=yes	181/261 (70.2%)	Aspect of RM that women put themselves in situations where they are likely to be attacked; Also BJW that victims get what they deserve

Research Questions

Research Question 1: How often is the victim described in the article (i.e., was there any information given about the victim)? Has this prevalence changed over the years?

Research Question 2: What are the most common rape myths found in the sample of articles? Has the prevalence of rape myths changed over the years?

Research Question 3: What types of just world beliefs are conveyed (e.g., by describe a victim's "negative character" or "her behavior after the crime")? What are the most common themes among these articles?

Sample

The sample consisted of articles from 29 states; Alaska, Alabama, Arkansas, California, Colorado, Connecticut, Washington DC, Florida, Georgia, Illinois, Iowa, Louisiana, Maryland, Massachusetts, Missouri, North Carolina, New Mexico, New York, New Jersey, Oklahoma, Pennsylvania, Rhode Island, South Carolina, Texas, Tennesse, Utah, Washington, West Virginia, and Wisconsin. Each state had at least one article included in the sample.

The sample of 261 articles included descriptions of 81 victims from 1987, 79 from 1997, and 101 from 2007. The number of victims varied because one article could discuss multiple victims, or an article could describe the crime but not the victim. Articles from 1977 were omitted, due to the lack of relevant articles available. The lack of articles reporting rapes in 1977 does not necessarily reflect a decrease in rapes during this year, nor does it reflect a small number of articles reporting such crimes. Conversely, it is likely that the database's archives do not contain as large a selection of articles from 1977 as they do for more recent years.

Results and Discussion

Research question 1 asked how often the victim was described in an article; specifically, if there was any information given about her. In 223 of 261 (85%) of the articles, the victim is described in at least minimal detail (e.g., providing her age). Pearson's Chi Square indicated that whether information was provided or not did not vary by year ($p > .05$).

Although information printed about victims has not increased over time, such information has not decreased either. Furthermore, the majority of articles did include at least minimal information about these women. This finding indicates that the victim and her behavior are still the main foci of newspaper reports of sexual assaults and rapes. The inclusion of victim characteristics may further imply victim blame. For example, a report describing a woman who willingly took a ride from her rapist is likely interpreted differently than report of a woman who was abducted by her attacker. In both cases, women were forcibly raped. However, stating that a woman chose to accompany her attacker implies a risky choice, further suggesting a certain level of victim responsibility. Additionally, characteristics irrelevant to the present crime (i.e., the victim was a recovering drug addict) suggests victim condemnation. Such negative characteristics detract from the other relevant facts of the crime, such as her injuries, or the attacker's behavior.

Research question 2 asked which rape myths were most common in the sample of articles, and if the prevalence of rape myths have changed over the years. The most often cited rape myths included when the victim was out at night (33.5%), was a friend or acquaintance of her attacker (19.2%), and if the author implied that the victim was alone at the time of her attack (70.2%). Statistical analyses indicate that the prevalence of these factors did not change over time. Although none of the trends were statistically significant, general trends over time revealed an increase from 1987 to 2007 in reports that the victim used alcohol and/or drugs, was at a party or bar, was a friend or acquaintance of her attacker, was wearing revealing clothing, and was flirting with her attacker (see Table 2).

Table 2. Rape Myth Frequencies

Rape Myths	1987	1997	2007
Flirting/Talking	N=1/81 (1.2%)	N=6/79 (7.6%)	N=7/101 (6.9%)
Clothing	N=1/81 (1.2%)	N=2/79 (2.5%)	N=4/101 (4%)
Alcohol/drugs	N=4/81 (4.9%)	N=11/79 (13.9%)	N=14/101 13.9%)
Late at Night	N=39/81 (48.1%)	N=23/78 (29.5%)	N=25/101 (24.8%)
Party or Bar	N=6/81 (7.4%)	N=10/79 (12.7%)	N=12/101 (11.9%)
Alone	N=7/81 (8.6%)	N=4/79 (5.1%)	N=7/101 (6.9%)
Implied Alone	N=58/81 (71.6%)	N=59/79 (74.7%)	N=64/101 (63.4%)
Previous Sexual Partner	N=5/81 (6.2%)	N=6/79 (7.6%)	N=4/101 (4%)

Some RMA variables appear to have increased within the 20 year period, although results were not statistically significant. Rape myths are defined by the cultural functions they serve, such as trivializing or justifying sexual violence against women (Abrams, Tendayi Viki, Masser, & Bohner, 2003). According to the results of this study, trends over time may indicate an increase in support of violence against women. However, if this is true, the legal system may be attempting to protect victims, despite the possible increase in rape myth acceptance. For example, instead of the traditional non-legal definition of "carnal knowledge (penile-vaginal penetration only) of a female forcibly and against her will," many states have develped rape laws that include broader definitions (Crowell & Burgess, 1996). These reforms include broadening the definition of penetration (now including vaginal, anal, and oral), focusing on the offender's behavior rather than the victim's level of resistance, and making the victim's prior sexual conduct inadmissible in court (Crowell & Burgess, 1996). These changes reflect a change in legal attitudes toward rape victims. By broadening the definition of rape, this also increases the number of "legitimate" rape victims, as more forcible sex acts have become illegal. Additionally, focusing on the offender's behavior, rather than the victim's, indicates a shift in perpetrator, versus victim, culpability. Instead of examining how victims could have prevented their attack, focusing on the attacker's behavior decreases victim blame. There seems to have been an increase in legal reform (regarding the legal definition of rape), however the present study did not find similar reforms in media reports of rape. Although the newspaper articles did not reflect an increase in reported rape myths, there was no observed decrease over time.

Research question 3 investigated the types of just world beliefs (i.e., describing a victim's "negative character" or "her behavior after the crime") contained in articles. Although there were not enough articles from 1977 to include in the previous statistical analyses, articles from this year were used for research question 3's qualitative analysis. Analyses revealed "negative character" themes of the victim's past use of drugs and alcohol, and that the victim willingly went with her attacker (i.e., hitchhiked). Common themes regarding the victim's behavior after the crime include her waiting to report the attack, if her story changed over time, and that she could not readily identify her attacker.

All of these factors may increase victim blame in rape cases; for instance, whether the victim willingly spent time alone with her attacker. This may explain why acquaintance and date rapes are harder for a prosecutor to get a conviction for than stranger rapes. For example, those who score high in rape myth acceptance believe that a woman who goes to the home or apartment of a man on their first date is willing to have sex (Burt, 1980). Several articles in the sample described victims who willingly went to their attacker's residence, or accepted a ride. Consequently, choosing to include this information when describing a rape may perpetuate rape myth acceptance.

In addition, describing the victim's behavior may support the belief in a just world. The primary component of just world beliefs is that people get what they deserve and that bad things only happen to bad people. Therefore, implying that a victim chose to put herself in a risky situation preserves an observer's sense of security that the same crime will not happen to them. In other words, rape myths serve to deny personal vulnerability, especially for women (Lonsway & Fitzgerald, 1995). A woman may think she has less of a chance of being attacked if she believes that certain behaviors encourage rape. For example, if "bad" women engage in "bad behaviors," such as walking alone at night, "good" women who do not go out alone should remain safe. In this case, rape myths help support just world beliefs, and vice versa.

One of the most detrimental effects of just world beliefs is how they can affect many areas of the legal system. If victims blame themselves, and feel they were somewhat deserving of the rape, they may be reluctant to report the crime to authorities. Police may be less willing to investigate an alleged rape, and prosecutors may be reluctant to prosecute rapes because they assume jurors will hold victims partially responsible. This may particularly likely in cases where the victim knew her attacker, such as in acquaintance or date rapes. Finally, jurors may wish to maintain their own sense of safety by blaming victims of rape. Jurors may presume that, if a woman acted inappropriately and was later raped, a similar crime would not happen to those who do act appropriately. Victim blame may help jurors feel safe, but can result in a low rate of rape convictions. Therefore, media reports that support just world beliefs may have a significant impact on legal actions against rapists.

Limitations

There are several limitations to the current study. First, the sampled articles include a small percentage of articles published in 1977, 1987, 1997, and 2007. Only some analyses utilized the 1977 data because of the small number of articles in that year. Researchers used one particular database, Lexis-Nexis, which may have had limited the quantity and type of archived articles available. Therefore, a large percentage of articles describing rapes may have been excluded, simply because a particular newspaper chose not to archive their articles in Lexix-Nexis. Second, the sample included newspaper articles, and did not contain other forms of media (e.g., magazine articles, transcripts from newscasts, commentaries). The use of rape myths may be either more or less prominent in these media outlets. Consequently, results from this study can not generalize to widespread media effects. Finally, the rape myth variables were taken from the original rape myth acceptance scale, published in 1980 (Burt, 1980). Using these rape myths may not account for changes in cultural norms in the past three decades. As a result of changing cultural norms and laws regarding sexual behavior, it is likely that there are additional rape myths that fit with current social conditions, but were not included in the current study. On the other hand, some myths that existed in 1980 may not be as prevalent in current society; thus we may have measured for a RMA variable that no longer is such.

Most importantly, this study only measured the presence of possible RMA and BJW variables. It did not measure whether readers actually perceive these to be RMA and BJW factors. That is, we are making an assumption that the factors in newspapers actually do increase RMA and BJW. For instance, we assumed that reading about a woman who was hitchhiking alone at night and took a ride from a man who later raped her will lead a reader to blame the victim. Future study is needed to test these assumptions. Despite the limitations, results from this study can help to inform the legal system how current rape myths that are reported in the newspapers may disadvantage sexual assault victims by encouraging readers to blame the victim.

CONCLUSION AND RECOMMENDATIONS

Promoting rape myth acceptance and just world beliefs can have serious consequences for rape victims. In order to avoid such risks, journalists should change their policies so as to not print RMA and BJW factors when reporting crimes of rape. Journalists can accomplish this by limiting what they print about victims. Many media outlets have policies that prevent reports that include the name of child victims. Similar policies could be adopted to protect rape victims that bar the media from reporting details about rape victims. This may lead to less victim blame in society, including victims, police, prosecutors, and jurors.

If the media reports fewer RMA and BJW details, then victims may feel less like they will be treated negatively in the news and by others (e.g., police). Due to ambiguous terminology and stereotypes about rape, some victims may be reluctant to report their rape (Hamby & Koss, 2003). For example, some women who describe sexual experiences as "forced sex" will not label those experiences as "rape" (Percy & Mayhew, 1997). Additionally, some women only label forced sexual encounters as "rape" if the attacker is a stranger, rather than an acquaintance or friend (Resnick, Kilpatrick, Dansky, Saunders, & Best, 1993). These may be reasons why victims wait to report their attack, will not readily identify their attacker, or may change their accounts of the attack over time. However, if the media includes this information in articles describing rapes, this can lead the public to doubt victims' honesty. Furthermore, such reporting supports the rape myth that a large percentage of women who report rape are lying, either to get back at the man they accuse, or to protect their reputation (Burt, 1980).

Victim blame may decrease prosecutors' confidence in pursuing cases against perpetrators and encourage jurors to focus on a victim's behavior, rather than the defendant's. Police may also be reluctant to investigate rapes in which they think the victim is partially to blame. Therefore, additional education regarding rape myths should be included in police and prosecutors training. Such training should consist of current rape myths held by society, and how such myths can be perpetuated by the media. If authorities are aware of potential biases, they may be less likely to use them when deciding whether to pursue rape crimes. Furthermore, when a rape case goes to trial, judges should encourage jurors to focus on the defendant's behavior, rather than the victim's (e.g., her character, clothing at the time of attack, past sexual history). Judges could also prohibit defense attorneys from using such information in their arguments. Consequently, such actions should result in an increased number of legal sanctions for rapists.

Even without policies such as these, there are steps journalists and other media reporters can take to neutrally describe crimes and their victims, without perpetuating rape myth acceptance. For instance, changes in legal definitions of rape may reflect the legal system's attempt to decrease victim blame. However, a change in how society views rape victims also needs to occur. Although this study did not reveal a statistically significant increase in the frequency of newspapers use of rape myths, the current use of *any* rape myth is still alarming (see Table 2). If there is a cultural norm of blaming rape victims through rape myth acceptance, jurors sitting on a rape trial will likely use these myths when making legal judgments. One possible way to decrease the norm of victim blame is for the media to carefully examine their use of rape myths, and focus less on the victim's behavior, and more on the actions of the perpetrator.

REFERENCES

Abrams, D., Tendayi Viki, G., Masser, B. M., & Bohner, G. (2003). Perceptions of stranger and acquaintance rape: The role of benevolent and hostile sexism in victim blame and rape proclivity, *Journal of Personality and Social Psychology, 84,* 111-125.

Burgess, A. W., & Holmstrom, L. L. (1974). Rape trauma syndrome, *American Journal of Psychiatry, 131*, 981-986.

Bohner, G., Siebler, F., & Schmelcher, J. (2006). Social norms and the likelihood of raping: Perceived rape myth acceptance of others affects men's rape proclivity. *Personality and Social Psychology Bulletin, 32,* 286-297.

Branscombe, N. R., Owen, S., Garstka, T. A., & Coleman, J. (1996). Rape and accident counterfactuals: Who might have done otherwise and would it have changed the outcome? *Journal of Applied Social Psychology, 26,* 1042-1067.

Burt, M. R., & Albin, R. S. (1981). Rape myths: Rape definitions and probability of conviction. *Journal of Applied Psychology, 11*, 212-230.

Burt, M. R. (1980). Cultural myths and supports for rape. *Journal of Personality and Social Psychology, 38,* 217-230.

Crowell, N. A., & Burgess, A. W. (1996). Understanding violence against women. National Academies Press.

Furnham, A., & Procter, E. (1989). Belief in a just world: Review and critique of the individual difference literature. *British Journal of Social Psychology, 28*, 365-384.

Gilmartin-Zena, P. (1994). Gender differences in college students' perceptions about rape: The results of a quasi-experimental research design. *Free Inquiry in Creative Sociology, 22,* 2-12.

Greene, E. (1990). Media Effects on Jurors. *Law and Human Behavior, 14*, 439-450.

Hallie, P. P. (1971). Justification and rebellion. In N. Sanford & C. Comstock (Eds.), *Sanctions for evil.* San Francisco: Josey-Bass.

Hamby, S. L., & Koss, M. P. (2003). Shades of gray: A Qualitative study of terms used in the measurement of sexual victimization. *Psychology of Women's Quarterly, 27,* 243-255.

Kramer, K. M. (1994). Rule by myth: The social and legal dynamics governing alcohol-related rape. *Stanford Law Review, 47,* 115-160.

Lerner, M. (1965). Evaluation of performance as a function of performer's reward and attractiveness. *Journal of Personality and Social Psychology, 1,* 355-360.

Lerner, M., J. & Simmons, C. H. (1966). The observer's reaction to the "innocent victim": Compassion or rejection? *Journal of Personality and Social Psychology, 4,* 203-210.

Lonsway, K. A., & Fitzgerald, L. F. (1995). Attitudinal antecedents of rape myth acceptance: A theoretical and empirical reexamination. *Journal of Personality and Social Psychology, 68,* 714-711.

Percy, A., & Mayhew, P. (1997). Estimating sexual victimization in a national survey: A new approach. *Studies on Crime and Prevention, 6,* 125-150.

Redman, S., & Taylor, J. (2000). Legitimate family violence as represented in the print media: Textual analysis. *Journal of Advanced Nursing, 56,* 157-165.

Resnick, H. S., Kilpatrick, D. G., Dansky, B. S., Saunders, B. E., & Best, C. L. (1993). Prevalence of civilian trauma and post traumatic stress disorder in a representative national sample of women. *Journal of Consulting and Clinical Psychology, 61,* 984-991.

Rubin, Z., & Peplau, L. A. (1975). Who believes in a just world? *Journal of Social Issues, 31,* 65-89.

Steblay, N. M., Besirevic, J., Fulero, S..M., & Jimenez-Lorente, B. (1999). The effects of pretrial publicity on juror verdicts: A meta-analytic review. *Law and Human Behavior, 23,* 219-235.

Tendayi Viki, G., & Abrams, D. (2002). But she was unfaithful: Benevolent sexism and reactions to rape victims who violate traditional gender role expectations, *Sex Roles, 47,* 289-293.

Workman, J. E., & Freeburg, E. W. (1999). An examination of date rape, victim dress, and perceiver, variables within the context of attribution theory, *Sex Roles, 41,* 261-277.

In: Contemporary Perspectives on Legal Regulation... ISBN 978-1-60741-161-1
Editor: Monica K. Miller

Chapter 4

RECENT JUDICIAL RULINGS IN VOLUNTARY UNDERAGE SEX CASES: ANALYSIS OF LEGAL CASE STUDIES AND POLICY IMPLICATIONS

Sarah D. Merz and Monica K. Miller
University of Nevada, Reno, Nevada, USA

ABSTRACT

Recently, legal cases involving consensual sex between minor females and young males have received national media attention. An analysis of eight high profile case studies revealed a variety of outcomes in consensual underage sex prosecutions. It compares and contrasts recent cases involving consensual sexual encounters. Results indicate that factors such as age disparity, marriage and pregnancy do not have uniform effects on sentences that young men receive. Psychologists can provide research on how to avoid such sentencing inconsistencies and suggestions for how psychologists can help policymakers create better laws are provided. For example, psychologists can help determine appropriate legal action for these young men, while also aiding lawmakers in weighing the potential economic consequences for minors involved in sex prosecutions.

The recent announcement of 16 year-old actress Jamie Lynn Spears' pregnancy has prompted some to examine how the legal system deals with voluntary underage sex ("Jamie Lynn Spears pregnancy raises legal questions," 2007). In Spears' hometown in Louisiana, it is illegal for a 17-19 year-old to engage in consensual sex with a minor, age 15-19, if the age disparity is more than 2 years. However, even though Spears has named the 19 year-old father of her unborn child, there has been no mention of possible legal action against him. The decision not to prosecute may be due to Spears' parental approval of the relationship, or that there is a pregnancy is involved. However, other young men have been legally sanctioned for similar acts.

Rates of teenage sex have declined in recent years (Kaiser Family Foundation, 2005), but other concerns remain, for instance teen pregnancies spiked in 2006 ("Report: Teen pregnancies up for first time in 15 years, 2008). Underage sexual behavior remains a popular discussion for lawmakers, policy makers, religious leaders and the media (see Colb, 2007; Levesque, 2001). Recently, the media has highlighted numerous cases involving teenage and young adult males convicted for voluntary sexual acts with minor females. Some cases receiving a great deal of coverage involve young men who are incarcerated for having voluntary sex with minors. Such cases have brought national attention to the laws regulating minors' sexual activity and have resulted in mixed public opinion with regards to their legitimacy and fairness (Mehta, 1998; Oberman, 2000).

Most states have statutory rape laws that punish adults who engage in sexual activity with minors; some also have laws that punish minors for having sex with other minors (Sutherland, 2003). Prosecutors also use other laws (e.g., commission of a lewd act) to prosecute those who have sex with minors. Almost all states set an age limit at which a person can legally "consent" to having sex (Levesque, 2000). Even if a young female under this age wants to have sex, she cannot legally consent to the act. Thus, the term "consensual" is used in this article to mean that the female wanted to have sex with the young male (as opposed to referring to "consensual" in the legal sense).

Laws governing underage sexual activity are designed in part to protect minors by communicating social values about sexual behavior. This philosophy is essentially a moral one; the judicial system punishes those who violate norms concerning appropriate sexual partners. Simply put, some lawmakers have determined that it is inappropriate for minors to have sex. Complexities arise, however, when the sexual act is consensual, the female gets pregnant, the couple marries, or there is little age difference between the partners. Due to differences in jurisdictions, prosecutors' discretion, and varying social and contextual factors (i.e., ages of both parties, whether the couple is married) these cases can result in disparate legal outcomes (e.g., prison time or probation) across cases. The purpose of this article is to summarize legal case studies, to determine what social and contextual factors might predict case outcome, and to suggest ways in which psychologists can help policymakers create better laws.

METHOD

The goal of data collection was to identify high profile legal cases involving consensual sex between minor females and teenaged or young adult males. Legal cases were found through an internet news search. Cases were chosen if they involved consensual activity between a minor female and a teenaged or young adult male, recently received media attention, and if the male has been legally charged from 2001 to 2007. Eight cases matched these criteria and all were chosen. Cases were coded for the following variables: age of both parties, relationship (i.e., marriage of the parties), whether a pregnancy occurred, and whether parents approved of the relationship. Each legal case study is summarized in Table 1.

Table 1. Summary of legal case studies

Defendant Name	Female Age	Male Age	Parental Permission	Marriage	Pregnancy	Outcome
Koso	14	23	yes	yes	yes	30 months prison
Dixon	15	18	no	no	no	15 months prison
Wilson	15	17	no	no	no	10 years prison; must register as offender (he has been released and doesn't have to register)
Boudreau	13	17	yes	yes	yes	1 year probation
Stellini	15	16	no	no	yes	6 mo court supervision, community service
Harer	15	17	unknown	no	no	1year probation; possibly removed from record
Dencs	13	18	no	no	no	10 years in prison
Tenant	16	27	yes	no	no	plead guilty to sexual misconduct (sentence pending)

Note. Outcome listed is maximum sentence.

Summary of Legal Case Studies Involving High Profile Underage Sex Prosecutions

These eight recent high profile legal case summaries illustrate the variety of ways that prosecutors have addressed underage sexual behavior. A 2005 Nebraska case involved a sexual relationship between 23 year-old Matthew Koso and his 14 year-old girlfriend. When she became pregnant, they decided to get married; however, they lived in Nebraska, where the age of consent to marry (with parental permission) was 17. Therefore, they crossed the state line to Kansas, where the age of consent to marry with parental permission was 12 (since this case, Kansas has changed the age to 16). With permission from the young woman's mother, the couple married and returned to Nebraska. Soon thereafter, Koso was arrested ("Man Weds 14-Year-Old," 2005). According to Nebraska law, a person commits sexual assault of a child if he or she "subjects another person fourteen years of age or younger to sexual contact and the actor is at least nineteen years of age or older" (Nebraska code §28-320.0145 (2006)). The pregnancy proved that they had engaged in sexual activity, and the marriage did not prevent the prosecution. Consequently, Koso was charged with first degree sexual assault and sentenced to 18-30 months in prison (Mabin, 2006).

In 2003, a Georgia case received national attention. Marcus Dixon, an 18 year-old male was sentenced to ten years in prison for aggravated child molestation for having consensual intercourse with a 15 year-old female. However, his sentence was overturned because the Georgia Supreme Court decided that the law was not intended to punish consensual sex between minors (*Dixon v. Georgia*, 2004). After this decision was handed down, Dixon was released, having spent 15 months in jail (Hart, 2004).

In 2005, another consensual sex case resulted in prison time for the defendant. Genarlow Wilson, 17, was accused of rape and aggravated child molestation for a consensual act of oral sex with a 15 year-old (Colb, 2007). A Georgia jury acquitted him of rape, but convicted him on the molestation charge. He received a ten year sentence, one year probation and is required to register as a sex offender for the rest of his life. Because Wilson engaged in oral sex (and not intercourse) with the minor, he could not benefit from the Dixon precedent (which only applied to intercourse). After the Wilson case, the Georgia legislature passed a bill, H.B. 1059, which limited the sentences in cases similar to Wilson's to one year of incarceration. However, this law could not benefit Wilson because it does not apply to those who were already convicted prior to the change in law (H.B. 1059, 2006). In March, 2007, a Georgia Senate committee approved a bill that would allow a judge to review underage sex cases such as Wilson's and adjust sentences that the judge rules are too harsh (SB 37; 2007). The bill proposed to amend O.C.B.A. § 17-10-1(f) would also allow for the review and adjustment of sentences that were handed down prior to the passage of the H.B.1059 (2006). The Georgia Senate did not vote on the bill in time for it to be passed in the 2007 session; thus, the bill was in limbo (Georgia General Assembly, 2007). However, the Georgia Supreme Court has since ruled that Wilson's sentence was cruel and unusual punishment. After serving more than 2 years in prison, Wilson was released and will not have to register as a sex offender ("Wilson released after two years behind bars for teen sex conviction," 2007).

More recently, in Florida, Tamas Dencs, 18, was sentenced to 8 3/4 years in prison for committing lewd and lascivious battery against his 13 year-old girlfriend (Swift, 2008). The minor's parents disapproved of their relationship when their daughter was 12, and obtained an injunction, barring Dencs from seeing her. After the minor's father found them having intercourse (by this time, the minor was 13), he reported Dencs to the police. Dencs also received an additional 1 ¼ years for violating the injunction to stay away from his girlfriend (Swift, 2008).

Not every case resulted in a lengthy prison sentence, however. In 1998, Chris Boudreau was 17 when he engaged in consensual intercourse with a 13 year-old female. She became pregnant and they married (Davis, 2001). The state attorney's office charged him with committing a lewd and lascivious act. After a lengthy legal battle, Boudreau's charge was reduced from a felony to a misdemeanor and he pleaded no contest to contributing to the delinquency of a minor. In 2001, Boudreau was sentenced to one year of probation (Davis, 2001).

Other teens also received relatively light sentences. In 2001, the state of Florida brought a case against 16 year-old Joseph Stellini (Levesque, 2001). Stellini and a 15 year-old female engaged in consensual intercourse and the young woman became pregnant. The state charged him with committing a lewd and lascivious act, which could have carried a sentence up to five years in prison. However, Stellini received a sentence of probation and community service (Levesque, 2001).

For some men charged with statutory rape crimes, their punishment remains uncertain. 17 year-old Brendan Harer was charged with four counts of statutory rape for having sex with a 15 year-old on four different occasions ("Police Briefs," 2007). In January, 2007, a Massachusetts judge sentenced him to a year of probation, but suspended the judgment. If Harer is not arrested in the next two years, the charges will be dismissed. Twenty-seven year-old Zachary Tenant of Connecticut recently plead guilty to "sexual misconduct," for having consensual intercourse with his 16 year-old girlfriend (Murphy, 2008). According to the district attorney, Tenant was allowed to plead guilty to this lesser charge because he had a "long standing relationship with the victim," and is also a friend of her family's. Both the family and the minor objected to Tenant going to prison (Murphy, 2008). At the time of this writing, his sentence has not been handed down.

As these legal case studies illustrate, young men have been charged with a variety of offenses, and have received a variety of punishments for what appears to be similar behavior (i.e., sexual behavior with a minor female). Some defendants received harsher punishments than others, despite similarities between the cases. The following analysis describes similarities and differences, and determines whether a variety of social and contextual factors (e.g., parental approval) may have played a role in sentencing.

Case Analysis

Factors that may have influenced the defendants' sentence severity include the age disparity between the partners, whether the couple had parental permission, whether or not they were married or if they had a child. Comparing cases based on these characteristics can clarify whether these factors may have played a role in determining severity of sentence.

Age of Partners

One of the most obvious factors potentially affecting outcomes in these cases is the age of both the female and male. It would seem logical that the punishment might increase as his age increases or the female's age decreases. In the eight case studies analyzed here, the females ranged in age from 13 to 15, and the males ranged in age from 16 to 27. The age of the female does not seem to be a consistent factor predicting the outcome of the case. Specifically, in cases in which the young man was sentenced to prison, the females were either 13, 14 or 15. In the cases in which the young men were not sentenced to prison, the females were 13 or 15. Thus, the cases with both the youngest females and oldest females were split between prison and non-prison sentences.

In contrast, the age of the male might somewhat predict case outcome. The young men who were sentenced to prison were 17, 18 or 23, while those who received other sentences were 16 or 17. Thus, the oldest was given a prison sentence and the youngest was given probation. However those in the middle (age 17 or 18) were split between parole (two young men) and prison (two young men).

Age Disparity

Although it would seem logical that age disparity might explain discrepancies among case outcomes, an analysis of the cases reveals that this is not necessarily the case. It might be predicted that cases with larger age disparities would receive longer sentences than cases in which there is less disparity. The age disparities in the cases in which the young men were sentenced to prison are 9 (Koso), 3 (Dixon), 5 (Dencs), and 2 (Wilson) years. The age differences for the young men who received other sentences are 4 (Boudreau), 1 (Stellini), and 2 (Harer) years. The defendant with the largest relationship age disparity (Tenant; 11 years) was allowed to plead guilty to a lesser charge, but he has not yet been sentenced. However, analyses of the other cases indicate that those with similar age disparities do not always have similar outcomes. In both the Wilson case and the Harer case, there was only a two year difference, yet Harer received probation and Wilson is served a two year sentence. Nevertheless, a large disparity (Koso) led to prison time, while the smallest disparity (Harer) led to probation. As this analysis demonstrates, the age difference between the man and the minor female may predict some outcomes, but is not a consistent determining factor in outcomes of cases.

Parental Approval

Another factor that could possibly affect the sentence is whether the minor's parents approved of the relationship. Although it is possible that judges are more lenient when the couple has the parents' approval, these cases indicate that the legal system does not consistently consider parental consent. Of the eight cases analyzed, only three young men clearly (Koso, Tenant, and Boudreau) had the approval of the young woman's parents. The families in these cases rallied behind the couples and asked the courts for leniency. In contrast, the minor's parents in the Stellini and Dencs cases did not approve of the relationship. The minor's guardians secured an injunction that prevented Dencs from seeing his girlfriend. Similarly, the parents in the Stellini cases took steps to keep him away from their daughter, even after the baby was born. The support or opposition to the relationship does not affect case outcome in these cases. Stellini and Boudreau received probation with no jail time, while Koso and Dencs were sentenced to prison. Because of these sentence inconsistencies, it appears that parental permission is another social factor that can not uniformly predict trial outcomes in these eight case studies.

Pregnancy

A factor that could potentially affect the sentence that a young man is given is whether the young woman is pregnant or has a child. Perhaps a pregnancy increases the perceived severity of the sexual act, leading a judge to give a harsher sentence. Koso, Boudreau and Stellini all had children with their minor girlfriends. However, Koso received prison, while other two received probation. Another possibility is that the young man's intent to support the mother and child could sway the court to avoid handing down a prison sentence. This does not seem to be the case, however. Koso (prison) and Bourdeau (probation) both showed intent (i.e., marrying the young woman) to support the mother and child, while Stellini (probation) did not. Thus, pregnancy does not have a uniform effect on sentence severity.

Marriage

The final factor that could potentially affect a case outcome is a marriage between the young man and his minor partner. It could be assumed that couples that are married may receive more sympathy from the courts. However, these cases do not support this conclusion. Koso received a harsher punishment (prison) than Boudreau (probation), although they were both married to their partners. None of the other young men were married to their partners.

Discussion

The eight legal case studies reported here indicate that prosecutors have targeted cases with many different characteristics. For instance, cases differed as to the age of the partners, the size of the age disparity and whether the couple was married or had a baby. This variety of cases also produced a diversity of legal outcomes. On one end of the spectrum, Genarlow Wilson who initially received a 10 year prison sentence and was initially required to register as a sex offender. At the other end of the spectrum, Brendan Harer was given a sentence of suspended probation that can be removed from his record if he does not get arrested in two years. The analysis of these legal case studies indicated that social and contextual factors such as pregnancy, age disparity, marital status, and parental approval do not necessarily predict the outcomes (e.g., prison, parole) in cases of consensual underage sexual activity. While age of the male and age disparity between partners were somewhat consistent with what might be expected (i.e., greater punishments in cases with older males and greater age disparities), not all cases fit these expectations.

It should be noted, however, that the aforementioned rulings include a small sample of high profile cases that have received large amounts of media attention. The media likely do not report many cases that would have fit the study's selection criteria. In addition, only a handful of states are represented in this analysis. Therefore, this sample may not reflect legal procedure or political climate nationwide.

Young men who have consensual sex with minors can face a variety of charges, including statutory rape. If convicted, defendants can face charges that range from probation to prison time. The age of each of the partners, the age disparity between the couple, whether the couple is married, whether the minor becomes pregnant and whether the couple has the support of the minor's parents are all factors that logically could affect the severity of a defendant's punishment. However, the inconsistencies in the aforementioned cases show that such factors do not consistently affect sentence outcomes.

These legal case studies highlight the differences between jurisdictions, judges, and legal responses to underage sex. Obviously, many young people have sex and are never prosecuted. Meanwhile, young males like Wilson spend time in prison and are treated as sex offenders. There seems to be no reliable way to determine what punishment, if any, a young man will receive. Thus, the law is sending mixed messages about whether underage sex is acceptable or not. These inconsistencies are just one of the legal dilemmas that such prosecutions raise.

Due to the media attention and heightened awareness of underage sex laws, critics have come to question the fairness of these laws (Reinhart, 2007). For instance, some deem it unjust to force these young men to register as sex offenders. They also cite studies indicating that, during adolescence, the parts of the brain responsible for impulses and judgment are still developing (Reinhart, 2007). Additionally, such laws can be unfair to young women. Because of the inconsistencies among state laws, it may be legal for a teenage girl to have sex with her boyfriend in one state, but illegal in another. Teens may not always be aware of their state's laws, leading to confusion about whether they are doing something illegal. These issues highlight some of the controversy over the prosecutions described above. Psychologists can play an important role in resolving some of this controversy.

Roles for Psychologists

Psychologists can help lawmakers make informed decisions regarding consensual sex cases. First, researchers can inform policymakers as to the most beneficial ways to address the behavior of these young offenders. In respect to juvenile offenders, advocates of less punitive measures claim that teen sex offenders are less likely to re-offend than those who commit sex crimes as adults (Reinhart, 2007). Many of the offenders are teenagers themselves and are engaging in consensual sex. For example, the Wilson case involved consensual sex between a 17 year-old and 15 year-old. Even though the minor female was only two years Wilson's junior, he was initially sentenced to ten years in prison and was required to register as a sex offender for the rest of his life. Just as the Supreme Court has determined that juveniles do not deserve the death penalty because of their immature brain development (*Roper v. Simmons*, 2005), perhaps they do not deserve to be permanently labeled as "sex offenders." Lawmakers in some jurisdictions have adopted this reasoning (Reinhart, 2007). For instance, in 2007, a group of Arizona lawmakers proposed a group of laws that would allow judges to bypass some mandatory punishments, such as requiring some young men to register as sex offenders. Supporters of the proposed laws acknowledge that teenagers often make poor sexual choices, but they should not be treated as sexual predators for having sex with their teenaged girlfriends. The proposed law would allow judges greater discretion to determine what should happen to such teenagers and young adults (Reinhart, 2007).

Research has indicated that the portion of the brain that controls logical reasoning is not fully developed in juveniles (e.g., Steinberg & Scott, 2003). Instead of relying on this immature part of the brain, juveniles rely on the part of the brain that controls emotions. This limited capacity reduces the criminal culpability for death penalty purposes. A similar argument can be made for considering juveniles to be less culpable for their sexual behaviors. Researchers can determine whether juveniles' limited ability to make reasoned judgments makes it legally appropriate to permanently label them as sex offenders.

Second, developmental researchers have yet to conduct research that would determine when adolescents are mature enough to consent to having sex (Levine, Wallach & Levine, 2007). States have adopted a variety of ages at which minors in their state can "consent" to sex. Four states set the age at 12; at the other extreme, two states set the age at 18 (Levesque, 2000). These laws represent a tremendous disparity, as a 12 year-old is developmentally quite different than an 18 year-old. Because adolescents mature at very different ages, it may be difficult to set a specific age for consent. Nevertheless, psychologists could help determine when the majority of adolescents are mature enough to make that decision. This would prevent the prosecution of individuals who are mature enough to consent, while still protecting those who are not mature enough.

Third, psychologists can help lawmakers weigh the potential economic consequences for the female. Sentencing a young man to jail may force his partner into economic hardship. This argument is particularly applicable when the minor has a child or is pregnant. Teenage mothers have lower rates of high school completion and are less likely to achieve higher levels of education (Mehta, 1998). Therefore, it would be useful to study whether having their boyfriends/husbands at home (instead of in prison) improve these conditions. If lawmakers consider these factors, such a decision would support the principles of therapeutic jurisprudence. Advocates of therapeutic jurisprudence encourage legal actors to maximize the law's therapeutic effects, and minimize its anti-therapeutic effects (Wexler, 1991, 1996; Winick, 1997).

Mandatory sentences do not allow for the judge to take into account the effects on the teenaged mother or child. To prevent possible anti-therapeutic effects, the law could give judges the ability to allow for leniency in cases in which the defendant is a father who intends to provide for his child. The recently proposed Arizona laws discussed above illustrate some lawmakers' desire for increased judicial discretion (Reinhart, 2007).

On the other hand, judicial discretion might cause discrepancies in outcomes because some judges would choose to be lenient, while others would not. These discrepancies could be perceived as unfair, as two young men could do identical acts but one goes to prison and the other is never even prosecuted. In order to avoid this, lawmakers may decide that judges should instead hand down mandatory sentences. For example, before the Georgia Supreme Court disallowed the law, Dixon was given an automatic ten year sentence ("Court Weighs Teenager's Sentence," 2004). Automatic sentencing laws do not allow the consideration of possible mitigating factors such as a small age disparity, marriage, pregnancy, or parental permission. Research is needed to determine what legal approaches are most therapeutic.

Finally, when creating laws that regulate underage sexual behavior, lawmakers may wish to consider public opinion. Psychologists are often employed to conduct such research. Public opinion differs as to which punishment fits the crime of engaging in sexual relations with a minor. Some argue that minors should never engage in sexual activity with adults, due to the risk of exploitation and coercion (Oberman, 2000). Supporters of this argument would likely disapprove of such relationships, regardless of the couple's circumstance (i.e., if the couple is now married, if the minor is pregnant, whether there is a small age disparity). This argument is based on the desire to protect the minor from abusive, damaging relationships. However, others argue that instead of protecting the minor, such punishments should be avoided because they cause teenaged mothers emotional suffering and economic hardship (Mehta, 1998). Clearly, public opinion is sharply divided among those who choose to speak out. It is often difficult to determine the overall public opinion because most people do not speak publicly about this sensitive issue.

Laws pertaining to underage sexual activity clearly communicate that the act of minors engaging in sexual relationships is wrong. Because this argument is morally based, it is impossible to prove its validity. Those who choose to speak out on the issue frequently have very strong opinions, which are often morally based. However, they may not represent the overall community sentiment. Thus, measuring the general public's opinion could reveal how the public feels these cases should be handled. Many factors are involved in determining the appropriate legal responses for illegal, underage sexual acts, and psychologists can aid lawmakers in making such decisions. Social psychologists can administer surveys to the public and present the results to lawmakers. Such research can help lawmakers, judges, and prosecutors make decisions based on the public's wishes.

Although there is some debate as to whether public opinion should play a role in lawmaking (see Finkel, 1995), there is evidence that basing laws on community sentiment would be beneficial. The public's willingness to accept legal decisions is influenced by the perceived fairness of the decision making procedures (Tyler & Rasinski, 1991). Based on the media response, some of the cases analyzed here have been perceived as unfair. For example, the Nebraska attorney general's office received nearly 340 letters and emails regarding the Koso case ("Man Weds 14-Year-Old," 2005). Of the 283 *out-of-state* letters, 72% were in support of the couple and 56% of the 56 *in-state* letters were defending Koso ("Man Weds 14-Year-Old," 2005).

Prosecutors who listen to public opinion could use this information to determine whom to prosecute. Because it is impossible to find and prosecute all cases of underage sex, prosecutors must make choices about whether to prosecute men who have sex with their minor girlfriends. These choices can sometimes be very difficult to make. They may also reflect a number of biases. For example, underage sexual behavior cases that result in pregnancies may be more likely to be prosecuted because of the emotional and financial burden placed on the minor female. However, if the young woman has abortion or gives the baby up for adoption, prosecutors may not be as likely to pursue the case. Relationships in which no pregnancy occurs and the parents do not object to the relationship might be even less likely to be prosecuted because law enforcement officers are unlikely to even discover the crime. Prosecution of seemingly "easy" cases such as these may lead people to question the fairness of the law. Such unequal enforcement is difficult to overcome, however if laws are based on public opinion, then they will be perceived as more fair and the public will be more likely to accept the legal decisions.

CONCLUSION

The current analysis of underage sex cases suggests that social factors such as pregnancy, marital status, age of partners, age disparity between partners, and parental approval do not necessarily predict legal outcomes. Psychologists can help remedy sentence inconsistencies and help determine the best way for the legal system to handle consensual underage sex cases. Researchers can inform courts about juveniles' cognitive abilities. This information can provide insight into whether the same punishments are appropriate for adults who engage in sexual activity with minors as well as for minors who engage in sexual activity with each other. Developmental research can also provide guidance to states trying to determine an appropriate age of consent. Furthermore, psychological research can help determine if the public favors solutions that promote therapeutic jurisprudence or solutions that are more punitive in nature. This information could help lawmakers enact laws that reflect public opinion. Such research can also help determine what, if any, contextual factors should be considered when judges sentence defendants.

The topic of teenage sexuality remains a controversial matter (see Colb, 2007; Levesque, 2001). Recent high profile cases involving consensual sex between young men and their minor partners have brought attention to this issue. Inconsistencies in legal outcomes for defendants have raised questions as to the fairness of laws punishing individuals for consensual sex. While some argue that sex with a minor is harmful, regardless of the contextual factors (Oberman, 2000), others assert that lenient punishments should be allowed in certain situations (Reinhart, 2007). This article suggests ways in which psychologists can help solve the current social issues of minors engaging in sexual activity and the inconsistencies in legal punishments for this behavior.

REFERENCES

Campos, C. (2007, March1). Bill allowing reviews of teen sex offenses moves forward. Atlanta Journal-Constitution. Retrieved March 16, 2007, from http://www.ajc.com/blogs/content/sharedblogs/ajc/georgia/entries/2007/03/01/bill_allowing_r.html

Colb, S. F. (2007).The harsh wages of sin: Why Genarlow Wilson is languishing in prison. Retrieved on February 23, 2007, from http://writ.news.findlaw.com/colb/20070110.htmsl

Court weighs teenager's sentence. (2004, January 21). Retrieved March 9, 2007, from http://www.cnn.com/2004/LAW/01/21/athlete.appeal.ap/index.html

Davis, C. (2001, April 26). Father avoids teen sex trial. St. Petersburg Times. Retrieved February 23, 2007, from http://www.sptimes.com/News/042601/TampaBay/Father_avoids_teen_se.shtml

Dixon v. Georgia, 596 S.E.2d 147 (Ga. 2004).

Finkel, N. J. (1995). Commonsense justice: Juror's notions of the law. Cambridge MA: Harvard University Press.

Georgia General Assembly (2007). Retrieved April 28, 2007 from http://www.legis.state.ga.us/legis/2007_08/sum/sb37.htm.

Hart, A. (2004, May 4). Child molesting conviction overturned in Georgia classmate case. New York Times. Retrieved February 23, 2007, from http://www.nytimes.com

H.B. 1059 (2006). Retrieved April 28, 2007 from http://www.legis.ga.gov/legis/2005_06/pdf/hb1059.pdf

Jamie Lynn Spears pregnancy raises legal questions. (2007, December 20). Retrieved June 7, 2008, from http://www.cnn.com/2007/SHOWBIZ/TV/12/19/spears.statutory.rape/index.html

Kaiser Family Foundation. (2005, January). Teenage sexual activity. Retrieved March 3, 2007, from http://www.kff.org/youthhivstds/upload/U-S-Teen-Sexual-Activity-Fact-Sheet.pdf

Levesque, R. J. R. (2000). Adolescents, sex, and the law. Washington, DC: American Psychological Association.

Levesque, W. (2001, May 12). Boy avoids felony in teen sex case. St. Petersburg Times. Retrieved February 23, 2007, from http://www.sptimes.com/News/051201/TampaBay/Boy_avoids_felony_in_.shtml

Levine, M., Wallach, L., & Levine, D. (2007). Psychological problems, social issues, and law (2nd Ed.). Boston: Allyn and Bacon.

Mabin, B. (2005, December 13). Koso pleads guilty to child sex charge. Lincoln Journal Star. Retrieved February 23, 2007, from http://www.journalstar.com/articles/2005/12/14/local/doc439f04051b59a828393930.txt

Man weds 14-year-old, faces charges. (2005, September 13). Retrieved February 23, 2007, from http://abcnews.go.com/GMA/story?id=1121138&page=1

Mehta, J. (1998). Prosecuting teenage parents under fornication statutes: A constitutionally suspect legal solution to the social problem of teen pregnancy. Cardozo Women's Law Journal, 5, 121-150.

Murphy, T. (2008, March, 5). Man pleads to lesser charge in underage sex case. Evening Sun. Retrieved June 1, 2008, from http://www.evesun.com/news/stories/2008-03-05/3831/Man-pleads-to-lesser-charge-in-underage-sex-case/

Nebraska code §28-320.0145 (2006).

Oberman, M. (2000). Regulating consensual sex with minors: Defining a role for statutory rape, Buffalo Law Review, 48, 703-779.

Police briefs sentinel & enterprise. (2007, January 30). Retrieved March 3, 2007, from http://www.sentinelandenterprise.com/ci_5118053

Reinhart, M. K. (2007, February 11). Legislatures try to ease laws for sex crimes by youths. East Valley Tribune. Retrieved March 16, 2007, from, http://www.eastvalleytribune.com/index.php?sty=83904

Report: Teen pregnancies up for first time in 15 years (2008, July 11). Cnn.com. Retrieved October 15, 2008 from http://www.cnn.com/2008/HEALTH/07/10/teen.pregnancy/index.html.

Roper v. Simmons, 543 U.S. 551 (2005).

S.B. 37 (2007). Retrieved April 28, 2007 from http://www.legis.state.ga.us/legis/2007_08/pdf/sb37.pdf

Steinberg, L., & Scott, E. S. (2003). Less guilty by reason of adolescence: Developmental immaturity, diminished responsibility, and the juvenile death penalty. American Psychologist, 58, 1-10.

Sutherland, K. (2003). From jailbird to jailbait: Age of consent laws and the construction of teenage sexualities. William and Mary Journal of Women and the Law, 9, 313-349.

Swift, A. (2008, April, 25). Teen sent to prison for 8 ¾ years for sex with young girlfriend. Naples News. Retrieved June 1, 2008, from http://www.naplesnews.com/news/2008/apr/25/teen-sent-prison-8-years-sex-young-girlifriend/

Tyler, T. R., & Rasinski, K. (1991). Procedural justice, institutional legitimacy, and the acceptance of unpopular U.S supreme court decisions: A reply to Gibson. Law & Society Review, 25, 621-630.

Wexler, D. B. (1991). Putting mental health into mental health law: Therapeutic jurisprudence. In D. B. Wexler, & B. J. Winick (Eds.), Essays in therapeutic jurisprudence (pp. 3–15). Durham, NC: Carolina Academic Press.

Wexler, D. B. (1996). Some therapeutic jurisprudence implications of the outpatient civil commitment. In D. B. Wexler, & B. J. Winick (Eds.), Law in a therapeutic key: Developments in therapeutic jurisprudence (pp.145-148). Durham, NC: Carolina Academic Press.

Wilson released after two years behind bars for teen sex conviction (2007, October 27). Retrieved June 7, 2008, from http://www.cnn.com/2007/US/law/10/26/wilson.freed/index.html

Winick, B. J. (1997). The jurisprudence of therapeutic jurisprudence. Psychology, Public Policy,and Law,3,184–206.

PART II: PSYCHO-LEGAL ANALYSES

Part II of this book presents four in-depth psycho-legal analyses of several issues relating to legal regulation of sexual behavior. The first chapter in this section investigates a possible role for courts that can help break the cycle of illegal prostitution. The second chapter investigates the unintended effects of good-intentioned laws, specifically laws prohibiting procreation. The third chapter in this section illustrates how the courts can use psychological research to make well-informed decisions, using the example of laws requiring parental notification for minor abortions. The final chapter offers a historical-social constructionist perspective to explain the perpetuation of masculinism as a function of the legal regulation of same-sex marriage laws, anti-sodomy legislation, and heart balm torts. All four chapters share the common theme of using the justice system to promote the well-being of those it affects.

In: Contemporary Perspectives on Legal Regulation...
Editor: Monica K. Miller
ISBN 978-1-60741-161-1

Chapter 5

USING THERAPEUTIC JURISPRUDENCE TO DESIGN A SPECIAL TREATMENT COURT TO ADDRESS ILLEGAL PROSTITUTION

Misty H. Sanchez and Monica K. Miller
University of Nevada, Reno, Nevada, USA

ABSTRACT

The crime of prostitution has become a social concern that needs to be addressed in alternative methods as opposed to punishment-only sanctions. Prostitution has existed for years, but this article is suggesting that the court needs to play a vital role in therapeutically addressing the issue of prostitution and what it does to an individual and community. By assessing the individual needs of the prostitute, the court could potentially act as a therapeutic agent and prevent the woman from continuing a life in prostitution. This article suggests the formation of a prostitution treatment court, based on the drug court model, in order to develop a specialty court to deal solely with prostitutes and their specific needs. The benefits of such a court not only help the prostitute herself, but enhance the community, ease the judicial system, and reduce prostitution related offenses, which improves public safety.

The crime and social conditions leading to prostitution have existed throughout history (Barry, 1995). Although prostitution is recognized as the oldest profession, not all of the women involved in prostitution want to continue with that profession, rather many feel stuck into that life in order to survive (Sterk, 2000). In recent years, the justice system has begun to address social concerns such as substance abuse and domestic abuse by attending to the individual needs of abusers (Casey & Rottman, 2000). This therapeutic approach, as opposed to a punishment-only approach addresses the underlying causes of crime instead of only punishing the criminal. For instance, special courts have been developed to address criminality through a holistic approach, which has yet to be used with prostitutes, but has lead to some insight into how the criminal justice system can address the needs of prostitutes. This holistic approach is about stopping the cycle of abuse by focusing not only on the defendant, but the victims and root causes of the crime. This approach is in line with the foundations of therapeutic jurisprudence that the law itself often functions as a therapeutic or anti-therapeutic agent. It urges awareness of the law's impact on emotional, physical, and social life, an area often ignored by the law and legal profession (Wexler & Winick, 2003).

This article will suggest that the application of therapeutic jurisprudence should be extended to include approaches to the issue of prostitution. Included in this article is the history of specialty courts, the applications of therapeutic jurisprudence, the specific needs of prostitutes, and the rationale for extending the services of specialty courts to prostitution.

History Of Therapeutic Jurisprudence

The nationwide growth in specialized or problem solving courts (e.g., drug courts, community courts, mental health courts, and domestic violence courts), raises questions about the role of the justice system (Mirchandani, 2005). In the past, the justice system has embraced punitive sanctions, but recently, the courts have made a shift to being therapeutic. Drug courts began appearing in the 1980s as one reaction to the dramatic rise in court caseloads involving drug offenses (Casey & Rottman, 2000). The first drug court was started by a Florida judge with the intent to systematically bring drug treatment to the criminal justice population entering the court system (Hora, Schma, & Rosenthal, 1999). A therapeutic perspective regards the law as a social force that produces behaviors and consequences (Wexler & Winick, 1996). In recent years, judges, courts, and state court systems have diverted from the traditional model of dispassionate and disinterested magistrate and have adopted a focus based on therapeutic jurisprudence principles (Casey & Rottman, 2000). This diversion from the traditional role of the court is one of many therapeutic principles that include a shift from simple adjudication to ensuring community well-being that concentrates on the law's impact on the individual. This perspective regards the law (rules of law, legal procedures, and roles of legal actors) as a social force that often produces therapeutic or anti-therapeutic consequences (Wexler & Winick, 1996). This concept of therapeutic jurisprudence was first used by Professor David Wexler in 1987 (Hora et. al, 1999).

The developers of this paradigm, David Wexler and Bruce Winick, state that therapeutic jurisprudence principles require legal actors (e.g., lawyers, judges) to consider the law's impact on emotional and social life and psychological well-being (Winick, 1997). "It is a multidisciplinary approach that seeks to bring insights from the behavioral sciences – psychology, social work, criminology and the like – into the law, the lawyer's office, and the courtroom" (Wexler & Winick, 2003, p. 54). Although therapeutic jurisprudence originally had limited applications, the evolution of the role of the justice system has allowed the concepts of therapeutic jurisprudence to be applied to numerous quality of life crimes. Specialty courts take a social problem approach to crime by seeking the root causes of crime within the individual, the society, and the larger culture (Mirchandani, 2005). In this new role of tackling social problems, the court allows legal officials to respond not only to individual troubles, but also to broader social issues of communities (Mirchandani, 2005). Though it is a relatively new approach to justice, this judicial shift has seen consistent growth in scholarly consideration and critique as well increased practical use (Slobogin, 1995). Therapeutic jurisprudence is a very individualized approach to deal with those that break the law. Rather than a one-size fits all approach to deal with these individuals, therapeutic jurisprudence looks at the individualized needs and helps with those specific needs. For example, one may need drug treatment and another may need housing, but in a therapeutic approach both needs would be met in order to help the individual. Although this approach assists the criminal, this does not mean that the criminal should not be punished, it merely means that some individuals should be considered to receive services in addition to punishment.

Applications of Therapeutic Jurisprudence

In this new era of the therapeutic court, numerous applications, such as drug courts, domestic violence courts, and gambling courts, have emerged (Casey & Rottman, 2000). Some of the therapeutic jurisprudence concepts in drug courts are as follows: a) early identification, assessment, and placement of eligible substance abusers; b) continuous judicial supervision during the individual's participation in the program; c) clear communication of program requirements to the individual and confirmation of the individual's agreement to comply; d) imposition of intermediate sanctions when program requirements are violated; and e) an emphasis on overcoming denial and promoting personal responsibility and self-esteem (Hora et al., 1999). Rather than focusing on punishment per se, most specialized programs provide services such as family counseling, restitution, employment training, and interventions with schools or employers to try to ameliorate sources of stress and failure (Binder & Geis, 1984). These concepts attempt to reintegrate offenders by providing a better overall quality of life, in order to ameliorate the need to commit crime. A strong development of interdependent ties between program participants and drug court officials, educational and occupational aftercare allow for a participant graduation ceremony that seals their arrest record. This also provides a clean slate, making it easier for the offender to secure a job (Miethe, Lu, & Reese, 2000).

Domestic violence courts were also formed on therapeutic jurisprudence principles, such as: a) positive potential interactions with victims to empower them; b) continuous judicial supervision; and c) counseling opportunities for the victims (Hartley, 2003). Similarly, gambling treatment courts began by examining the "unnoticed, unattended, and unlooked into root causes of many crimes within gambling addiction" (Hinshaw, 2005, p. 338)

Each of these specialized courts target different concerns, but yet all share a basic organizing theme of a desire to improve the outcomes for victims, litigants, defendants, and communities (Berman & Feinblatt, 2001). With documented success on therapeutic jurisprudence approaches in the courts, the continuum of care should be extended to include prostitution.

Defining the Prostitution Problem

The problems associated with street prostitution affect both the prostitute and her community, thus making prostitution a good candidate for a problem-solving court (Buffalo Prostitution Task Force, 1999). The innovation of problem-solving courts should extend to prostitution in order to address this population's needs and to benefit society as a whole

(Berman & Feinblatt, 2001). Rather than simply process people arrested for prostitution, a problem-solving court tries to determine what kinds of social services can be tapped to help women put prostitution behind them (Cauvin, 2003).

Prostitution is a crime with repeat offenders whom are continually receiving punitive sanctions, which does not address the underlying social issues that accompany prostitution. O'Leary and Howard (2001) define prostitution as "the exchange of money or something of value, including drugs or shelter, or other survival needs – for sexual activity. Sexual activity includes vaginal sex, anal sex, oral sex, and manipulation of another person's genitals for purposes of sexual arousal" (pg. 3).

The majority of prostitution offenses are misdemeanors. The prostitute typically would spend a day or two in jail, be sanctioned to community service, or be required to pay fines (Berman & Feinblatt, 2001). Typically, the prostitute does not receive any services or counseling. This creates a continuous cycle of crimes and arrests in which the prostitute is arrested for solicitation is adjudicated, does minor time, then goes right back to prostituting on the street (Berman & Feinblatt, 2001). An intervention, based on the principles of therapeutic jurisprudence, could stop this punitive-only approach and better meet the needs of prostitutes. Similar to other problem-solving courts, if treated in a therapeutic manner, prostitution treatment court could reduce repeat offenses and address various social issues that contribute to prostitution. In order to address the issue of prostitution, it is important to address the needs of prostitutes.

Needs of Prostitutes

Women enter into prostitution for many reasons, which need to be addressed before this crime can be tackled. A research study conducted in Chicago, found that "girls and women in prostitution have been found to be addicted to alcohol and drugs, suffer serious physical problems, are frequently homeless...have serious mental health problems, including posttraumatic stress disorder and depression" (O'Leary & Howard, 2001, pg. 29). With these root problems, many women are unable to exit prostitution. Most of the women have no or little employment skills, so there is a definite need for treatment services for this population. The Problem-Orientated Guides for Police Series called *Street Prostitution* suggests that understanding factors that are known to contribute to the problem will help guide local analysis questions, determine effectiveness measures, recognize key points of interventions and select an appropriate set of responses for particular problems (Scott, 2001). Experts have recognized that the key root causes of prostitution are employment issues, mental health, substance abuse, and housing issues. For example, Sterk (2000) reported that some prostitutes explanation for becoming involved in prostitution include having a history of sexual abuse, having grown up without love from the adults in their lives, and needing money. Rather than addressing prostitution as a crime, a prostitution treatment court will address the conditions that lead a woman into a life of prostitution.

Employment Needs

Since most prostitutes have few employment skills, a life of prostitution is a quick way to earn a living (Scott, 2001). In a study conducted on 50 incarcerated prostitutes, fifty-six percent were high school dropouts and had few economically practical alternatives to street prostitution (Norton-Hawk, 2001). The majority (62%) lacked even vocational training (Norton-Hawk, 2001). Eighty-two percent had held a legal job for at least a brief period but this employment rarely paid more than minimum wage and prostitution provided much higher pay than the legitimate job market (Norton-Hawk, 2001). Typical explanations given by respondents were, ''I have an eighth grade education and don't have any other way to make a living;'' ''we do it for the money;'' and ''People must live'' (Norton-Hawk, 2001, pg. 406). Without financial stability, a prostitute is forced to stay on the streets in order to earn money. For example, one prostitute planned on leaving the life of prostitution by securing employment, however because she lacked any marketable job skills, she was unsuccessful in locating employment in the legitimate job market (Norton-Hawk, 2001). She was frustrated with her lack of success and one night she decided to turn just one trick—just enough to get her by; one night and one trick became three tricks until she was again working full-time (Norton-Hawk, 2001). This is a typical scenario for the life of a prostitute. Legitimate employment is a critical need for prostitutes in order to leave the life of prostitution. With a specialty court in place to assist prostitutes, the court can facilitate looking for employment, providing vocational training for a career, and even with smaller assistance such as help writing a resume and job interviewing skills. In order to help a woman have financial stability outside of prostituting, employment needs have to be met within this court, in addition to a myriad of other needs.

Mental Health Needs

Some street prostitutes typically need mental health treatment if they are to quit prostitution. Historically, prostitutes have endured violence, trauma, and mental health issues (Raphael & Shapiro, 2002). Raphael and Shapiro's study (2002) illustrated how a sample of women had run away from home for various reasons, grew up in households with loss of life, separation from caretakers, domestic violence, substance abuse, and prostitution. Many prostitutes also grew up in single family households, and half of these women had witnessed a parent, usually her mother, being victimized by domestic violence (Raphael & Shapiro, 2002). Because of these experiences, the primary mental health issue common among prostitutes is posttraumatic stress disorder (PTSD). The American Psychiatric Association (1994) states

> "PTSD can result when people have experienced extreme traumatic stressors involving direct personal experience of an event that involves actual or threatened death or serious injury; or other threat to one's personal integrity or witnessing an event that involves death, injury, or a threat to the physical integrity of another person; or learning about unexpected or violent death, serious harm, or threat of death or injury experienced by a family member or other close associate" (pg. 308).

This common diagnosis among prostitutes is found to be linked to the following: first, most people working as prostitutes have a history of childhood physical and sexual abuse (Belton, 1992). Second, adult prostitutes often suffer sexual and other physical violence (Hunter, 1993). Third, the presence of dissociative symptoms, which often occur in conjunction with PTSD, has been noted among prostitutes (Vanwesenbeeck, 1994). Given the extent of violence in their lives and the presence of dissociative symptoms, women prostitutes would most likely experience PTSD, and are therefore in need of mental health counseling. El-Bassel and colleagues (1997) found significantly more psychological distress among women who used drugs and who also prostituted than among drug-using women who did not prostitute. Farley and Kelly (2000) interviewed prostitutes about receiving services, one prostitute said, "I wonder why I keep going to therapists and telling them I can't sleep and I have nightmares. They pass right over the fact that I was a prostitute and I was beaten with 2x4 boards, I had my fingers and toes broken by a pimp, and I was raped more than 30 times, why do they ignore that" (pg. 37). A lack of attention to women's experiences of violence and sexual abuse has resulted in repeated failures of the health care system for women. This study found that prostitutes generally lacked access to social and medical services, which were available to others whom were not prostitutes (Weiner, 1996). Essentially, fear of arrest and social contempt made it difficult for prostitutes to seek medical treatment.

This article is an example of how prostitution is currently handled in the judicial system; this article suggests that the violence and psychological distress resulting from prostituting is a public health concern. Within the context of a treatment court, any intervention attempting to reduce risk behavior among prostitutes must also address the psychological ramifications of violence (Raphael & Shapiro, 2002). The current judicial process does not address a prostitute's needs, so any mental health concerns would need to be incorporated into a prostitution treatment court. In addition to mental health issues of prostitutes, a major issue continuing women in prostitution is substance abuse.

Substance Abuse Needs

The lifestyle of a prostitute typically includes the use of illicit drugs and alcohol (Weiner, 1996). "Street prostitution and street drug markets are often closely linked, supporting and reinforcing one another. Many street prostitutes use illegal drugs. Many female serious drug users turn to prostitution at some point to finance their habit. Some prostitutes develop drug habits before turning to prostitution, while others start using drugs as part of the street prostitution lifestyle" (Scott, 2001, pg. 10). When prostitutes are using drugs, street prostitution becomes less predictable and more dangerous (Scott, 2001). Whether drug abuse tends to precede prostitution or whether drugs follow entering prostitution to numb the pain of working as a prostitute is unclear. A national report estimates that as many as 95-99% of prostitutes have substance abuse issues (Genesis House, 1998).

Due to the high correlation between drug use and prostitution, adequate substance abuse treatment is necessary to treat this population. If drugs and prostitution go hand in hand, treating the drug use could aid women and help them quit prostitution. The Chicago study mentioned above reported that only a small percentage of women stated they never used alcohol and drugs during prostitution activities and most women stated that they increased their usage in one way or another during the prostitution activity (Raphael & Shapiro, 2002).

Drug use not only affects the prostitute, but in many instances, also affects the community. For example, a prostitute might leave syringes and other paraphernalia on the ground that becomes unsightly and potentially hazardous that affects the entire community (Scott, 2001). Treating prostitutes' substance abuse issues is a major concern and a service that needs to be provided by a specialty treatment court. Without addressing the substance abuse needs, a prostitute will never be able to change her lifestyle. In addition to mental health and substance abuse needs, many prostitutes need stable housing.

Housing Needs

Scott (2001) reported that the most urgent need of girls and women escaping prostitution was housing. The Homeward Bound Fact Sheet (2001) reports that many prostitutes seek shelter in abandoned buildings or homes of partners, pimps, or customers, because they do not have a safe, affordable place of their own. Unfortunately, these places can be abusive (Homeward Bound, 2001).

Access to safe and affordable housing can be a viable form of escape and a first step on a road to recovery (Homeward Bound, 2001). To treat the problem of prostitution, affordable housing should be provided to therapeutically address all the causes and needs of prostitutes. To address homelessness in this population, a specialty treatment court, and policymakers in general should follow this suggestion offered by Homeward Bound (2001):

> "the definition of who is homeless should be expanded to include those who are trapped in systems of prostitution. Subsequently, an already critical lack of affordable housing seems even more critical, especially when characterized as part of a solution to assist those surviving and fleeting violent and abusive systems or as a preventative measure that decreases vulnerability. Collective advocacy around affordable housing development should also include representation of those who are trapped in systems of prostitution" (pg. 1)

With such a service provided to those women as part of prostitution treatment court, the cycle of prostitution would hopefully be stopped. Having her basic shelter needs met allows a woman to focus on other issues of and substance abuse treatment and employment. With individual needs met, the community would be an additional stakeholder in a prostitution treatment court.

Community Needs

Concern regarding prostitution extends well beyond the personal issues of the prostitute's life; it is also a public health concern (Weiner, 1996). In the 1990s a focus on the spread of HIV shifted attention away from the inaccessibility of health care for women in prostitution in the United States (Lawless, Kippax, & Crawford, 1996). Of the 206 prostitutes sampled in the Chicago study, almost 22% responding reported being HIV positive, 5.9% of the sample refused to answer or said they did not know if they were or not (Raphael & Shapiro, 2002). Although HIV exists in this population, prostitution has not been demonstrated to be a primary means of HIV transmission (Farley & Kelly, 2000). This is due largely to the fact that most street prostitution sex acts are oral rather than vaginal, most prostitutes insist that clients use condoms, and transmission is more difficult from female to male (Weitzer, 1999). This is less true of drug-dependent prostitutes (Farley & Kelly, 2000). Farley and Kelly (2000) found that drug use decreased condom use because when women needed money for drugs, they were more willing to accede to johns' demands for unsafe sex. Nevertheless, HIV transmission is a concern for the community. With a population riddled with a severe medical condition, a specialty treatment court needs to not only lend support for medication and doctor's fees, but needs to educate prostitutes about how to reduce the further spread of such infectious diseases. By educating prostitutes on HIV and other infectious diseases, all of society benefits from a specialized treatment approach to prostitution. Reducing prostitution will also reduce drug use, homelessness, and the social ill of prostitution. The reduction of these social ills improves the general standard of living in society. Another major benefit to society is that this saves the government money because the judicial system, jails, and healthcare system would not be used for prostitutes, once prostitution is reduced.

Working Toward a Therapeutic Court

In order for these women to leave the life of prostitution, these services need to be recognized and delivered to prostitutes. Interviews with prostitutes suggest that services needed are: employment, housing, mental health treatment, substance abuse treatment, and medical attention. Meeting these needs will benefit the prostitute and society (El-Bassel et al., 1997). An example of such a model to address those specific needs of prostitutes is the Hartford Community Court Model (Sviridoff, Rottman, Ostrom, & Curtis, 1997). Midtown Community Court posed a fundamental challenge to traditional assumptions about the role of American courts in dispersing justice and, in particular, about how they should relate to the community. Specialty court process defendants with a wide range of nonviolent public nuisance complaints, such as: public drinking, prostitution, solicitation, illegal gambling, and graffiti (Sviridoff et al., 1997). In this model, defendants arrested for prostitution may be eligible for the Prostitution Protocol, a program of intensive counseling and education designed to show women involved in prostitution that alternatives exist (Sviridoff et al., 1997). In this program, participants attend weekly and individual sessions addressing topics of physical and emotional care, stress reduction and avoidance, self-esteem, goal setting, and achieving success (Sviridoff et al., 1997). After needs assessment identifies what services are needed, then referrals are made to the appropriate agencies. According to court officials of the Hartford Community Court, none of the prostitutes who have completed the program have returned to prostitution (Sviridoff et al., 1997). This example illustrates the benefits of a prostitution court. It is unfortunate, however that such courts are rare.

With all their needs addressed by a prostitution treatment court, prostitutes could potentially change their lives. By facilitating access to a range of social services to help prostitutes address problems that contribute to their behavior, including drug abuse, mental illness, homelessness, and lack of education or job skills, prostitution can be dealt with in a therapeutic manner. With the current criminal justice system not addressing prostitutes' needs, it is becoming a revolving door of justice. Many women are incarcerated on prostitution-related charges or drug offenses and released to an unstable environment and then return to prostitution (Homeward Bound, 2001). A prostitution treatment court's goals should shift from the current atmosphere of simply punishing prostitutes. Rottman and Casey (2000) suggest that "the court should be a teaching place, women who fall into the prostitution and drug-ridden lifestyle need something other than time behind bars, they should be taught morals, values, the court is not the classroom, that's why there's so much recidivism" (pg. 15).

Policy Suggestions for Developing Prostitution Treatment Courts

In order to adopt therapeutic approaches to prostitution, a specialty court must have five essential elements: 1) immediate supervision; 2) non-adversarial adjudication; 3) hands-on judicial involvement; 4) treatment programs with clear rules and structured goals; and 5) a team approach that brings together the judge, prosecutor, defense counsel, treatment provider, and correctional staff (Casey & Rottman, 2000). This approach allows defendants to learn what is expected and understand that participating in the program will take considerable effort, but can succeed in turning their lives around (Casey & Rottman, 2000). A prostitution treatment court is a specialized court with the responsibility of addressing prostitutes' needs. A prostitution treatment court should offer comprehensive supervision, treatment services, immediate sanctions and incentives, and undertaking of her individualized needs. In such a court, prostitute offenders are treated holistically and are smoothly reintegrated into society. The offender who enters the judicial system because of a criminal offense benefits from the enhanced supervision provided by the specialty court system. Not only do offenders benefit, but public safety is also strengthened through the monitoring and accountability that occurs in specialty courts (Hinshaw, 2005). By using the success of drug courts as a model, therapeutic jurisprudence should be extended to prostitution. This application will assist this new court with the theoretical background needed to understand the goals and principles upon which prostitution treatment courts should operate (Hinshaw, 2005).

The differences between conventional court and a prostitution treatment court would begin well before any cases reached the courtroom. Similar to drug courts, a prostitution court would include a rigorous, inter-agency plan (Berman, 2003). This would include bringing the defense attorney and local prosecutor together to determine which defendants are eligible to participate in the program and to designate a pre-arranged system of graduated sanctions and rewards with which to respond to participants' progress in treatment (Berman, 2003). Another component of this specialty court also means that representatives of the court will have to work with drug treatment providers, probation departments, and police in advance to establish protocols for reporting back to the court. After the eligibility criterion has been established, all participants would agree to a formal treatment plan that stipulates the length of treatment, the treatment modality, and the consequences she faces if she fails to comply with court orders (Berman, 2002).

Once a prostitute is in the program, she would be rigorously monitored by probation officers and court staff, regularly reporting to the court, and submits to frequent drug and alcohol testing. All specialty courts share an underlying premise that courts should do more than just process cases (Berman, 2002). As opposed to traditional court cases where the judge, prosecutors, and defense try to complete all persons on the docket as quick as possible, a specialty treatment court allows for extended and individualized lengths of time for individuals. A prostitution treatment court would allow for enough individualized attention and maintain an intense level of supervision.

By distancing the specialty courts from the traditional courts, these problem-solving courts all attempt to use the authority of the judiciary in new ways and are characterized by a number of unique elements. A problem-solving court focuses on a team approach to decision making, referrals to treatment and other social services, ongoing judicial monitoring, direct interaction between litigants and judge, community outreach, and a proactive role for the judge inside and outside of the courtroom (Farole, Puffett, Rempel, & Byrne, 2005). This approach varies from the traditional in a positive manner for all players in the justice system. Traditional litigation approaches can yield distinctly unsatisfactory outcomes when applied to these non-traditional issues, such as prostitution. The systematic failure of the revolving door of justice is all too common in such cases. Knipps and Berman (2000) note a negative outcome of this approach, "if the justice system is viewed as a revolving door for petty offenders, citizens may see little point to reporting low-level crime, police view enforcement efforts as futile, and offenders themselves may perceive little downside to repeat offending" (pg. 9). A specialty prostitution treatment court would address the needs in a manner that traditional courts do not.

In order to have a successful prostitution court, the specific needs of the clients' would need to be addressed and fulfilled. To be successful outside of the life of prostitution, a client would need to gain job training and skills. Such a program must address the lack of economic opportunities (Norton-Hawk, 2001). Existing welfare-to-work programs should be utilized to facilitate movement back into the legal economy. This would involve developing job skills as well as the attitudes necessary to become a reliable and productive employee (Norton-Hawk, 2001). By working with court staff and/or case managers, the client (i.e., the prostitute) would be able to gain access to vocational rehabilitation and job training. The woman could be ordered by the court to complete job training and a participant could be required to fill out job applications and/or secure employment in order to maintain a positive status in the court.

In order to address the mental health needs of a prostitute, psychological testing would need to be in place. As mentioned above, many prostitutes suffer from PTSD and psychotherapy should be provided that takes into consideration the aberrant backgrounds and lifestyles of these women (Norton-Hawk, 2001). Innovative programs should be developed along the lines used by groups such as Alcoholics Anonymous. A Prostitutes Anonymous program could be based on the 12-step AA model (Norton-Hawk, 2001). In addition to counseling, any mental health medications would be prescribed to those requiring them. A prostitution court enables a judge and court staff to ensure that the client is following through with mental health and medication recommendations. For example, court staff could be required to watch participants take medications and guarantee compliance with doctor's appointments.

Even if a client has sufficient job training and is receiving counseling, unless the cycle of addiction is broken, a majority of these women will return to prostitution in order to finance their drug and/or alcohol habits (Scott, 2001). With as much as 95-99% of prostitutes having an addiction problem, drug counseling and participation in Alcoholics Anonymous or Narcotics Anonymous would need to be a substantial component to a prostitution court. In order to ensure a client's sobriety, another component of the court would be to include random drug and alcohol testing. Again, being a participant in this court could ensure that a client follows through with orders of the court in relation to drug counseling and testing.

Another major need of this population is to address the issue of housing. The court could work with community agencies to assist with housing costs, shelters, and housing assistance programs. One such mental health court program incorporates state funded housing slots for its participants with the greatest need for housing (Mental Health Court, 2003). As long as participants remain in compliance of the court, they are available to live in state-funded housing throughout the time participating in court. A case manager or court staff would be responsible to ensure that the participant is transitioned from state-funded housing into housing they are responsible for paying prior to leaving the court program. The goal would be to guarantee that the prostitute has aftercare plans that include housing and a legitimate method to pay for that housing.

In order to fulfill the community and medical needs of the prostitutes, the prostitution treatment court would need to address this issue. With public health being the biggest community concern, this court would need to provide adequate medical attention for prostitutes. With the great majority of the women having multiple problems arising from their unhealthy lifestyles, few receive regular medical attention (Norton-Hawk, 2001). In addition to any HIV and STD information, the most basic medical knowledge about proper nutrition, female anatomy, and pregnancy is pertinent for a prostitute to receive. Health assessment, informative lectures, and birth control counseling will improve the health and well-being of the women, their families, and the public at large (Norton-Hawk, 2001). By addressing this need through the court, prostitutes hopefully would gain the knowledge needed to make better informed decisions on a healthy lifestyle, not only for themselves for but also for their families. This need is a larger community issue that can be addressed with the formation of a prostitution court.

Any other services needed for the individual prostitute would be addressed within the context of the prostitution court. The rationale for such a highly integrated program is to ensure that all areas of the prostitutes' life is addressed and hopefully altered in order to potentially reduce future offending. By addressing each and every individualized need of the prostitute, the court gives every opportunity for a positive change. This change can have long-term benefits for the prostitutes, her family, and the community in which she lives.

CONCLUSION

Previously used specialty courts have proven very successful in other regions of the United States, providing a prime example for a prostitution treatment court. According to a community court study, evaluators found that the Midtown Community Court helped reduce local crime, improved compliance with alternative sanctions and enhanced public confidence in courts (Knipps & Berman, 2000). In addition to successfully reducing recidivism and bettering a defendant's quality of life, specialty courts have shown to be cost efficient as opposed to traditional courts. The financial benefits have proved to be a guiding factor for the rationale of problem-solving courts (Wolfe, 2005). For example, in a California drug court, a traditional court processing ranges from $5,000 to $19,000 per participant. On average, a specialty court can save from about $3,200 to over $19,000 per participant (Wolfe, 2005).

Judiciaries around the country are embracing a new way of business, one that emphasizes partnerships with stakeholders in and outside the courts, improved community access to the justice system, greater accountability for offenders and better community outcomes, such as increased safety and improved public confidence (Wolfe, 2005). A specialty prostitution treatment court would benefit all stakeholders; the community, the justice system, and the offender. Not only would all needs be assessed and services delivered, but a treatment court could save taxpayer's money and reduce crime. A prostitution treatment court would seek the goals of addressing the defendant's problems and to improve public safety, which would all contribute to bettering society and addressing the specific population's needs. This therapeutic approach would help prostitutes build a better life and help society address a number of social problems.

REFERENCES

American Psychiatric Association (1994). *Diagnostic and statistical manual of mental disorders,* 4th ed. Washington DC: American Psychiatric Press.

Barry, K. (1995). *The prostitution of sexuality.* New York University Press: New York.

Belton, R. (1992). *Prostitution as traumatic reenactment,* 8th Annual Meeting of International Society Traumatic Stress Studies, Los Angeles CA Oct. 22, 1992.

Berman, G. (2002). *Judges and problem-solving courts.* Center for Court Innovation. Retrieved November 24, 2007 from: www.courtinnovation.org

Berman, G. & Feinblatt, J. (2001). Problem-solving courts: A brief primer. *Law and Policy, 23*(2) 125-140.

Binder, A. & Geis, G. (1984). Ad populum argumentation in criminology. *Crime and Delinquency, 30*, 309-333.

Buffalo Prostitution Task Force (1999). *Workable solutions to the problems of street prostitution in Buffalo.* Retrieved November 24, 2007 from: http://www.popcenter.org/problems/street_prostitution/PDFs/Workable%20Solutions.pdf

Casey, P. & Rottman, D. (2000). Therapeutic jurisprudence in the courts. *Behavioral Science Law, 18*, 445-457.

Cauvin, H. (2003). City's prostitution court targets defendants for aid. *Washington Post.* Retrieved November 21, 2007 from: http://www.walnet.org/csis/news/usa_2003/washpost-030515.html

El-Bassel, N., Schilling, R., Irwin, K., Faruque, S., Gilbert, L., Von Bargen, J., Serrano, Y., & Edlin, B. (1997). Sex trading and psychological distress among women recruited from the streets of Harlem. *American Journal of Public Health, 87*(1), 66-70.

Farole, D., Puffett, N., Rempel, M., & Byrne, F. (2005). Applying the problem-solving model outside of problem-solving courts. *Judicature, 89*, 40-43.

Farley, M. & Kelly, V. (2000). Prostitution: A critical review of the medical and social sciences Literature, *Women & Criminal Justice, 11*(4), 29-64.

Genesis House, *Fact sheet* (1998). Retrieved December 15, 2006 from: www.icasa.org/docs/prostitution.doc

Hartley, C. (2003). A therapeutic jurisprudence approach to the trial process in domestic violence felony trials. *Violence Against Women, 9*(4), 410-437.

Hinshaw, C. (2005). Taking a gamble: Applying therapeutic jurisprudence to compulsive gambling and establishing treatment courts. *Gaming Law Review, 9*(4), 333-342.

Homeward bound 2001: The facts behind the faces: A policy paper from the Chicago coalition for the homeless. Retrieved September 9, 2008 from: www.chicagohomeless.org/files/Archive/factsfigures/housingwrap.pdf

Hora, P., Schma, W., & Rosenthal, J. (1999). Therapeutic jurisprudence and the drug treatment court movement: Revolutionizing the criminal justice system's response to drug abuse and crime and America. *Notre Dame Law Review, 74*(2), 439-538.

Hunter, S. (1993). Prostitution is cruelty and abuse to women and children. *Michigan Journal of Gender and Law, 1*, 1-14.

Lawless, S., Kippax, S. & Crawford, J. (1996). Dirty, diseased, and undeserving: The positioning of HIV positive women. *Social Science and Medicine, 43*(9), 1371-1377.

Knipps, S. & Berman, G. (2000). New York's problem-solving courts provide meaningful alternatives to traditional remedies. *New York State Bar Journal, 72*(5), 8-10.

Mental health court learning sites (2003). Office of Justice Programs, U.S. Department of Justice. Retrieved November 20, 2007: http://consensusproject.org/downloads/Reno_snapshot.pdf

Miethe, T., Lu, H. & Reese, E. (2000). Reintegrative shaming and recidivism risks in drug courts: Explanations for some unexpected findings. *Crime and Delinquency, 46*(4), 522-541.

Mirchandani, R. (2005). What's so special about specialized courts? The state and social change in Salt Lake's City domestic violence court, *Law and Society Review, 37*, 379-418.

Norton-Hawk, M. (2001). The counterproductivity of incarcerating female street prostitutes. *Deviant Behavior, 22*(5), 403-417.

O'Leary, C & Howard, O. (2001). The prostitution of women and girls in metropolitan Chicago: A preliminary prevalence report center for impact research. Retrieved June 15, 2008 from: http://www.issuelab.org/click/download2/prostitution_of_women_and_girls_in_metropolitan_chicago_a_preliminary_prevalence_report/7446prostitutionreport.pdf

Raphael, J. & Shapiro, D. (2002). *Sisters speak out: The lives and needs of prostituted women in Chicago,* Center for Impact Research. Retrieved October 20, 2007 from: http://www.impactresearch.org/documents/sistersexecutivesummary.pdf

Rottman, D. & Casey, P. (2000). Therapeutic jurisprudence and the emergence of problem-solving courts. *National Institute of Justice Journal, 3,* 12-19.

Scott, M. (2001). *Street prostitution.* Problem-Oriented Guides for Police Series No. 2, U.S. Department of Justice, Office of Community Oriented Policing Services.

Slobogin, C. (1995). Therapeutic jurisprudence: Five dilemmas to ponder. *Psychology Public Policy and Law, 1*(1), 193-219.

Sterk, C. (2000). *Tricking and tripping : Prostitution in the era of AIDS.* Social Change Press: New York.

Sviridoff, M., Rottman, D., Ostrom, B., & Curtis, R. (1997). *Dispensing justice locally: The implementation and effects of the midtown community court.* Alexandria, Virginia: State Justice Institute.

Vanwesenbeeck, I. (1994) *Prostitutes' well-being and risk.* VU University Press, Amsterdam.

Weiner, A. (1996). Understanding the social needs of street walking prostitutes. *Social Work, 41*(1), 97-105.

Weitzer, R. (1999). Prostitution control in America: Rethinking public policy. *Crime, Law and Social Change, 32,* 83-102.

Wexler, D. & Winick, B. (1996). *Law in therapeutic key: Developments in therapeutic jurisprudence.* Carolina Academic Press: North Carolina.

Wexler, D. & Winick, B. (2003). Putting therapeutic jurisprudence to work. *ABA Journal, 89*(54), 54-57.

Winick, B. (1997). The jurisprudence of therapeutic jurisprudence. *Psychology, Public Policy and Law, 3*(1), 184-206.

Wolfe, R. (2005). *California's collaborative justice courts.* Justice Council of California, Administrative Office of the Court. Retrieved June 18, 2008 from: http://www.courtinfo.ca.gov/programs/collab/documents/California_Story.pdf

In: Contemporary Perspectives on Legal Regulation... ISBN 978-1-60741-161-1
Editor: Monica K. Miller

Chapter 6

Legal Restrictions on Procreation: Therapeutic Jurisprudence Suggests Alternatives that Avoid Unintended Legal, Health, and Gender-Based Consequences

Monica K. Miller [*] ***and Lorie L. Sicafuse***
University of Nevada, Reno, Nevada, USA

Abstract

Judges have issued probation or parole restrictions forbidding procreation, often because the person abused a child. Though well-intentioned, the restrictions come with legal, health, and ethical challenges. Specifically, procreation restrictions may infringe on individuals' Constitutional rights to privacy, bodily autonomy, and reproduction. They may burden women more than men because it is harder for women to hide a pregnancy; they could also encourage violence or abortion. Not only may procreation restrictions result in a host of unintended negative consequences, but they also fail to address the issues that bring parents into the legal system. Consequently, procreation restrictions are unlikely to be an effective solution to the complex problem of parental delinquency. Rather than administering potentially unconstitutional sanctions, judges and other legal professionals should consider viewing parental delinquency through the lens of therapeutic jurisprudence. Legal professionals adopting this perspective may address the economic, social, and mental health issues that underlie parental delinquency while maintaining due process and other important justice principles. This article discusses the history, intent, and usage of procreation restrictions. It identifies the potential negative outcomes that may result from procreation restrictions, and proposes therapeutic alternatives that may be more effective in addressing parental delinquency. It is concluded that the potential side effects of procreation restrictions and therapeutic alternatives to these sanctions should be carefully considered and studied. Ultimately, approaching cases of parental delinquency from the perspective of therapeutic jurisprudence may result in the prolonged well-being of both parents and children.

---

[*] Monica K. Miller was a fellow for the American Association of University Women while writing this article.

In February, 2006, 20-year-old Jaclyn Helsel was arrested after placing the dead body of her newborn son in a trash can outside of her apartment complex. Ms. Helsel, who had given birth to another child only 7 months earlier, failed to seek medical care for the premature infant who died approximately 10 minutes after birth. In an apparent effort to protect the well-being of potential future children, a Florida judge refused to release Ms. Helsel from jail until she agreed to refrain from sexual intercourse. Additionally, Ms. Helsel was ordered not to associate with any male over the age of 15 without supervision ("Judge to mom," 2006). While these restrictions may seem unusual, Ms. Helsel is not alone. Judges in many states have issued probation or parole restrictions that forbid sexual intercourse or procreation (e.g., *In the matter of BobbiJean P.*, 2007; *Krebs v. Schwarz*, 1997; *State v. Kline*, 1998). While many similar restrictions are ordered due to the parent's abusive behavior, unfavorable lifestyle, or failure to financially support the child, other procreation restrictions are issued in less extreme cases. In October, 2006, 26-year-old Mandy Nelson was sentenced to three years of probation for forgery. As part of her probation, Missouri Judge Daniel Kellog ordered the mother of three to refrain from having more children ("Mo Judge," 2006). Though the sentence (i.e., restrictions on sexual behavior or procreation) imposed for these two women are similar, their crimes are very different. While Ms. Helsel's crime was directly related to the safety of children, Ms. Nelson's crime had nothing to do with child safety and was arguably a less serious crime. These examples illustrate a variety of situations in which judges have issued orders restricting individuals' sexual and procreative behavior.

Although restrictions are intended to protect current and potential children from harm, the rulings in such cases come with serious legal and health-related challenges that should be carefully considered (see also, Miller, in press). First, procreation restrictions may infringe on women's Constitutional rights to privacy, bodily autonomy and reproduction. There are also health concerns; for instance a woman may feel she must undergo an invasive medical procedure, such as implanting of birth control devices or an abortion, to avoid violating the judge's orders. Importantly, these rulings create unequal burdens for men and women. It is harder for women to hide a pregnancy violation than it is for men to hide paternity. More generally, procreation restrictions are problematic because they fail to address the underlying problems that brought the individual into the legal system in the first place. Consequently, procreation restrictions may fail to decrease parental delinquency and result in a host of unintended consequences for both parents and children.

Therapeutic jurisprudence, "the study of the role of law as a therapeutic agent" (Wexler, 1995, p. 220), offers promising alternatives to procreation restrictions. Rather than attempting to solve complex social problems through extreme legal sanctions, therapeutic jurisprudence proposes that the law be administered in a manner that maximizes therapeutic outcomes (Winick, 1997). In adopting this approach, judges and attorneys may address the underlying causes of parental delinquency without condoning illegal behaviors.

This article will first discuss the major legal decisions regarding the permissibility of procreation restrictions, focusing especially on the challenges associated with such restrictions from a health and well-being standpoint. Next, it will present potential antitherapeutic consequences of procreation restrictions and examine the problem of parental delinquency from the perspective of therapeutic jurisprudence. It is concluded that, although these restrictions may be ordered with good intentions, they also come with a host of negative side effects. The overall outcomes, especially for mothers and children, should be thoroughly considered and studied. Despite the lack of definitive outcomes, it is likely that the risks posed by procreation restrictions outweigh the intended benefits. Instead, legal professionals should consider therapeutic alternatives to procreation restrictions.

Notable Examples of Procreation Restrictions

As the two cases described in the introduction illustrate, procreation restrictions may be ordered in response to a variety of delinquent behaviors. However, most procreation restrictions have involved crimes closely related to children. Specifically, courts have issued restrictions because of the parents' abuse or failure to support children financially.

Abuse and Neglect

The most common reason courts have restricted procreation is due to abuse or neglect. Appeals courts have sometimes upheld such restrictions. Kenneth Krebs was convicted of sexually abusing his daughter and, as a condition of his probation, Krebs was ordered to seek permission from his probation officer prior to engaging in a sexual relationship (*Krebs v. Schwarz,* 1997). When Krebs appealed this ruling, the Wisconsin Court of Appeals upheld the probation restriction because the restriction did not constitute a *complete* ban on his right to procreate; Krebs only needed to seek permission from his probation officer before having sex. The court determined that the restriction was not overly broad, was reasonably related to his rehabilitation, and was generally related to the protection of the public.

Temporary procreation restrictions were also upheld in *State v. Kline* (1998). While serving 36 months probation for criminal mistreatment, Tad Kline abused his two and a half year old daughter by screaming obscenities at her, throwing her in her crib, and breaking her leg. In 1990, Mr. Kline and his wife Krista had their parental rights to their first child terminated after Mr. Kline broke his son's arm and inflicted multiple bruises. During his probation revocation hearing, the court imposed an additional condition to Mr. Kline's probation: He was not to father additional children until completing drug counseling and anger management treatment. Citing concern for the children's safety and the temporary nature of these restrictions, the Oregon Court of Appeals upheld this condition.

Other courts have found procreation restrictions unconstitutional. In 2001, Kristie Trammell, who had twice been convicted of child abuse, was put on probation after her abuse led to the death of her infant son (*Trammell v. State*). The trial court judge forbid her from becoming pregnant as part of her parole restrictions; however, the appeals court rejected the restriction because it did not serve a rehabilitative purpose. Similarly, the appeals courts in *People v. Pointer* (1984) rejected a procreation restriction, holding that the condition was overbroad and was not intended to rehabilitate the mother. Ruby Pointer had placed her two children on a strict macrobiotic diet, which consisted largely of grains, beans and vegetables. Although a doctor determined that her son's health was in extreme jeopardy, she refused medical care for him. The doctor called the authorities, and she was convicted of abandonment and neglect. Pointer was ordered not to conceive another child during her during her five-year probation period, an order that was struck down by higher court. Other courts have also rejected procreation restrictions imposed on mothers (see, e.g., *People v. Ferrell*, 1995; *People v. Zaring*, 1992; *Rodriguez v. State*, 1979; *State v. Mosburg*, 1989).

Financial Support

Procreation restrictions have also been ordered for parents who fail to support their children financially. In the landmark case of *State v. Oakley* (2001), David Oakley had fathered nine children by four mothers and had not paid child support for 120 days, a felony in Wisconsin. The judge sentenced Oakley to five years of probation and ordered him not to father any children until he could demonstrate ability to support his existing children and a future child. The Wisconsin court upheld the restriction; thus, the restriction due to his failure to financially provide for his children was acceptable.

Other courts have come to a different conclusion, however. In 2004, a judge forbade Stephanie Pendleton from having more children until she could demonstrate her ability to provide for her existing children, who were in foster care (*In re BobbiJean P.*, 2004). The judge stated that "She should not have yet another child which must be cared for at public expense before she has proven herself able to care for other children" and determined that "The court must balance individual privacy rights with the state's overriding interest in protecting children and limiting the financial and societal burden created by caring for neglected children." While also suggesting concern for the child's physical welfare, the judge clearly demonstrated her concern for the child's financial well-being. The New York appeals court overruled the judge in 2007, finding that she had exceeded her authority (*In the matter of BobbiJean P.*, 2007).

Similarly, the Ohio appeals court rejected a procreation restriction resulting from a parent's inability to pay $38,000 in child support, finding that the restriction was overbroad because the judge's order did not state whether the restriction could be lifted if the debt was paid (*State v. Talty*, 2004). Most recently, in 2005, a New York judge forbade a mother, known in court documents as Judgette W. from having more children because she had "demonstrated that…she will not or cannot reasonably … provide for the child's needs financially, by any legitimate means" and did not have "the ability to care physically, emotionally or financially for [the baby]" because she was addicted to drugs and homeless (Ertelt, 2005; *In re V.R.*, 2004). Six of Judgette's children were in foster care and one lived with an aunt. The judge's hope was that the restriction would help Judgette improve her life, including her financial situation.

In sum, child abuse, drug use, and failure to pay child support are serious social issues with the potential to cause children immeasurable harm. Many judges feel that procreation restrictions are justified responses to such situations. Nevertheless, it is important to consider the challenges associated with these restrictions. Only after considering both the positive and negative effects can a judgment be made as to the utility of procreation restrictions.

Issues Associated with Procreation Restrictions

Although intended to protect current and potential children, procreation restrictions pose a variety of legal and health-related issues (e.g., Miller, in press), which disproportionately affect women. Each of these issues is discussed to provide a fuller picture of the potential effects of procreation restrictions.

Legal Consequences

The first consequence presented by procreation restrictions poses a legal dilemma. Despite taking precautions, a woman could conceive a child. In such a case, the legal system would be faced with hard choices (Miller, in press). Punishing this probation or parole violation could mean sending her to prison for having a child. Such an outcome would contradict the very reasons for the restriction, which include protecting children from being financially unsupported. The state would, in many cases, have to support the child through foster care as long as the mother is imprisoned. On the other hand, if there were no consequences for this violation, the legal system would send a message that violations of parole and probation orders are not a serious matter. Therefore, a violated restriction presents the courts with a legal dilemma with seemingly no positive outcome.

Another legal issue associated with these prohibitions involves their enforcement. Enforcing restrictions on sexual relationships or procreation requires the courts to have knowledge of a defendant's sexual activity and pregnancy status. While it is typically obvious if a woman becomes pregnant, it is particularly difficult for legal actors like probation officers and judges to know whether a man's partner has become pregnant. Even more difficult is the monitoring of restrictions on sexual behavior (as in *Krebs v. Schwarz,* 1997).

Procreation restrictions can also violate an individual's Constitutional rights to privacy, bodily autonomy, and reproduction. The U.S. Supreme Court recognized the importance of fundamental "privacy" rights in *Griswold v. Connecticut* (1965) and *Eisenstadt v. Baird* (1972) stating, "if the right of privacy means anything, it is the right of the individual, married or single, to be free from unwarranted governmental intrusion into matters so fundamentally affecting a person as the decision whether to bear or beget a child" (p. 453). Similarly, procreation restrictions could infringe on the right to bodily autonomy. In 1891, the U.S. Supreme Court noted that "no right is held more sacred...than the right of every individual to the possession and control of his own person, free from restraint or interference of others, unless by clear and unquestionable authority of law" (*Union Pacific Railway Co. v. Botsford,* 1891, p. 251). In this case, the court refused to force an individual to submit to an unwanted medical examination. Whether a procreation restriction similarly infringes on the individual's right to be "free from restraint," and whether the court deciding procreation restriction cases has "clear and unquestionable authority of the law" is not clear, as the situation has not been addressed by the Supreme Court.

Along the same lines, the right to refuse medical treatment is long-standing in the country's history and reinforced by the U.S. Supreme Court (*Cruzan v. Director of the Missouri Health Department,* 1990). However, the coercive nature of procreation restrictions may lead individuals to feel they have no choice but to be sterilized, have an invasive procedure, or take hormonal birth control pills. In these cases, an individual's right to be free from unwanted medical procedures and treatments is potentially violated.

Additionally, procreation restrictions may violate an individual's reproductive freedoms. The U.S. Supreme Court has declared that the government cannot infringe on an individual's right to procreate (*Skinner v. Oklahoma,* 1942). In *Skinner,* a state law mandated the permanent sterilization of repeat criminals. The Court concluded that this violated the defendant's fundamental rights, and found the law unconstitutional. Similarly, an argument could be made that procreation restrictions also violate this right. Typically, courts uphold procreation restrictions as long as they are provisional (unlike the sterilization required by the law in the *Skinner* case). For some of the defendants, however, the restriction is essentially permanent. In theory, a parent who is ordered not to have any children until she pays tens of thousands of dollars in child support could technically still have children once this payment is made. In reality, she may never be able to pay this debt; thus, the restriction is essentially permanent. As such, both procreation restrictions and sterilization are permanent restrictions on the right to bear children.

Finally, because procreation restrictions may infringe upon an individual's fundamental rights, they are subject to the strict scrutiny standard of judicial review (Epps, 2008). Consequently, any imposition of procreation restrictions must not only be justified by a compelling government interest, but also be narrowly tailored and the least restrictive means of achieving this interest. Although the protection of children is unquestionably a compelling government interest (Epps, 2008), they are unlikely to be an effective means of accomplishing this goal. Moreover, permanent and essentially permanent procreation restrictions may be conceptualized as overly broad. Most significantly, a variety of less restrictive alternatives may be imposed to further the compelling government interest of child protection. In the case of *People v. Pointer* (1984), the court identified routine pregnancy testing, prenatal monitoring, and termination of parental rights as less restrictive alternatives to procreation restrictions. The failure of procreation restrictions to meet strict scrutiny standards furthers the notion that such sanctions may be unconstitutional.

Health-Related Consequences

Procreation restrictions potentially conflict with the state's interests in promoting citizens' health and well-being (Miller, in press). If individuals do not wish to abstain from sexual behavior, they must utilize birth control. The most effective means of contraception involve medical procedures, hormones, or both (US Department of Health and Human Services, 2005). Like all invasive procedures, sterilization and Norplant may result in medical complications, a few of which are potentially severe. Popular forms of hormonal contraception such as birth control pills come with side effects like blood clots and stroke; Depo-Provera injections can result in a loss of bone density and may increase the risk of bone fractures and osteoporosis (US Department of Health and Human Services, 2005).

If a woman becomes pregnant, she faces a difficult dilemma. The way she chooses to solve the dilemma could affect her health and well-being. Facing imprisonment, some women may feel that their only choice is to have an abortion. Not only do abortions performed by qualified medical professionals pose serious health risks such as infection, blood clots, and death, but women who feel forced to terminate a pregnancy may experience serious, long-term emotional problems (Planned Parenthood, 2008). Further, the majority of women who are ordered to refrain from having children have serious financial problems.

Women unable to pay for abortion procedures offered by legitimate medical providers may turn to less qualified individuals for services or perform a self-induced abortion.

Alternatively, a woman could choose to hide her pregnancy by starving herself so that her probation officer does not notice the pregnancy, or she could go into hiding. In these instances, she would be unlikely to get prenatal care, which can be detrimental to the fetus (Sovinski, 1997). Such a choice could also have a negative effect on the mother's emotional and social well-being.

In addition, such restrictions may have negative effects on the well-being of children born to individuals with procreation restrictions (Miller, in press). For example, when a parent is imprisoned, it conflicts with the state's interests in providing for children. If the parent is working, her wages can be garnished, providing at least some support for her children. However, if she violates her probation restriction by having another child, she will be incarcerated and unable to support any of her children (McCanna, 2003). Children raised in poverty are at risk for a variety of health-related problems stemming from poor living conditions and lack of quality nutrition and healthcare. Enforcement of this probation restriction ensures that none of her children will be supported, an outcome that is counter to the intended purpose of the restriction.

Further, a child who has knowledge that her existence led to her parent's punishment could experience mental anguish (McCanna, 2003). In such scenarios, parents are unable to bond with their children while imprisoned. The children would likely be sent to foster care, and parents may not ever regain custody. This transition into foster care is associated with a host of negative outcomes. Children in foster care may be especially vulnerable to further abuse and neglect, and the majority of children in foster care experience feelings of fear, sadness, confusion, and stress. Parental separation coupled with a history of maltreatment increases children's susceptibility to posttraumatic stress disorders, depression, and social problems (Bruskas, 2008). These outcomes could be counter to the state's interests in protecting children's health and well-being. This list of health-related consequences illustrates some of the difficulties surrounding procreation restrictions, and many of these consequences are more likely to affect women.

Disproportionate Effects on Women

The discussion above demonstrates that there are various legal and health-related consequences associated with procreation restrictions. Unfortunately, women are at greater risk of experiencing these consequences than are men. Procreation restrictions are potentially discriminatory because they are more likely to have legal implications for women than for men (see also, Miller, in press). Women are more likely to be "caught" violating a procreation restriction, and are thus more likely to face legal consequences. A probation officer would likely be unaware of a man's violation unless he fathers a child and his partner seeks child support or reports his infraction to authorities. On the other hand, a woman with a procreation restriction cannot as easily hide a pregnancy.

Women also bear more health risks than men. In order to take personal responsibility for preventing pregnancy, most men can use condoms to prevent violating their restriction, but women typically have to do something more invasive like take medication, get sterilized, or get Norplant or an IUD implanted. Although there are less obtrusive birth control methods available for women, these are typically less effective and pose a greater risk of accidental conception. The most common birth control methods for women are more invasive and pose greater health risks than the most common birth control methods for men. If a pregnancy does result, a woman may feel as if she must have an abortion in order to avoid a violation and going to prison. She may even obtain an illegal abortion, fearing that her probation officer will find out about her pregnancy. A man who has a procreation restriction would not be faced with this difficult choice. Moreover, men may be less susceptible to the emotional trauma women may experience when they feel forced to terminate a pregnancy.

A special consequence concerns female partners of men with procreation restrictions, who are especially at risk for abuse. In such cases, the man may fear going to prison because of the pregnancy. He may become violent or force the woman to have an abortion. Additionally, men with procreation restrictions may be especially likely to have a history of violent and abusive behavior (e.g., *State v. Kline*, 1998), increasing their partners' risk of being victimized in cases of unintended pregnancy. Hopefully, such cases are rare. Nevertheless, this is an important consideration for judges to ponder when determining what restrictions to impose.

As these examples illustrate, women are especially affected by procreation restrictions. While the legal and health-related dilemmas affect men, they are particularly troublesome for women. Because of these issues, the utility of such restrictions is questionable. As an alternative to the imposition of potentially ineffective and unconstitutional sanctions, judges should consider the merits of viewing these legal issues through the lens of therapeutic jurisprudence.

Therapeutic Alternatives to Procreation Restrictions

Procreation restrictions are intended to protect future children from harm and to motivate delinquent parents to "turn their lives around." Not only are procreation restrictions such as these unlikely to yield these desired outcomes, they do not address the underlying behavioral, emotional, health, social, and employment problems that brought the individual into the courtroom (Miller, 2006). Further, procreation restrictions do not tackle broader issues of violence, homelessness, and drug abuse that underlie parental delinquency. Because procreation restrictions are overly simplistic solutions to very complex problems, they are unlikely to be effective at influencing behavior or creating positive changes. In applying therapeutic jurisprudence to cases that may typically elicit the administration of procreation restrictions, judges should address the underling issues that brought the parents into the legal system, resulting in more therapeutic outcomes for both parents and children. Attention to the underlying problems is the best way to achieve the positive outcomes for parents and children.

Therapeutic jurisprudence proposes that judges and attorneys should recognize that their actions and decisions can have therapeutic or antitherapeutic consequences (Casey & Rottman, 2000). The conceptualization of therapeutic jurisprudence as a practice reform rather than a law reform contributes to its discretionary nature and broad scope. Drawing on social science research and principles, judges and attorneys must carefully consider the aspects of each case in order to maximize therapeutic outcomes without subordinating due process or other justice values (Casey & Rottman, 2000). In cases of parental delinquency, judges and attorneys adopting this perspective must recognize the underlying causes of deviant behaviors to ensure the law is administered in a therapeutic manner.

The Antitherapeutic Consequences of Procreation Restrictions

Judges order defendants to refrain from having more children based on the belief that such restrictions are in the best interest of future children, and possibly current children and the parent. However, these decisions cannot be considered therapeutic, as they fail to address the factors that led these defendants to violate the law. Simply put, restrictions to do not teach abusive parents how to control their anger, help drug abusers stop using drugs or help unskilled parents find higher paying jobs that would enable them to financially support their children. These issues may be particularly difficult to address for women, who may have an especially difficult time finding a job or a drug rehabilitation program that can accommodate the needs of a mother or pregnant woman. Not only does the failure to acknowledge these issues lead to antitherapeutic consequences, but it also may increase the likelihood that these restrictions will not be followed. For example, a woman who continues to live in poverty, abuse drugs, and engage in prostitution may be less likely to have access to birth control, be more likely to be in an impaired mental state and be more likely to engage in sexual activity than a mentally stable woman with economic resources. Thus, the administration of procreation restrictions may not prevent intended or unintended pregnancy.

The potential antitherapeutic consequences of procreation restrictions may extend beyond the parents to their existing and future children. First, procreation restrictions do not address the primary factors that perpetuate child maltreatment: Poverty, drug abuse, mental illness, and lack of parenting skills (Asawa, Hanson, & Flood, 2008). Consequently, the administration of procreation restrictions may not prevent child abuse and neglect. Second, restrictions typically do not provide mothers with any education regarding child development and parenting. This lack of knowledge coupled with the admonition that a defendant is unfit to bear children may lead to a further decline in parental self-efficacy, which has been linked to child abuse and neglect (Jones & Prinz, 2005). Third, the fallibility of birth control methods, the overrepresentation of single mothers in the legal system, and the possibility of non-adherence to procreation restrictions increases the likelihood that pregnant mothers with dependant children will face incarceration. The temporary loss of their mother robs children of the stable and continuous environment necessary for healthy development (Brooks, 1999). Finally, a child who was conceived to a parent with a procreation restriction may experience potentially devastating psychological consequences related to immense guilt over her mother's incarceration. These examples demonstrate that procreation restrictions do little to help, and may even harm existing and future children.

As previously mentioned, the maintenance of due process and legal principles is a pre-requisite to any application of therapeutic jurisprudence. Ironically, ordering procreation restrictions violates the legal values that therapeutic jurisprudence strives to uphold. Aside from infringing upon Constitutional rights, procreation restrictions undermine the principles of procedural justice: That the law should be administered in a fair, ethical, and respectful manner (Tyler, 2006). This violation is particularly observable in the Mandy Nelson case. Not only did Ms. Nelson express shock and confusion regarding her sentence ("Mo Judge," 2006), but her crime (forgery) was not directly related to her parenting ability. Further, Ms. Nelson had already undergone a sterilization procedure prior to her trial ("Mo Judge," 2006). As a result, Ms. Nelson may feel that her sentence was unfair; certainly the sentence was not in accord with the principles of therapeutic jurisprudence or procedural justice. In contrast, judges who opt to view parental delinquency through the lens of therapeutic jurisprudence may maximize the therapeutic consequences of their decisions without subordinating legal precepts.

Applying Therapeutic Jurisprudence to Cases of Parental Delinquency

Any given legal imposition may have therapeutic consequences for one defendant and antitherapeutic consequences for another (Wexler, 1995). Thus, judges and attorneys must rely on previous experience, social science research, and interdisciplinary consultants when considering the law from a therapeutic perspective. Therapeutic jurisprudence may be applied to a broad range of legal decisions, but it is most commonly utilized in individual cases and in specialized (e.g., drug and family) courts. Although the practice of therapeutic jurisprudence varies according to the characteristics of the case, a variety of judicial decisions may help to address the issues that brought delinquent parents into the legal system and maximize the likelihood of therapeutic outcomes for both parents and children. Consistent with the tenets of therapeutic jurisprudence, judges administering such decisions must not minimize the severity of delinquent behaviors and encourage defendants to accept responsibility for their harmful actions (Edwards & Hensley, 2001; Hartley, 2003).

The complex social issue of poverty underlies the behaviors of many parents who have been ordered to refrain from having children. David Oakley was unable to pay child support (*State v. Oakley*, 2001), Stephanie Pendleton was unable to financially support her children (*In re BobbiJean P.*, 2004), and Judgette W. resorted to prostitution as a means of survival (Ertelt, 2005). Although judicial decisions may have limited potential to modify the social structural factors that contribute to poverty, a combination of court-ordered interventions may help delinquent parents develop the necessary skills to escape destitution. For example, a judge may order delinquent parents to attend general job training and money management classes, complete community service, and obtain a GED or high school diploma. When coupled with accessibility to job placement services, such judicial actions may not only help ameliorate financial difficulties but also increase defendants' compliance with restitution orders.

Drug abuse, a common theme in cases involving procreation restrictions (e.g., *In re Bobbijean P.*, 2004; *In re V.R.*, 2004; *State v. Kline*, 1998) and a significant predictor of child maltreatment (Asawa et al., 2008) has been successfully addressed utilizing therapeutic jurisprudence principles. Senjo and Leip (2001) found that supportive court monitoring and the establishment of a positive relationship between judges and defendants were linked to the successful completion of court-ordered intensive drug treatment programs. Epps (2008) maintains that court-ordered programs targeting parents with substance abuse problems are promising alternatives to procreation restrictions. Programs focused on delinquent parents in Nevada and Illinois have demonstrated success in increasing treatment completion rates and in reuniting parents with their children. Consistent with the principles of therapeutic jurisprudence, both programs emphasized advocacy, encouragement, and accountability (Epps, 2008). In cases of parental delinquency, legal professionals must consider the value of court-ordered drug treatment programs and administer such orders from a therapeutic perspective.

A lack of parenting skills and knowledge of child development are perhaps the primary causes of child abuse and neglect (Asawa et al., 2008), and remain at the forefront of many cases involving procreation restrictions (e.g., *People v. Pointer*, 1984; *Trammel v. State*, 2001). Ordering delinquent parents to attend parenting classes may dramatically increase the potential for therapeutic outcomes for both parents and children (Lederman & Osofsky, 2004), and anger management training may help parents respond to misbehaviors in an appropriate and caring manner. Following such interventions with regular home visitations from social workers has proven an effective means of preventing child maltreatment in many cases (Asawa et al., 2008).

Many cases involving procreation restrictions are likely further complicated by mental illness. Psychopathology is a common theme in many instances of child maltreatment. In examining 206 court records of seriously abused and neglected children, Taylor et al. (1991) found that 84% of parents in these cases had been diagnosed with a DSM III mental disorder. Often, mental illness accompanies many of the underlying factors that contribute to parental delinquency. Ruby Pointer's decision to place her children on a strict macrobiotic diet illustrates the effects of inadequate knowledge regarding child development and nutrition. However, Ms. Pointer's behaviors may have also been influenced by mental illness. According to her physician, Ms. Pointer suffered an "altered state of reality" and reportedly had an extreme fear of chemicals (*People v. Pointer*, 1984). Because therapeutic jurisprudence is primarily concerned with the law's impact on mental and physical health (Winick, 1997), legal professionals adopting this approach must carefully consider the mental status of parental delinquents that appear in court. Specifically, these individuals should be strongly encouraged to utilize mental health assessment and treatment services provided by the court. In cases that have established a direct link between parents' mental health and child maltreatment, judges may order defendants to undergo psychological counseling.

Because the majority of the above interventions are court-ordered and defendants are held accountable for their actions, these applications of therapeutic jurisprudence to the problem of parental delinquency maintain due process and other important justice principles. However, in cases involving female defendants, legal professionals and social services must recognize the specific challenges women face in overcoming the issues that lead to parental delinquency. Court-ordered drug treatment programs must accommodate pregnant women; job placement services should focus on finding flexible employment for single mothers. Providing child care referrals would assist mothers in completing community service and educational requirements. Additionally, due to the prevalence of mental illness among defendants in cases involving procreation restrictions and the strong association between stress, depression, and child maltreatment (Asawa et al., 2008), therapeutic principles mandate that courts provide mental health services to delinquent parents. Accessibility to psychological counseling coupled with sanctions that address the underlying causes of delinquency may establish the optimal foundation for the development of therapeutic outcomes.

Conclusion

Judges who impose procreation restrictions likely feel that the restrictions are beneficial. There is no doubt that child abuse, drug exposed-babies, and financially unsupported children are major social issues that need to be addressed. Nevertheless, the potential consequences considered here illuminate the problems that procreation restrictions create (see also, Miller in press). These side effects are particularly problematic because they disproportionately affect women. Consequently, it is important to weigh the potential costs and benefits associated with procreation restrictions. Social scientists should carefully study the effects of such restrictions, noting both the positive and negative outcomes. To date, there is no definitive research that explains the effects of these restrictions. Nevertheless, it is likely that the risks posed by procreation restrictions outweigh the intended benefits.

Approaching cases of child maltreatment, parental drug abuse, and other forms of parental delinquency from the perspective of therapeutic jurisprudence is an attractive alternative to the administration of legally problematic procreation restrictions. Not only does the application of therapeutic jurisprudence to such legal issues uphold individuals' Constitutional rights and justice values, but it also addresses the underlying factors responsible for delinquent behavior. By drawing on experience and social science research, legal professionals utilizing therapeutic jurisprudence may impose appropriate sanctions to help ameliorate the consequences of poverty, drug abuse, and poor parenting skills. Ultimately, viewing parental delinquency through the lens of therapeutic jurisprudence may lead to prolonged well-being of both parents and children- the outcomes that procreation restrictions strive for but fail to achieve.

REFERENCES

Asawa, L. E., Hansen, D. J., & Flood, M. F. (2008). Early childhood intervention programs: Opportunities and challenges for preventing child maltreatment. Education and Treatment of Children, 31(1), 73-110.

Brooks, S. L. (1999). Therapeutic jurisprudence and preventative law in child welfare proceedings. Psychology, Public Policy, and Law, 5(4), 951-965.

Bruskas, D. (2008). Children in foster care: A vulnerable population at risk. Journal of Child and Adolescent Psychiatric Nursing, 21(2), 70-77.

Casey, R., & Rottman, D. B. (2000). Therapeutic jurisprudence in the courts. Behavioral Sciences and the Law, 18, 445-457.

Cruzan v. Director of the Missouri Health Department, 497 U.S. 261 (1990).

Edwards, W., & Hensley, C. (2001). Restructuring sex offender sentencing: A therapeutic jurisprudence approach to the criminal justice process. International Journal of Offender Therapy and Comparative Criminology, 45(6), 646-662.

Eisenstadt v. Baird, 405 U.S. 438 (1972).

Epps, F. A. (2008). The right responsibility: Does the right to procreate include the responsibility to parent? Ohio Northern University Law Review, 34, 85-133.

Ertelt, S. (2005). Judge orders woman not to have more children, rules out abortion. Retrieved September 13, 2008 from www.lifenews.com/state825.html.

Griswold v. Connecticut, 381 U.S. 479 (1965).

Hartley, C. C. (2003). A therapeutic jurisprudence approach to the trial process in domestic violence felony trials. Violence Against Women, 9(4), 410-437.

In re Bobbijean P., 2004 WL 834480 (N.Y. Fam. Ct. 2004).

In re V.R., 2004 WL 3029874 (N.Y. Fam. Ct. Dec. 22, 2004).

In the matter of BobbiJean P., 842 N.W.S.2d 826 (NY 2007).

Jones, T. L., & Prinz, R. J. (2005). Potential roles of parental self-efficacy in parent and child adjustment: A review. Clinical Psychology Review, 25, 341-363.

Judge to mom: "No more sex" (2006, March 31). *WESH News*. Retrieved September 13, 2008, from http://www.wesh.com/news/8392209/detail/html

Krebs v. Schwarz, 568 N.W. 2d 26 (Wis. Ct. App. 1997).

Lederman, C. S., & Osofsky, J. D. (2004). Infant mental health interventions in juvenile court. Psychology, Public Policy, and Law, 10(1), 162-177.

McCanna, K. E. (2003). A hot debate in the summer of 2001: State v. Oakley's excessive intrusion on procreative rights. Indiana Law Review, 36, 857-881.

Miller, M.K. (in press). Legally Restricting Procreation: The challenges, dilemmas, and unequal effects of the judicial trend on men and women. Women's Policy Journal of Harvard.

Miller, M. K. (2006). Avoiding policies that unnecessarily harm women, children and society: Promoting comprehensive justice. Restorative Directions Journal, 2, 75-89.

Mo judge tells woman: No more pregnancies (2006, October 18). *Associated Press*. Retrieved November 28, 2008, from http://www.stltoday.com/stltoday/news/stories/nsf/missouristatenews/story/6098E92F9A19636F8625720B004D909A?OpenDocument

People v. Ferrell, 659 N.E.2d 992 (Ill. App. Ct. 1995).

People v. Pointer, 199 Cal. Rptr. 357 (Cal. Ct. App. 1984).

People v. Zaring, 10 Cal. Rptr. 2d 263 (Cal. Ct. App. 1992).

Planned Parenthood (2008). Abortion Procedures. Retrieved August 15, 2008, from http://www.plannedparenthood.org/health-topics/abortion/abortion-procedures-4359.htm.

Rodriguez v. State, 378 So. 2d 7 (Fla. Dist. Ct. App. 1979).

Senjo, S. R., & Leip, L. A. (2001). Testing and developing theory in drug court: A four-part logit model to predict program completion. Criminal Justice Policy Review, 12(1), 66-87.

Skinner v. Oklahoma, 316 U.S. 535 (1942).

Sovinski, C.J. (1997). The criminalization of maternal substance abuse: A quick fix to a complex problem. Pepperdine Law Review, 25, 107-139.

State v. Kline, 963 P. 2d 698 (Or. Ct. App. 1998).

State v. Mosburg, 768 P.2d 313 (Kan. Ct. App. 1989).

State v. Oakley, 629 N.W. 2d 200 (Wis. 2001).

State v. Talty, 814 N.E. 2d 1201 (Ohio 2004).

Taylor, C. G., Norman, D. K., Murphy, J. M., Jellenik, M., Quinn, D., Poitrast, F. G., et al. (1991). Diagnosed intellectual and emotional impairment among parents who seriously mistreat their children: Prevalence, type, and outcome in a court sample. Child Abuse & Neglect, 15, 389-401.

Trammell v. State, 751 N.E.2d 283 (Ind Ct. app. 2001).

Tyler, T. R. (2006). Restorative justice and procedural justice: Dealing with rule breaking. Journal of Social Issues, 62(2), 307-326.

Union Pacific Railway Co. v. Botsford, 141 U.S. 250 (1891).

US Department of Health and Human Services (2005). Birth Control Methods. Retrieved September 13, 2008, from http://www.womenshealth.gov/faq/birthcont.htm

Wexler, D. B. (1995). Reflections on the scope of therapeutic jurisprudence. Psychology, Public Policy, and Law, 1(1), 220-236.

Winick, B. J. (1997). The jurisprudence of therapeutic jurisprudence. Psychology, Public Policy, and Law, 3(1), 184-206.

In: Contemporary Perspectives on Legal Regulation...
Editor: Monica K. Miller

ISBN 978-1-60741-161-1

Chapter 7

THE LAW AND THE PSYCHOLOGY OF PARENTAL NOTIFICATION: IMPLICATIONS FOR POLICY AND FUTURE RESEARCH

Alicia Summers and Monica K. Miller
University of Nevada, Reno, Nevada, USA

ABSTRACT

Parental notification laws, which require minors to inform their parents of their intent to obtain an abortion, remain a controversial issue within the United States. State courts have offered varied rulings when determining the constitutionality of parental notification clauses (*Ayotte v. Planned Parenthood of Northern New England,* 2006). Many states require that minors notify their parents before obtaining an abortion. However, there is not a consensus as to whether parental notification is the best approach for both teens and parents. In order to address this complex issue, both legal and psychological considerations must be addressed. First, a history of parental notification laws and cases is presented, using examples of recent judicial decisions. Psychological research that can inform the issue is addressed, such as developmental issues in adolescent's decision-making and communication. For example, research has shown that adolescents have reasoning abilities and decision-making skills that are as good as adults. This suggests that teens can make the decision alone. However, research has also discovered that states with parental notification laws have lower minor abortion rates. Arguments for and against parental notification are presented and implications for future research are addressed.

According to the National Abortion Federation (2007), every year, one million teenagers become pregnant, and the vast majority (78%) of these pregnancies are unintended. Of these pregnancies, more than one third choose to have an abortion. Minors often face more obstacles than adults when attempting to have an abortion. One potential obstacle is that of parental involvement. At present, 36 states have parental involvement laws currently in effect, seven states have parental involvement laws which are not in effect, and seven states and

Washington, D.C. have no parental involvement laws (Planned Parenthood, 2007). Parental involvement laws require parental consent or parental notification before a minor can get an abortion. It is the latter that will be the focus of the current article, although many issues discussed are relevant to both forms of parental involvement.

Parental notification laws are controversial, both from a legal and a psychological perspective. At present, 15 states have these laws, although, in four of the states, the laws are not currently in effect (Planned Parenthood, 2007). These 15 states do not include New Hampshire, which had a recent parental notification case, *Ayotte v. Planned Parenthood of Northern New England* (2005), make it to the Supreme Court, before being remanded to the lower court for decision. The state legislature made a decision in June of 2008 to repeal the law, becoming the first state to repeal a law requiring parental notification prior to minor girls obtaining an abortion (Belluck, 2007). This is just one of many legal cases which have surrounded the ongoing legal debate regarding parental notification.

Proponents and opponents of the laws debate over its validity both on legal and psychological grounds. The main legal arguments for parental involvement are that it protects the rights of the parents and ensures that minors are fully aware of their options (Ellerston, 1997). The main legal arguments against parental involvement are that it infringes on the rights of the minor, impedes access to competent medical care, and can delay abortions, which increases medical risks (Ellerston, 1997). In addition to legal arguments, several psychological arguments have arisen. Proponents of the law argue that parental involvement offers support to minors during a stressful event, facilitates family unity, and promotes responsible sexual behavior among minors (Ellerston, 1997). Proponents also argue that minors are not capable of making good decisions. Opponents of the law argue that it increases the birthrate by deterring minors from abortion, traumatizes minors, and can lead to emotional or physical abuse (Ellerston, 1997).

The current article seeks to inform the debate by examining legal issues that have arisen over the years, as well as psychological research which can inform the ongoing controversy over the impact and necessity of such laws. Policy recommendations and directions of future research will also be addressed.

THE LEGAL ISSUES

In the historic *Roe v. Wade* (1973) case, the United States Supreme Court determined it was unconstitutional for a state to restrict a woman's access to an abortion. However, this case failed to address the rights of minors to obtain an abortion. In recent years, courts across the nation have been faced with determining the constitutionality of parental notification clauses in state abortion laws. In general, such laws require a minor to notify one or both parents before obtaining an abortion (e.g., *H.L. v. Matheson,* 1981). However, these laws also require a judicial bypass procedure to be in place, whereby a judge can grant a minor permission to get an abortion without the consent of her parents if she meets certain criteria (*Bellotti v. Baird*, 1979). The issue has sparked much controversy, with several states weighing in on the issue. In the 2005-2006 session, another case reached the US Supreme Court (*Ayotte v. Planned Parenthood of Northern New England*, 2005). The Supreme Court did not rule on the case, but sent the decision back to the lower courts and asked them to consider including a medical exception to the parental notification law; otherwise the entire law in unconstitutional. This section will present a history of parental notification laws and examples of recent judicial decisions.

Supreme Court Cases in which the Law has been Challenged

The courts have long agreed that parental authority in their own household is the foundation of American society (*Ginsberg v. New York*, 1968; *Hodsgon v. Minnesota*, 1990). However, in 1976, the Supreme Court held that parents may not veto their child's decision to have an abortion; the court also noted that it is permissible to encourage an unmarried pregnant minor to seek advice or help from her parents in making such an important decision (*Planned Parenthood of Central Missouri v. Danforth*, 1976). The Supreme Court has addressed both parental consent of minor abortion and parental notification of minor abortion.

In the case of *Bellotti v. Baird* (1979), the Supreme Court decided the constitutionality of a parental consent statute in Massachusetts that required consent of both parents, unless there was a medical emergency. The Court found that the statute was unconstitutional because it did not allow for an appropriate judicial bypass. It did not allow for a minor who was mature to bypass the consent process, it did not allow for a minor who showed it was in her best interest to bypass the consent process, and it did not allow for prompt judicial bypass (*Bellotti v. Baird*). The *Bellotti* case set the standard for judicial bypasses or waivers required in parental notification or consent cases. In addition to the *Bellotti* case, the Supreme Court has also ruled on parental notification statutes.

Since *Bellotti,* the Supreme Court has upheld several parental notification statutes (*H.L. v. Matheson,* 1981; *Lambert v. Wicklund,* 1997; *Ohio v. Akron Center for Reproductive Health,* 1990). For example, in *Akron*, the Court reversed a decision which had invalidated an Ohio statute that required parental notification prior to a minor's abortion. The Court held that the notification was constitutional because it allowed for a bypass if her parents had abused her, she was mature enough to make the decision herself, or it was in her best interest not to notify her parents. In contrast, in *Hodgson v. Minnesota* (1990), the Supreme Court ruled that a Minnesota law requiring both parents to be notified of a minor's abortion was unconstitutional because the requirement of two-parent notice was not reasonably related to state's interest. However, the separate judicial bypass provision was considered constitutional. This line of cases demonstrates the Supreme Court's insistence on having proper procedures in place that allow a minor to get an abortion without parental consent or notification under some circumstances.

Ayotte V. Planned Parenthood of Northern New England

One of the most recent Supreme Court case is that of *Ayotte v. Planned Parenthood of Northern New England* (2006). In 2003, New Hampshire passed a law that forbids doctors from performing abortions on minors under the age of 18 unless the parent has been notified 48 hours prior. The law, however, did not include any exception which would account for situations in which delaying the abortion could be dangerous to the woman's health. Planned Parenthood of Northern New England challenged the law, claiming it was unconstitutional because it did not include an exception for medical emergencies which may endanger the woman.

The district court issued an order preventing the law from taking effect because it did not have the exception for medical emergencies. New Hampshire appealed the case to the U.S. Court of Appeals, which affirmed the district court's decision. Kelly Ayotte, the Attorney General of New Hampshire, requested that the U.S. Supreme Court review the case. The Supreme Court, however, remanded the case to the appeals court, and insisted the legislature find a solution regarding a medical provision or repeal the law. In June of 2008, the state decided to repeal in the law.

In addition to the few Supreme Court cases in the area of parental involvement and minor's abortion, several cases have been decided at the state level. Often, these cases are a result of abortion practitioners challenging new laws. However, juveniles and school officials have also challenged the laws. These challenges can make significant legal changes in the system. The following are just a few recent challenges to parental notification and consent laws.

State Cases in Which an Abortion Law is Being Challenged

On the state level, there have been multiple cases challenging the parental notification laws. These laws have been challenged by abortion practitioners, juveniles, and schools.

Challenges by Abortion Practitioners

Primarily, parental notification laws are challenged by abortion practitioners. Abortion practitioners challenge the laws because they are interested in preserving the right of females to choose to have an abortion.

Nova Health Systems v. Fogarty

In 2002, Nova Health Systems, the owner of a medical clinic in Oklahoma that provides (among other services) abortions, challenged the constitutionality of an Oklahoma statute that stated that any person who performed an abortion on a minor without parental consent or knowledge could be held liable for costs incurred (*Nova Health Systems v. Fogarty, 2002*). Nova argued that the statute violated their rights of due process and equal protection and the minor's rights to privacy and equal protection. Due to the vagueness of the statutes, Nova began to require parental consent prior to an abortion and had to turn away several minors because they did not have consent. As such, Nova argued that this statute was detrimental to them and their clients.

Despite the fact that other states have parental consent and parental notification laws in place and provide medical exception when the minor's life or health is at risk, the court agreed that the lack of a health exception in the Oklahoma statute made it "constitutionally infirm" (*Nova Health Systems v. Fogarty, 2002*). As the Oklahoma statute did not meet the specific requirements that had already been established by the Supreme Court, the law was found to be unconstitutional. Additionally, the statute was too vague, not clearly specifying the degree of parental consent or notification required for a minor. In the end, the court ruled that the parental consent and notification statute was unconstitutional for three reasons. First, it did not have a judicial bypass option. Second, it lacked a medical emergency exception. Finally, it was too vague, which left it open to much interpretation.

Following the 2002 ruling of unconstitutionality, Oklahoma legislators amended the statute. The new law required that abortion providers notify the minor's parent in writing 48 hours prior to performing the abortion. The law also required the provider to give information to abortion clients concerning medical risks and the fetus development at least 24 hours prior to the abortion. Once again, Nova Health Systems challenged the constitutionality of the new abortion law (*Nova v. Edmondson,* 2005). However, the court has ruled this time against Nova and has upheld the constitutionality of the new parental notification law.

North Florida Women's Health and Counseling Services v. State

In 1999 in Florida, the Parental Notice of Abortion Act went in effect. The act required a minor to notify a parent of her decision or prove to the court that she is mature enough or that the notification would not be in her best interest before she can get an abortion. Immediately following the passing of the act, women's rights groups, women's clinics and several physicians moved to block its enforcement. Those opposed to the statute contested that it was unconstitutional and violates a minor's rights (*North Florida Women's Health and Counseling Services v. Florida,* 2003).

The North Florida Women's Health and Counseling Services (NFWHCS) argued that the act violated the due process rights of the physicians, it was unconstitutionally vague in terms of definition of medical emergency and reasonable effort to notify, and that it burdened the rights of minors' confidentiality if they have to report sexual abuse as a reason for not involving parents. The circuit court agreed with NFWHCS and filed a temporary injunction, blocking the enactment of the law. The State immediately appealed the decision. In district court, the decision was reversed. When it reached the Florida Supreme Court, it was determined that the statute was, in fact, unconstitutional.

In response, the Florida legislature enacted an amendment to the earlier parental notice of abortion act whereby, notwithstanding a minor's right to privacy, a parent or guardian must be notified before a minor decides to terminate her pregnancy. The amended act guaranteed the privacy of the minor, but still required notification, and allowed for medical exceptions and a judicial bypass option. This became effective on June 30, 2005 (*Womancare of Orlando v. Agwunobi,* 2005). Under the new act, parental notice is not required if there exists a medical emergency, parents waive notice in writing, the minor is married, the minor has dependent children or the minor has petitioned the court for a waiver. As this case meets the bypass requirements as established in *Bellotti*, the court denied the plaintiffs' request to block the act. As such, the Parental Notice of Abortion Act is now effective in Florida.

Planned Parenthood of Idaho v. Wasden

Similar challenges to the parental notification laws have also occurred in Idaho. In 2000, the state of Idaho passed legislation that required parental consent prior to performing an abortion on minors (*Planned Parenthood of Idaho v. Wasden,* 2005). According to the legislature, pre-abortion consent is waived in the event of a medical emergency, but post-abortion notification is required in these cases. Planned Parenthood challenged the law. The legislature passed amendments to the law, which Planned Parenthood again challenged. The Courts found four parts of the law to be unconstitutional. Those include 1) a restriction on where the minor could file a judicial bypass waiver, 2) giving minors only two days to appeal a decision, 3) a requirement that the judge who hears the bypass plea to report criminal activity, as all sex with minors is considered a criminal act in Idaho, and 4) the requirement to notify parents following a medical emergency abortion. The court held that the rest of the law was constitutional and upheld the remainder of it. Both parties were dissatisfied and appealed this decision.

The United States Court of Appeals for the Ninth District heard the case and by unanimous vote, found the entire law to be unconstitutional because it did not allow for an adequate medical emergency exemption or for mature minors to bypass the process (*Planned Parenthood of Idaho v. Wasden*, 2005). As such, Idaho has no parental involvement law in practice to date.

Overall, the majority of concerns with the laws are focused on the ability of the law to ensure that appropriate measures are in place to ensure the privacy and rights of the minor, as well as the rights of the parents. All of the challenges focus on important aspects of the laws that need to be in place, such as appropriate measures for judicial bypass, exceptions for medical emergencies and measures to ensure that it is not an undue burden for minors.

JUVENILE CHALLENGES TO LAW

Not only have practitioners challenged notification and consent laws, minors have also challenged the laws. Most of the challenges to the law occur in the form of an appeal to a rejected petition for a judicial bypass. These challenges are considered on a case by case basis and judges must make determinations without concrete criteria as to what it means to be mature and informed. Challenges have been both successful and unsuccessful. For example, an Ohio youth, Jane Doe, petitioned the Hamilton County Juvenile Court in Ohio to have an abortion without parental consent on the grounds that she was mature enough to make that decision (*Jane Doe v. Hamilton County Juvenile Court*, 2005). The court denied her application and she appealed. The Ohio Court of Appeals reversed the lower court's decision, determining that the minor was sufficiently mature enough to have an abortion without parental notification.

The Appeals court's decision that the minor was mature and well informed came from a variety of evidence that the minor presented during the bypass hearing. Some of the facts that may have played a role in this decision are that the minor had a 3.2 grade point average, had been accepted to college for the fall, had been working between 26 and 35 hours a week while going to school to pay for her college in the fall, and had received counseling regarding her decision about options for her pregnancy including abortion and adoption options. Additionally, the minor acknowledged the risks of abortion including that she knew that death was a risk. She also noted that she would be 18 in about two months and could have the abortion then, but mentioned to the court that the risks increased if she waited that long to have an abortion. The minor also noted that she believed her parents would not support her decision and she believed her father would make her leave home and would not provide financial assistance to her, in which case she would be unable to attend college as planned. The court considered the evidence and determined that she was both well-informed and mature enough to make this decision on her own (*Jane Doe v. Hamilton County Juvenile Court*, 2005).

Other challenges have not been successful. The case of *Jane Doe 2 v. Court of Appeals of Colorado* (2007) is a prime example. A 16 year-old girl petitioned the court to bypass parental notification. The minor indicated she did not think her mother would understand her decision. The judge rejected the minor's request for a judicial bypass based on the assumption that the child did not demonstrate maturity. She was unwilling to communicate with her mother or consult other adults, she had not discussed the issue with a doctor and only exhibited minimal understanding of the risks inherent in having an abortion. The appeals court agreed.

A second case which was unsuccessful was that of *in re: Jane Doe v. Ohio* (2007). The minor had petitioned the court to bypass parental notification, but the judge was not sufficiently assured that the minor was mature enough to make the decision. This was her third pregnancy, she had had to repeat a grade in school, was often in trouble for fighting, and had had her last abortion only three months prior. The appeals court agreed with the lower courts decision.

In sum, it appears that the challenges by juveniles focus specifically on the judicial bypass procedure. Minors who are able to demonstrate maturity, either via their grades or their ability to demonstrate an understanding of the risks inherent with abortion, seem to be more able to successfully challenge the judicial bypass.

School Districts Challenging Parental Notification Laws

In addition to parental notification laws for minor abortions, laws have also been challenged that require schools to notify parents if they become aware of a minor who is pregnant. In November of 2002, the Port Washington, New York District Superintendent of Schools issued a memorandum outlining the responsibilities of the staff to report a minor's pregnancy to her parents (*Port Washington Teacher's Association v. Board of Education of the Port Washington Union Free School District*, 2006). By March of 2004, Port Washington Teacher's association along with several other organizations filed a complaint on behalf of themselves and their female students saying that this policy violated the students' rights to privacy, due process, and equal protection. In September, the plaintiffs filed for a preliminary injunction. In addition to the concern that the policy violated student's rights, was the concern that failure to comply with the policy could cause the faculty at the school to lose their jobs.

The district court determined that the policy did not violate any constitutional principles or state statutes. Unlike parental notification and parental consent laws which must contain a judicial bypass, the Supreme Court has never ruled on a mandatory reporting policy which requires parental notification when a minor is pregnant. As such, there are specific precedents to determine whether it is unconstitutional, and thus the injunction could not be granted for that reason (*Port Washington Teacher's Association v. Board of Education of the Port Washington Union Free School District*, 2006). In regards to the concern that school staff may lose their jobs for failure to comply with the policy, the court found that this is not a concern, based primarily on the testimony of Dr. Gordon, the superintendent of schools, who testified that he had no intention of disciplining staff who failed to comply with the policy. In sum, the court found that in this case, the parental notification bypasses required based on previous Supreme Court rulings (see *Bellotti*) are not required in mandatory reporting to parents of minor's pregnancy.

In sum, parental involvement laws have been challenged in several states with varying results. While abortion practitioners most commonly challenge these laws, juveniles and school systems have also challenged laws. These cases are often decided on the basis of vagueness (see *Nova v. Fogarty*, 2002), or because they do not have the requisite judicial bypass system (as established by *Bellotti*), or there is a violation of due process (see *Womancare v. Agwunobi*, 2005). As these cases indicate, judges analyze statutes from a legal standpoint only, while psychological aspects are ignored. However, many of the arguments for and against parental notification are psychological in nature. It is important, therefore, to examine the relevant research which can shed light on the debate.

THE PSYCHOLOGY OF PARENTAL NOTIFICATION

The psychology of parental notification is just as complex as the legal issues surrounding it. The American Psychological Association (APA, 2000) directly opposes parental involvement laws. In its official stance, the APA has discredited many of the psychological claims made by those who support these laws. First of all, according to the APA, most adolescents consult their parents or another adult concerning contraceptive and abortion decisions even without these laws in place, making these laws unnecessary in most cases (Blum, Resnick, & Stark, 1987). Secondly, there is much empirical data to support that adolescents are competent to make decisions concerning their reproductive health care on their own (Wiethorn & Campbell, 1982). The APA also points to a number of inadvertent, adverse consequences of these laws including possible stress and anxiety while seeking a judicial bypass, health problems and added expense stemming from delay in medical services, and possible illegal abortions that could be obtained as a consequence of the restricted access to abortion. In order to best address the complexity of this issue, arguments for and against parental notification are discussed in terms of relevant research. Family functioning and communication, adolescent decision-making ability, changes in sexual behavior, and psychological/physical consequences are all addressed.

Family Functioning and Communication

Those who support parental involvement laws cite research that shows that parental knowledge and the discussion that follows has a beneficial effect on adolescents. Whitaker, Miller, May, and Levin (1999) interviewed black and Hispanic teens aged 14 to 17 concerning past parent-teen discussion about sex. They found that parent-teen discussion increased the likelihood of later teen-partner discussion and it also increased condom use. Later, Wilson, and Donenberg (2004) conducted a small pilot study that video taped parents and their adolescent children having discussions about sex. They found that parental control and direction was linked to reduced sexual risk-taking. In this way, parental discussion can have a profound beneficial impact on an adolescent.

Opponents of parental involvement laws argue that most teenagers already include a parent in their decision-making. Many articles support this assertion. In a general review of the literature, Lewis (1987) mentions that the majority of minors consult a parent, usually the mother and this is especially true if the adolescent is either younger or is conflicted over her decision. About 60% of the adolescents say that their parents knew that they were going to a sexual health clinic (Jones, Purcell, & Singh, 2005). Consistent with earlier research (Lewis, 1987), there was also an indication that a greater percentage of the younger adolescents said their parents knew about their attendance at a sexual health clinic, 76% for 15 year olds as apposed to 60% overall (Jones et al.). Another study, focusing on black, urban teens who sought a pregnancy test at a clinic, found that of those who tested positive for that pregnancy test, 91% had consulted a parent before deciding what to do and another 4% consulted another adult (Zabin, Hirsch, Emerson, & Raymond, 1992). Further research supports the fact that teens discuss pregnancy decisions with their parents, as 61% of interviewed teens said that one or both parent knew about their planned abortion (Henshaw & Kost, 1992). Nearly all of the teenagers said that someone had helped them with the decision, and about 81% said they had consulted someone over 21. Of those who did not tell their parents, 30% said that they had experienced violence, feared violence or feared being kicked out of the home (Henshaw & Kost).

Having the discussion with parents may not be as important as the quality of the parent-minor discussion. Research has found that parent-teen discussions were only effective if parents were open, skilled and comfortable (Whitaker et al., 1999). Support for this research is found in a later study which indicated that frequency of discussion matters less than quality of discussion (Wilson & Donenberg, 2004). One aspect of quality that is important is the emotional tone of the conversation (Furstenberg, Herceg-Baron, Shea, & Webb, 1984). Parental involvement laws cannot possibly have an impact on the emotional tone or quality of the discussion; they can only ensure that there is a discussion. Thus, in light of this research, these laws may not be very useful in helping the adolescent with this difficult decision.

Even if parental involvement laws encourage involving the family, it is unclear if this has any effect on family communication. Interviews with adolescents at family planning clinics found that the number of mothers who knew that the adolescent was going to the clinic rose over time but the number of discussions did not change (Furstenberg et al., 1984). Thus, parents' knowledge of the pregnancy did not stimulate any discussion. Researchers also found that minors who did discuss their attendance at the clinic with their mothers were no more effective at using birth control than were the minors who did not discuss sex with their mothers.

In sum, it appears that facilitating family unity and communication may not be a valid reason to continue the parental involvement laws. As the majority of minors already discuss abortions with their parents, the law seems to be a moot point. Further, requiring notification to parents does not mean that positive conversations, which would be beneficial to the child, are going to occur. The discussions may not have any impact on the minor.

Changes in Sexual Behavior

Another argument for and against parental involvement law is that it will change sexual behavior. Those in favor of the law indicate it will increase positive sexual behaviors (i.e., decreased pregnancy), while those opposed to the law indicate it may have adverse consequences such as increasing the birth rate or delaying abortions until the minors are at increased risk for medical problems. The research on sexual behavior has found mixed results.

Research examined the rate of abortion per 100 residents for 15-17 year olds in over 30 states across the country in 1989 and 1992 (Altman-Palm & Tremblay, 1998). They found that minor abortion rates lowered in states that had parental involvement laws and that pregnancy and abortion rates rose slightly in states with out these laws (Altman-Palm & Tremblay). They also concluded that these abortion rates were not affected by crossing state lines as this was an uncommon practice. A second study, examining data from 11 states across the country, found that abortion rates went down following parental involvement laws for both 15-17 year olds and 18-19 year olds (Tomal, 1999). An investigation following Minnesota's implementation of a parental notification law also found that abortion rates declined for adolescents aged 15 to 19 (Rogers, Baruch, Stoms, & DeMoya, 1991). Rogers et al. (1991) interpreted the abrupt drop in abortions and births to indicate that the law encouraged adolescents to practice pregnancy avoidance. Similar results were found with a Texas study, indicating a drop in abortion rates among 15 to 17 year olds following implementation of the laws (Joyce, Kaestner, & Colman, 2006). According to these research studies, the parental notification laws may be effective in reducing the number of adolescent abortions.

Despite these positive findings of decreases in abortions, there is concern that that the parental notification laws increase births and increase the number of minors traveling to other states in order to get an abortion. Ellertson (1997) studied the effects of involvement laws on birthrate, in-state abortion rate, odds of interstate travel and odds of late abortion in Minnesota, Missouri, and Indiana and found results contradicting those mentioned above. Although in-state abortion rates for minors fell in all states after parental involvement laws were implemented, the laws also appeared to increase the odds of traveling to another state to have the abortion instead (Ellertson). This increase of interstate travel may even account for the entire abortion rate decline for at least Missouri. An examination of abortions and births prior to and following the April 1981 implementation of a Massachusetts parental involvement law found that half as many minors obtained abortions in the state during the 20 months following the law than they did prior to it. However, they found that 1,800 minors traveled to the four surrounding states to get an abortion, which accounts for the reduction in abortions (Cartoof & Klerman, 1986). Other studies also indicate that parental involvement laws increase interstate travel by abortions, by around 32% (Henshaw, 1995). Thus, these laws may only appear to be effective. When considering interstate travel, the effect is lost.

The research on parental notification laws impact on birth rates is somewhat mixed. One study indicated that birth rates declined along with abortion rates following implementation of a parental involvement law (Klitsch, 1991). Other studies indicate that the birth rate increases (Joyce et al., 2006; Tomal, 1999). Still others indicate that there is no impact on birthrate (Ellerston, 1997; Rogers et al., 1991). At present, it is unclear as to whether the parental involvement laws have any impact on the number of minor births.

The research does indicate that these laws may encourage dangerous behavior. For example, interviews with minors at a Planned Parenthood clinic found that a majority of minors would stop contraceptive services if they had to notify their parents (Reddy, Fleming & Swain, 2002). Another 11% would delay or discontinue sexually transmitted disease testing and almost 100% indicated that they would stop using some sexual health services but at the same time remain sexually active. The laws may also encourage risky abortion behavior, such as delaying the abortion until the minor reaches 18. Several researchers have indicated that parental involvement laws may make the minor delay the abortion past the first trimester (Ellertson, 1997; Henshaw, 1995). After the enforcement of the parental consent law, adolescents were 10-20% more likely to have the abortion after the first trimester (Henshaw, 1995). The later the abortion procedure is conducted, the more risk to the pregnant female (Gans Epner, Jonas, & Seckinger, 1998). The procedures used change further along in the pregnancy, becoming more invasive, which increases the risk for complications. The risk of mortality also increases consistently with the gestational age of the fetus (Gans Epner et al.). In sum, dangerous behavior, such as unsafe sex and riskier later stage abortions may be potential consequences of parental notification laws.

Adolescent Decision-Making Ability

A major argument in the debate regarding parental involvement is that adolescents are not capable of making these decisions on their own. There is, however, some research which discredits this assumption. For example, Weithorn and Campbell (1982) examined informed treatment decisions by age. They used a legal test of competency to evaluate decision-making for both medical and psychological treatments. They examined four ages of participants, (9, 14, 18 and 21) and found that 14 year olds did not differ from adults when it came to decision-making competency, although the nine year olds differed from adolescents and adults. Another study administered tests to examine the reasoning development and moral judgment of women, aged 12 to 25, seeking an abortion. They broke up the women into three age groups, 12-14, 17-19, and 23-25 and found that only those in the youngest group, 12-14, differed when it came to reasoning abilities as measured by sentence completion, defining issues, and moral judgment measures (Foster & Sprinthall, 1992). These measures were not specific to abortion decisions, but to more general moral reasoning abilities. A final study, examining feelings of invulnerability among middle class adults, their teenage children, and a comparison group of high risk adolescents found that all groups showed feelings of invulnerability, especially for events that participants felt they had some sort of control over, such as pregnancy (Quadrel, Fischhoff & Davis, 1993). Also, the minors that were not considered high risk showed less invulnerability than their parents did. This research supports the notion that adolescents make similar decisions to adults.

However, those who argue in favor of parental involvement laws also point to research that maintains the assumption that adolescents have a decreased ability to make decisions. Although the APA cites numerous examples of research that shows that adolescent decision-making abilities is on par with adults, these examples do not specifically address the abortion decision itself. Some research indicates that abortion decisions are very different from various other kinds of decisions (Finken & Jacobs, 1996). Researchers investigated the consultation patterns (i.e., who they consult) for adolescents aged 18 to 20 when making abortion, medical, interpersonal, and future oriented decisions. If abortion decisions were similar to either of the other types of decisions, then their consultation patterns should also be similar. However, abortion decisions had statistically different consultation patterns (i.e., these individuals consulted different people or in different order than for other decisions) and thus the applicability of studies investigating adolescent decision-making in other contexts has been called into question. This questionability of adolescents' abilities to make decisions must also consider adolescents abilities to perceive risk. Adolescents see significantly less risk than adults in involvement in various activities such as taking drugs or driving drunk (Cohn, Macfarlane, Yanez, & Imai, 1995). Therefore, minors may not fully understand risks associated with abortions, as they do not seem to fully appreciate risk as an adult would.

In sum, the research on adolescent decision-making is somewhat mixed. There is much research to support the notion that adolescent decisions are comparable to decisions that an adult would make. Yet, the research did not specifically examine an abortion decision. As abortion decisions may be different than other types of decisions, it is unclear how equitable minors and adults are in this decision-making capacity. Further, minors do not seem to have the same understanding and appreciation of risk that adults do. If judges in judicial bypass cases are supposed to make sure that adolescents demonstrate an understanding of the risks, it may be difficult to determine how deep their understanding of risk really goes.

Psychological/Physical Consequences

A final consideration is the psychological and physical consequences that a minor might experience in relation to having an abortion. One concern of proponents of the law is that minors may not have family support in their time of stress, which could have dire psychological consequences. Supporters point to possible psychological problems that could follow an abortion, the belief that adolescents may be more susceptible to these psychological affects and the belief that parents, acting as social support, may be able to alleviate these problems. Research examining psychiatric admission rates of women 90 days and four years following either an abortion or childbirth found that women who had an abortion were at a greater risk of psychiatric admission compared to those who gave birth, especially during the first 90 days (Reardon, Cougle, Rue, Shuping, Coleman & Ney, 2003). Abortion may have other negative psychological affects as well (Major, Cozzarelli, Cooper, Zubek, Richards, Wilhite, & Gramzow, 2000). A longitudinal study questioned women who came for an abortion, one hour prior to the abortion, one hour after the abortion, one month after the abortion and two years after the abortion. Although most felt satisfied with their decision, negative emotions increased and decision satisfaction declined over time. Although severe psychological problems were rare, women who were younger had a greater negative psychological reaction (Major et al.). This is supported by later research which found that minors were particularly susceptible to psychological distress following an abortion (Quinton, Major, & Richards, 2001). A comparison of minors who had an abortion with adults who had one, at one month and two years following an abortion found that minors felt less satisfied with their abortion decision and felt they had benefited less from it. It does appear that minors may be more susceptible to negative psychological reactions to abortion. Additionally, as proponents argue, parents may be uniquely suited to provide much needed social and emotional support (Adler et al., 1992).

There is also research which indicates that serious negative effects of abortion are rare, and there may even be more positive psychological affects of abortion. Interviews with women just before they received a pregnancy test, and one day and one month following the test, found that, at the time of the testing, those who chose abortion had more negative and less positive feelings surrounding the experience (Cohan, Dunkel-Schetter, & Lydon, 1993). Yet, at one month following this, the differences between the two groups disappeared; thus, abortion may simply be a brief stressor. Abortion has not been associated with significant psychopathology and at times it can be a milestone in an adolescent's life; the first time they take responsibility for their own lives. The most common feeling expressed is relief and at the best outcomes are connected with independent but supported decisions (Stotland, 1996).

There is also research that indicates that abortion is no more psychologically taxing than pregnancy (Zabin, Hirsch, & Emerson, 1989). Interviews with adolescents found that adolescents who had an abortion were no more likely to have psychological problems or experience stress and anxiety than adolescents who carried their pregnancy to term. Other research indicates that adolescents may feel less comfortable with a decision to have an abortion but demonstrate no other psychological differences from individuals over 18 who decide to have an abortion (Pope, Adler, & Tschann, 2001). Thus, these researchers found little evidence for psychological problems in minors either alone or as compared to adults.

It should also be noted that parents may not have a significant impact on whether an adolescent adjusts well to an abortion. Martin (1973) conducted interviews with girls aged 14 to 20 at the time of an abortion. There was no significant difference in adjustment between those who had the abortion with or without parental knowledge; nor was there any difference in adjustment between those whose mother influenced the decision or not. Thus, a parent may not really help reduce the possible psychological affects of an abortion.

Opponents of parental notification argue that there are also risks to the child when they are forced to tell their parents. Interviews with minors who were seeking abortions found that 30% said that they had experienced violence, feared violence or feared being kicked out of the home (Henshaw & Kost, 1992). Parental reactions differ depending on how they found out about their daughter's pregnancy. The risk of violence may be particularly enhanced if the parent does not find out from the child that she is pregnant (Henshaw & Kost, 1992). For example, there was increased anger, a higher rate of violence, and much less support from parents if they had found out about the abortion from a source other than their daughter (Henshaw & Kost, 1992). As abortion providers would be required to notify the parents, this could lead to greater risk for violence in the home. Pregnant minors who chose not to abort may also be at higher risk for domestic or family violence. A study of pregnant minors (under 18) found that almost 10% reported physical abuse, and of those 40% reported being hit during their pregnancy (Berenson, San Miguel, & Wilkinson, 1992). Therefore, it is important to consider the negative consequences both of telling the parents and not telling the parents.

In sum, the psychological factors related to parental notification can inform the ongoing debate, although much of the research is somewhat mixed. It appears that parental involvement laws may reduce the number of minor abortions, but it is may also delay abortions causing unnecessary risks to the adolescents, may encourage adolescents to cross state lines to get an abortion and may increase birth rates. While minor parenting is not addressed herein, the research on it is rarely of the positive nature. The psychological research also indicates that adolescents are comparable to adults in decision-making capacity and that the negative psychological and physical consequences are no more than what would be expected with child birth, and may occur with or without parental involvement. These findings clearly indicate a need for empirically based policy changes and more research in the area.

Policy Recommendations

Parental notification laws are clearly controversial. While the evidence listed above indicates the pros and cons of the laws, it does not provide a ready solution. Therefore, several remedies (either in part or in whole) are proposed which would address some of the concerns. Viable solutions include training and education of judges, modification of the current laws, and replacement of the current laws with more supported techniques which would focus on preventing teenage pregnancy.

Training Judges

One possible solution is to better train judges. Judges, although legal experts, are not psychologists. They are rarely trained in adolescent development, or in the possible psychological consequences that go along with abortion decisions. Using the psychological evidence presented herein, it is possible to design a training curriculum for judges which would allow them to better understand the complexities of making a decision about allowing a minor to obtain an abortion without parental notification or consent. Possible topics for judicial training could include psychological research on adolescent cognitive development, differences in adolescents' perception of risk, indicators of psychological resilience, indicators of susceptibility to domestic violence, and indicators of susceptibility to mental health issues. Education on these issues can help judges make a more informed decision. Further, it may be important to educate judges on the impact of parental notification laws and the reality of parental response. Although, ideally parents would be supportive of their child, this may not be the case. Overall, an enhanced training program would be ideal to facilitate decision-making.

Modification of the Current Laws

The deficiencies in the law indicate that the current law could be modified to achieve better results. One way this could occur is if there are set standards for the judicial bypass in terms of what it means to be mature, understand risks, and be in the best interest of the child. Maturity, understanding, and best interest are all ambiguous terms. This makes it difficult for judges to determine if the adolescent should be allowed a bypass or not. Checklists of questions could be designed which would address these three areas. A maturity checklist might, for example, include questions about school performance, having a job, attitude toward parents, or attitude toward sexual behaviors. If the adolescent does well in school, maintains a part time job, shows appropriate respect for her parents and acknowledges her mistakes, she might be considered mature. An understanding assessment checklist could likewise be constructed which lists all the information that judicial officers want pregnant minors to know before determining that they are making an informed decision. In this way, the judge can ensure the minor knows the risks of abortion, what the procedure entails, and how it might impact their physical and emotional health. Best interest can be assessed by examining the child's current and past history, self-reported vulnerability to domestic violence, and reasons for not telling parents. In addition, the court can examine the parent's past history to see if there are reported incidents of domestic violence or child abuse that may impact that child's welfare. A panel of psychologists and judges could easily ascertain appropriate checklist items used to make standardized decisions.

A second way that the law might be amended is through requiring a counselor or doctor to evaluate the minor to determine if she should receive a bypass. Psychologists and psychiatrists, in particular, should be well equipped to ascertain emotional and cognitive maturity, as well as trained to identify potential psychological reactions that the minor might encounter following an abortion. This provider would be able to discuss the issue thoroughly with the minor, make sure that she understands the risks, and make an informed decision regarding whether the minor should obtain the bypass. If funding is a concern, psychologists may consider doing the work pro bono, as lawyers often do. These two methods should ensure that both minor and parents rights are protected while still allowing some minors access to abortion services.

Alternatives to the Law

A final, and slightly more extreme, solution is to do away with the laws altogether. Different laws could be suggested to take their place or the government could invest in alternative methods to achieve the desired goals. If replacement of the law is desired, one method which might be effective is to require counseling instead of requiring parental notification. Counselors can ensure that the adolescent is made aware of the psychological and physical consequences of having an abortion and the medical risks involved. Required counseling also ensures that the minor has an opportunity to discuss her concerns and feelings in a supportive environment. The counselor may also screen for potentially serious mental health/psychological distress concerns, which can then be addressed with the minor. In fact, requiring a pre and post counseling session would further assist the minor as she would have someone to discuss this difficult decision with before and after she has had the procedure.

Of course, there are also other alternatives which do not involve parental consent. If the goal is to promote family unity, promote positive sexual behavior, and reduce minor pregnancy, there are other viable methods available. The APA suggests a number of other more supported techniques that focus on prevention of minor pregnancy including counseling programs, peer support programs, community based efforts, and programs to promote better family communication.

A final consideration is to modify the existing state of sexual education in the United States. Currently, most states stress abstinence only sex education with little focus on contraceptive usage. This may be because the government allocates considerable funds to those who teach abstinence only education. According to a five-year analysis of the abstinence only programs, there are few short term and no long-lasting positive outcomes from the abstinence only curriculum (Hauser, 2004). When compared to other countries with pragmatic and sex positive government policies, the United States has the worst sexual health related statistics, including the highest rate of minor births, minor abortions, and one of the lowest rates of contraceptive use (Weaver, Smith & Kippax, 2005). It appears that the sexual education taught in most schools is ineffective. Perhaps a better approach is needed in order to change minor sexual behaviors.

The current laws are not meeting their desired goals. Although minor abortion rates have dropped, so have abortion rates of 18 and 19 year olds (Rogers et al., 1991), of which the law should not impact. Perhaps there are fewer minors having abortions overall, yet there are still many unplanned minor pregnancies, indicating the law is not effective in promoting positive sexual behavior. Changes in the law could increase consistency, which may appease legal concerns, and create a more standardized way to determine if adolescents should receive a bypass. Or, better still, new policies and programs should be put into place, which directly target the goal of promoting positive sexual behavior.

Conclusions and Directions for Future Research

The issue of parental notification helps identify some deficiencies in the current state of research. Future research should specifically address the comparability of abortion decisions of minor adolescents with older adolescents. If the legal age to make the decision is 18, then it should be determined if younger females have different decision-making capabilities than older females. New research should also examine the direct impact of the parental notification laws by examining attitudes of minors toward the laws, minor behaviors, and the minors perceived consequences of the laws. This will allow researchers to better understand how the law is directly impacting the youth. The impact of the parental notification laws can also be examined by exploring alternatives which may also explain the drop in abortion rates to determine if parental involvement laws are the deciding factor. Researchers might also consider making interstate comparisons. In some states, a 16 year old can get an abortion, while the age is 18 in other states. Researchers could compare outcomes (i.e., a 16 year old immature minor who could not get a bypass in one state versus any 16 year old who could in another) and help to set an optimal age that minors are "mature" enough to make this decision, possibly an age that will be consistent across states. Finally, research should be conducted which ascertains the impact of the suggested alternative programs which target sexual behavior. If there is concrete research that indicates that these programs are effective, then the programs should be instituted on a larger scale so that minors across the nation can benefit from them.

In sum, parental notification remains a controversial topic. While some researchers indicate that adolescents may have the cognitive ability to make an informed decision, others argue that they do not. The debate is further complicated by differing state laws, which may make it desirable to go to another state in order to obtain an abortion. More research must be conducted to inform the ongoing debate and to help change or modify existing policies so that minors achieve optimal physical and psychological outcomes.

References

Adler, N. E., David, H. P., Major, B. N., Roth, S. H., Russo, N. F., & Wyatt, G. E. (1992). Psychological factors in abortion: A review. *American Psychologist, 47*, 1194–1204.

Altman-Palm, N., & Tremblay, C. H. (1998). The effects of parental involvement laws and the AIDS epidemic on the pregnancy and abortion rates of minors. *Social Science Quarterly, 79*, 846-862.

American Psychological Association (2000). Parental Consent and adolescent reproductive health care. What does the research say? Available online at www.apa.org/ppo/issues/pparentalconsent.html.

Ayotte v. Planned Parenthood of Northern New England, 546 U.S. 320 (2006).

Bellotti v. Baird, 443 U.S. 622 (1979).

Belluck, P. (June 8, 2007). New Hampshire to Repearl Parental notification law. The New York Times. Retrieved online July 17, 2008 from www.nytimes.com.

Berenson, A.B., San Miguel, V. V., & Wilkinson, G. S. (1992). Prevalence of physical and sexual assault in pregnant adolescents. *Journal of Adolescent Health, 13*, 466-469.

Blum, R. W., Resnick, M. D., & Stark, T. (1987). The impact of parental notification law on adolescent abortion decision-making. *American Journal of Public Health, 77*, 619-620.

Cartoof, V. G., & Klerman, L. V. (1986). Parental consent for abortion: impact of the Massachusetts law. *American Journal of Public Health, 76*(4), 397-400.

Cohan, C.L., Dunkel-Schetter, C., & Lydon, J. (1993). Pregnancy decision-making: Early - predictors of stress and adjustment. *Psychology of Women Quarterly, 17*, 223-239.

Cohn, L.D., Macfarlane, S., Yanez, C. & Imai, W. K. (1995). Risk-Perception: Differences Between Adolescents and Adults. *Health Psychology, 14*, 217-222.

Ellertson, C. (1997). Mandatory parental involvement in minors' abortions: Effects of the laws in Minnesota, Missouri, and Indiana. *American Journal of Public Health, 87*(8), 1367-1374.

Finken, L. L., & Jacobs, J. E. (1996). Consultant choice across decision contexts: are abortion decisions different? *Journal of Adolescent Research, 11*, 235–260.

Foster, V. & Sprinthall, N. A. (1992). Development profiles and adolescents and young adults choosing abortions: Stage sequence, decalage, and implications for policy. *Adolescence, 27*(107), 655-673.

Furstenberg, F. F., Jr., Herceg-Baron, R., Shea, J., & Webb, D. (1984). Family communication and teenager's contraceptive use. *Family Planning Perspectives, 16*, 163-169.

Gans Epner, J. E., Jonas, H. S., & Seckinger, D. L. (1998). Late-term abortion. *Journal of the American Medical Association, 280*, 724-729.

Ginsberg v. New York, 390 U.S. 629 (1968).

Hauser, D. (2004). Five years of abstinence-only-until-marriage education: Assessing the impact. *Title V State Evaluations*. Available online from www.advocatesforyouth.org.

Henshaw, S. K. (1995). The impact of requirements for parental consent on minors' abortions in Mississippi. *Family Planning Perspectives, 27*(3), 120-122.

Henshaw, S. K., & Kost, K. (1992). Parental involvement in minors' abortion decisions. *Family Planning Perspectives, 24*(5), 196-207, 213.

H.L. v. Matheson, 450 U.S. 398 (1981).

Hodsgon v. Minnesota, 497 U.S. 417 (1990).

In re: Jane Doe v. Ohio, 2007 Ohio 3495 (2007).

Jacobs, J. E., Greenwald, J. P., & Osgood, D. W. (1995). Developmental differences in baserate estimates of social behavior and attitudes. *Social Development, 4*(2), 165-181.

Jacobs, J. E., & Ganzel, A. K. (1993). Decision-making in adolescence: are we asking the wrong question? *Advances in Motivation and Achievement, 8,* 1–31.

Jane Doe 2 v. Court of Appeals of Colorado, 166 P.3d 293 (2007).

Jane Doe v. Court of Appeals of Ohio, Hamilton County Juvenile Court, 2005 Ohio 1559 (2005).

Jones, R., Purcell, A., & Singh, S. (2005). Parent-child relations among minor females attending U.S. family planning clinics. *Perspectives on Sexual and Reproductive Health, 37*(4), 192-201.

Joyce, T., Kaesnter, R., & Colman, S. (2006). Changes in abortions and births and the Texas parental notification law. *New England Journal of Medicine, 354*(10), 1031-1038.

Klaczynski, P. A., Byrnes, J. P., & Jacobs, J. E. (2001). *Journal of Applied Developmental Psychology, Volume 22, Issue 3, May-June 2001, Pages 225-236*

Klitsch, M. (1991). Teenage abortions fell after Minnesota imposed parental notification law. *Family Planning Perspectives, 23*(5), 240.

Lambert v. Wicklund, 520 U.S. 292 (1997).

Lewis, C.L. (1987). Minors' competence to consent to abortion. *American Psychologist, 42*, 84-88.

Martin, C. D. (1973). Psychological problems of abortion for the unwed teenage girl. *Genetic Psychology Monographs, 88*, 23-110.

Major, B., Cozzarelli, C., Cooper, M. L., Zubek, J., Richards, C., Wilhite, M., & Gramzow, R. (2000). Psychological responses of women following first trimester abortion. *Archives of General Psychiatry, 57*, 777-784.

National Abortion Federation. (2003). Teenage women, abortion, and the law. Available online at http://www.prochoice.org/pubs_research/publications/downloads/about_abortion/teenage_women.pdf.

North Florida Women's Health and Counseling Services v. State (FL) 866 So. 2d 612 (2003 Fla.)

Nova v. Edmondson, 373 F. Supp. 2d 1234 (2005 Okla.).

Nova Health Systems v. Gandy, 388 F. 3d 744 (10th Cir. Okla., 2004).

Ohio v. Akron Center for Reproductive Health, 497 U.S. 502 (1990).

Planned Parenthood. (2007). Laws requiring mandatory parental involvement for minors. (2007). Retrieved online July 17, 2008 from www.plannedparenthood.org.

Planned Parenthood of Central Missouri v. Danforth, 428 U.S. 52 (1976).

Planned Parenthood of Idaho v. Wasden, 376 F.3d 908 (9th Cir. 2003).

Pope, L. M., Adler, N. E., & Tschann, J. M. (2001). Postabortion psychological adjustment: are minors at risk? *Journal of Adolescent Health, 29*(1), 2-11.

Port Washington Teacher's Association v. Board of Education of the Port Washington Union Free School District, 2006 U.S. Dist. LEXIS 1904 (2006).

Quadrel, M. J., Fischhoff, B., & Davis, W. (1993). Adolescent (In)vulnerability. *American Psychologist,* 48, 102-116.

Quinton, W. J., Major, B., & Richards, C. (2001). Adolescents and adjustment to abortion: Are minors at greater risk? *Psychology, Public Policy, and Law,* 7(3), 491-514.

Reardon, D. C., Cougle, J. R., Rue, V. M., Shuping, M. W., Coleman, P. K., & Ney, P.G. (2003). Psychiatric admissions of low-income women following abortion and childbirth. CMAJ, 168 (10), 1253-1256.

Reddy, D. M., Fleming, R., & Swain, C. (2002). Effect of mandatory parental notification on adolescent girls' use of sexual health care services. *Journal of the American Medical Association, 288*(6), 710-714.

Roe v. Wade, 410 U.S. 113 (1973).

Rogers, J. L., Baruch, R. F., Stoms, G. B., & DeMoya, D. (1991). Impact of the Minnesota Parental Notification Law on abortion and birth. *American Journal of Public Health, 81*(3), 294-298.

Stotland, N. L. (1996). Conceptions and misconceptions: Decision about pregnancy. *General Hospital Psychiatry, 18,* 238-243.

Tomal, A. (1999). Parental involvement laws and minor and non-minor teen abortion and birth rates. *Journal of Family and Economic Issues, 20,* 149-162.

Weaver, H. Smith, G., & Kippax, S. (2005). School-based sex educational policies and indicators of sexual health among young people: a comparison of the Netherlands, France, Australia and the United States. *Sex Education, 5*(2), 171-188.

Weithorn, L. A., & Campbell, S. B. (1982). The competency of children and adolescents to make informed treatment decisions. *Child Development, 53,* 1589-1598.

Whitaker, D. J., Miller, K. S., May, D. C., & Levin, M. L. (1999). Teenage partners' communications about sexual risk and condom use: The importance of parent-teenager discussions. *Family Planning Perspectives, 31*(3), 117-121.

Wilson, H. W., & Donenberg, G. (2004). Quality of parent communication about sex and its relationship to risky sexual behavior among youth in psychiatric care: a pilot study. *Journal of Child Psychology and Psychiatry, 45*(2), 387-395.

Womancare of Orlando v. Agwunobi, 448 F. Supp. 2d 1293 (N.D. Fla. *2005*).

Zabin, L. S., Hirsch, M. B., & Emerson, M. R. (1989). When urban adolescents choose abortion: effects on education, psychological status and subsequent pregnancy. *Family Planning Perspectives, 21*(6), 248-255.

Zabin, L. S., Hirsch, M.B., Emerson, M. R., & Raymond, E. (1992). To whom do inner city minors talk about their pregnancies? Adolescents' communication with parents and parentsurrogates.*FamilyPlanningPerspectives,24*(4),148-154,173.

In: Contemporary Perspectives on Legal Regulation...
Editor: Monica K. Miller
ISBN 978-1-60741-161-1

Chapter 8

LAW, SEX, AND THE CULTURAL REPRODUCTION OF MASCULINISM: A HISTORICAL-SOCIAL CONSTRUCTIONIST ACCOUNT OF THE LEGAL REGULATION OF SEXUAL BEHAVIOR IN AMERICA

Jose H. Vargas and Alexandra E. Sigillo
University of Nevada, Reno, Nevada, USA

ABSTRACT

The transmission of cultural norms and values is predicated on several factors that exist at the intersection of the social, psychological, and historical. Most notably, social research has demonstrated that cultural reproduction proceeds successfully to the extent that effective legal institutions and social control mechanisms are established and sustained. This research suggests that although male values and ideology have relatively clear historical origins, the survival of those values and ideology is largely contingent on the psychological endorsement of masculinism by individuals, as well as on the communication of implicit and explicit masculine philosophies across a network of legal institutions. A historical-social constructionist perspective is offered to explain the perpetuation of masculinism as a function of the legal regulation of human sexuality. This perspective posits that legal systems successfully disseminate, socialize, and reproduce masculinism among the American populace when influential individuals endorse (psychologically) and institute (structurally) certain moral ideologies conducive to the "normalization" of male-dominated social orders and conventional forms of sexual behavior.

The production and transmission of cultural norms and values (i.e., cultural reproduction) are predicated on a multitude of psychological, sociological, and historical contingencies. Cultural and cross-cultural scholars, for instance, have linked cultural reproduction to parenting practices (Rudy & Grusec, 2001), nationalism and national identity (Billig, 1995), interpersonal and social communication (McIntyre, Lyons, Clark, & Kashima, 2004), and the formation of historically embedded social structures (Schooler, 2007).

Although contemporary social science has succeeded in identifying these essential cultural mechanisms, theory and research also seem to lend credence to the contention that the degree to which cultural reproduction proceeds successfully depends largely on the establishment, maintenance, and effectiveness of legal institutions and other social control systems (e.g., ingroups and ingroup norms and expectations; Chiu & Hong, 2006; O'Reilly & Chatman, 1996). The extant literature indicates that social control systems serve several functions, such as fostering commitment to group-level norms and enhancing individual-level participation (Grenier & Hogler, 1991). Thus, in order to appreciate the complexities associated with the reproduction of male-dominated social orders in American culture, it is imperative to understand the differential roles that people, institutions, and societal norms play within this social control process.

In American culture, the reproduction of *masculinism*—defined as a collection of male-oriented ideologies about human nature, male superiority, and the appropriateness of human behavior—manifests as a corollary of the interactions that occur between interrelated networks. These networks are comprised of persons, organizations, and social and legal prescripts, all of which are embedded within specific histories and socio-environmental contexts. As such, theory and research support the position that morally-driven individuals (e.g., certain politicians and legislators), legal systems, and gender norms reproduce and normalize male-oriented social orders over subsequent generations (e.g., Jost & Kay, 2005; Kay, 2000; Khan, 1996; Murray, 2007).

Premised primarily on the principles of a *historical-social constructionist* perspective of human behavior (see Conrad & Schneider, 1981, for a similar framework), we contend that opportunities for the reproduction of masculinism within contemporary American culture are systematically constructed through an interrelated network of individuals (e.g., law-makers), societal institutions (e.g., religious, legal, and marital), and social control mechanisms (e.g., gender norms, roles, and stereotypes). That is, to the extent that legal institutions successfully disseminate, socialize, and reproduce masculinism among the American populace, morally-driven individuals must first advocate a particular moral ideology that justifies the existence of a male-dominated status quo. Moreover, both socially influential and non-influential individuals within society must be willing to accept the system's ideology (i.e., system justification; Jost & Burgess, 2000; Jost & Kay, 2005; Jost, Pelham, Sheldon, & Sullivan, 2003). This ideology, in turn, acts as a catalyst that allows for the "normalization" of male-dominated social orders via the legal regulation of human sexuality.

To support this thesis, a social psychological analysis of three classes of legislation is offered. First, it is argued that state-level marriage restriction laws indirectly regulate human sexual behavior through the institution of marriage, where sexual activity between partners is traditionally expected. Second, anti-sodomy legislation is framed as evidence of *de facto discrimination*, a practice in which laws regarding permissible sexual behavior are differentially applied to socially stigmatized groups (i.e., gays) to their disadvantage, and to the advantage of the existing social order. Finally, two domains of "heart balm" tort legislation (i.e., *wrongful seduction tort* and *alienation of affections tort*) are discussed and it is argued that their historical origins rest mainly on specious assumptions about male sexual aggression and female sexual naïveté. However, before further elaboration on these classes of legislation, a brief discussion of the historical-social constructionist framework is first warranted in order to properly contextualize the remainder of this analysis.

The Politics of Definition and Moral Entrepreneurship: A Historical-Social Constructionist Perspective

In order to properly conceptualize the links between the perpetuation of masculinism and legal systems in terms of a historical-social constructionist model, two related concepts require elaboration: the *politics of definition* and *moral entrepreneurship*. The politics of definition (Conrad & Schneider, 1992) can best be described as a morally- and emotionally-driven societal-level conflict in which ideologically-inconsistent groups compete to legitimize valued ingroup "designations." For the most part, these designations reflect group-specific interpretations about the nature of social others and reality. In the course of this conflict, individual crusaders promote their respective ingroups' moral codes within the larger society's influential institutions. Often, these "moral entrepreneurs" attempt to confer legitimacy onto their ingroups' designations by framing ingroup-inconsistent designations in a negative light (Conrad & Schneider). That is, through a process of moral entrepreneurship (or "claims-making"), moral entrepreneurs come to advance assertions that associate ingroup-inconsistent values and acts with deviance. As a result, ingroup-inconsistent behaviors labeled as "deviant" come to serve as socially constructed symbols that reinforce the ideology that ingroup-consistent behaviors are natural and normative, and that ingroup-inconsistent behaviors must be regulated or eliminated.

The opportunities to advocate for one's position are not equally distributed, however. This is because social groups in American society tend to be unequal along certain dimensions, such as social status, educational attainment, and physical health. Consequently, the opportunities to successfully promote, legitimize, and (eventually) institutionalize a particular set of designations are likely to be disproportionately available to those individuals in society who have been socially, politically, or economically well-established (Conrad & Schneider, 1992). The same is true with respect to opportunities to devalue and eliminate ingroup-inconsistent designations. In short, although the struggle to promote and legitimize ingroup-level designations does give rise to individual crusaders willing to advocate for the institutionalization of valued ingroup norms, the politics of definition seem to assure that a monopoly on moral entrepreneurship would remain under the control of those individuals who have historically been in positions of social advantage. This further suggests that the social movements of dominant groups may be reactive in nature, and are likely to be motivated primarily by desires to safeguard existing social orders (see Mueller & Dimieri, 1982, for extensive research on reactive versus proactive social movements).

If this is the case, there may be some cause to suspect that the perpetuation of masculinism, at least in contemporary America, reflects a type of cultural by-product or social construction. In fact, there is historical precedence to indicate that white males (especially since the era of European colonization) have endorsed a belief that they are superior in comparison to other social groups (Duerst-Lahti, 2002; Hall, 2004). From a historical-social constructionist framework, masculinism appears to be predicated on the institutionalization of male-oriented values that have been in existence—socially, economically, and politically—for centuries. Thus, the cultural reproduction of masculinism is posited to be a function of three historically-bounded and interrelated networks: 1) male-dominated moral entrepreneur networks, 2) social institutions (e.g., legal, marital, and religious), and 3) cultural prescripts and designations (e.g., gender norms and expectations). To support this position, a social psychological analysis of three classes of legislation—marriage restriction laws, anti-sodomy laws and "heart balm" torts—is presented. The analysis offered here suggests that a truly comprehensive description of the cultural reproduction of masculinism is contingent upon a framework that links the differential roles of persons, organizations, and cultural prescripts to their specific histories and social contexts.

MARRIAGE RESTRICTION LAWS AND THEIR CONNECTION TO HETEROSEXISM

As an initial illustration of this thesis, consider state-level *marriage restriction laws*, defined here as laws that limit marriage to heterosexuals only, whether explicitly or implicitly. In terms of social psychological phenomenon, it is interesting to note that while general acceptance of gay relationships and marriages has improved across most international spheres in recent years, American acceptance of such relationships has been less forth coming by comparison (Brewer & Wilcox, 2005; Grossman, 2005; Schmitt, Lehmiller, & Walsh, 2007). Theoretically, the pervasiveness of this form of *heterosexism* (i.e., the belief in the normalcy or superiority of the heterosexual lifestyle) within American society can be partially attributed to the efforts of politically powerful moral entrepreneurs (e.g., religious fundamentalists, certain conservative politicians, conservative communities) who support traditional and stereotypically masculine assumptions about the "true nature" of family, marriage, and gender roles (Brewer & Wilcox). Thus, in American culture, the reproduction of heterosexism and masculinism is likely to be conditional on the efforts of Americans who support patriarchal family structures and salient sexual divisions of labor (Colb, 2006), many of which share their historical origins in the Judeo-Christian tradition.

At a deeper level of specificity, the social psychological motives underlying the institutionalization of marriage restriction within the legal sector are complex and ambiguous. Unlike gender and racial minorities, whose social categorization is solely predicated on visually salient physical features (i.e., sex traits and skin tone, respectively), the features that "justify" the construction of heterosexual and non-heterosexual social categories are not so readily visible. Further, these features are not as consistent as the physical attributes that have come to justify concepts such as race or gender. By comparison, the features that tend to demarcate heterosexuals from gays, lesbians, bisexuals, and transgender individuals (GLBTs) are grounded less in physical cues and more in perceived behavioral differences. Because the primary features which separate heterosexuals from GLBTs are behavioral in nature (e.g., sexual preference and sexual activity), it must follow that marriage restriction laws are motivated, at least in part, by heterosexuals' disapproval of these acts. In this regard, the legal regulation of sexual behavior is very subtle and indirect. In short, the underlying aim of marriage restriction legislation is not to prevent gay sexual activity, per se, as the enactment of sexual behavior is not contingent on one's martial status. Rather, marriage restriction appears to protect the traditional nuclear family structure that forms as a consequence of sex.

Marriage restriction laws are enacted to ensure that men and women marry each other because there is a cultural expectation that sex, procreation, and child-rearing will occur within the familial institution. In this regard, the reproduction of masculinism is facilitated when children who are raised within traditional families are socialized to value heterosexual-based ideals. Put differently, marriage restriction precludes the enactment of non-heterosexual acts within a traditional familial institution that is both valued by the heterosexual majority and understood by that majority as an arena where children are socialized into mainstream culture. Viewed in these terms, the enactment of homosexual activity, within an institution that has been socially constructed to be heterosexual in its structure, presents an immediate threat to the social identities of the heterosexual and masculine majorities (Schmitt et al., 2007). Within a social context where an aim is to protect traditional and masculine social structures, the construction of marriage restriction laws appears to be not only warranted, but also "justified" and "rational."

Arguably, the perpetuation of masculinism appears to be facilitated when erroneous assumptions about the nature of family, gender, and marriage come to restrict the notion of the "ideal family" to a heterosexist model permissive of social inequity. It should be noted, however, that the extent to which masculinism is reproduced within the American culture is not solely dependent on the endorsement and legitimization of inaccurate heterosexist assumptions. Rather, the production and maintenance of male ideology necessitate that those assumptions, once institutionalized, be differentially applied across various societal groups in ways that attempt to control threats likely to undermine the established male social order. Thus, differential application manifests in numerous forms for American GLBTs, as in marriage restriction laws that inevitably deny them the same legal marriage rights and protections that have been bestowed to heterosexual Americans.

Interestingly, a similar phenomenon is evident within the context of anti-sodomy legislation. The next section expands on the notion of differential application by relating the phenomenon to the history of American anti-sodomy laws. Here, differences in the administration of laws, across socially desirable and undesirable groups, play pivotal roles in the reproduction and maintenance of masculinism.

Threats to Masculinism and Anti-Sodomy Laws: The Purpose of Differential Application

Given that the maintenance of any group ideology cannot proceed effectively in the absence of social control mechanisms (e.g., group norms; O'Reilly & Chatman, 1996), it would be reasonable to posit that the reproduction of male ideology may require the differential application of laws as a means of addressing perceived threats to masculinism. In other words, the persistence of masculinism is not simply a function of the moral entrepreneurs who endorse the moral philosophy. Rather, to reproduce masculinism successfully within the larger society, it is imperative that social control systems (e.g., legal systems) be established to enforce the moral code of the male-dominated majority. Moreover, these systems must also frame non-masculine values as "deviant" vis-à-vis the values of the male social order (i.e., deviance designation; see Conrad & Schneider, 1992, for more on this concept). In this context, social control systems serve the dual-purpose of legitimizing the moral ideology of the majority and regulating any perceived threats to that ideology. Interestingly, this social construction process is evident in the case of anti-sodomy legislation.

During the time when American anti-sodomy laws were enforceable, at least two legal maneuvers aided in perpetuating the male social order. First, some anti-sodomy laws were constructed to exclusively target gay individuals (Fradella, 2002). Second, other anti-sodomy laws were constructed to be neutral *in principle*, but their enforcement *in practice* was often disproportionately geared toward the gay subsets of the American populace (a practice known as *de facto discrimination*; Colb, 2002; Fradella, 2002). Thus, males engaging in sodomy with their female partners were unlikely to be penalized under most anti-sodomy laws, while gay partners engaging in the same sexual act were commonly targeted for prosecution. The long history of differential application in the U.S. prompted many lawsuits by gays, as in the famous *Lawrence v. Texas* (2003) case. Prior to the *Lawrence* case, Texas' anti-sodomy law explicitly criminalized homosexual intercourse, even though heterosexual couples were permitted to engage in similar sexual activities, such as sodomy. In *Lawrence*, the U.S. Supreme Court determined that Texas' anti-sodomy law was unconstitutional as it violated the due process clause of the Fourteenth Amendment. The Court's decision also overturned one of its previous rulings, which had upheld the constitutionality of a Georgia anti-sodomy law that criminalized private oral and anal sex between consenting adults, regardless of their sexual orientation (see *Bowers v. Hardwick*, 1986). Consequently, states are no longer allowed to establish anti-sodomy legislation, primarily because it is permissible for adults of all sexual orientations to engage in private, consensual sex (Perkinson, 2007).

Arguably, the male social order, through the differential application of anti-sodomy laws, was reproduced in at least two ways. First, the creation of laws that targeted gays provided an institutional context wherein perceived threats to male ideology (i.e., homosexuality and non-masculinity) could be legally controlled. These laws, in turn, produced a context wherein the means to those ends could be socially validated, legitimized, and enacted with limited resistance. Second, the legal endorsement of anti-sodomy laws promoted a moral philosophy tolerant of the negative stigmatization of gay Americans and accepting of heterosexism (Fradella, 2002). Although the *Lawrence* decision suggests that de facto discrimination toward gays is declining, there is also no guarantee that this trend will persist in other areas of American law. Thus, masculinism may continue to permeate into the American legal system, affecting the design of other laws and the treatment of other social groups. Further, contemporary beliefs in the superiority of male status may continue to reinforce the social construction of historically-bounded and traditional status differentials between males and non-males; a process that sociologists refer to as *status construction* (Johnson, Dowd, & Ridgeway, 2006; Ridgeway, 2006; Ridgeway, Boyle, Kuipers, & Robinson, 1998). The next section discusses how status differences between men and women have been portrayed in American law and how these laws have also contributed to the reproduction of male ideology.

"Heart Balm" Torts as Social Controls over Feminism: On Personhood and Property

Though it is interesting to observe that the perpetuation of masculinism has been driven, in part, by the stigmatization of GLBTs and by the legal regulation of their sexual behavior, historical evidence suggests that women have also been long-time targets of legislation aimed at preserving male-oriented ideology (Kay, 2000; Khan, 1996; Murray, 2007). Arguably, this phenomenon is quite salient within the context of so-called "*heart balm*" tort laws. The term "heart balm" tort makes reference to a collection of laws that were originally enacted as a legal strategy to protect a father's interest in his daughter's chastity or to protect a person's interest—usually those of the husband—in his spouse's affections (Graham, 2008; Grossman, 2003b).

Because the moral entrepreneurship underlying heart balm legislation was primarily guided by men, the original impetuses of these laws were founded largely on specious notions about male and female sexuality. Traditionally, males have been socialized to value assertiveness, competition, and aggression while females have been socialized to value ingenuousness, innocence, and sincerity (Eder & Parker, 1987). Similarly, within interpersonal relationships, some men and women behave in ways that imply that men are able to claim women as a type of "property" or personal possession.

The unfortunate cultural by-products of heart balm torts were the inevitable relegation of female-status within the American legal sphere and the construction of state laws that treated women more like *property* rather than as *persons* (Grossman, 2003a). Accordingly, the present analysis suggests that this is evident in at least two types of legislation: wrongful seduction and alienation of affections torts. These topics are reviewed in turn.

Wrongful Seduction Tort

According to wrongful seduction tort law, individuals can be legally penalized if they are found guilty of seducing, deceiving, or enticing unmarried persons (usually women) to engage in sexual intercourse. On the surface, the law presents itself as a benign attempt by religious and legal institutions to secure the sanctity of marriage by sanctioning "lustful" individuals. However, wrongful seduction tort facilitated the perpetuation of masculinism primarily because the underlying purpose of the law centered on compensating fathers whose daughters were "wrongfully seduced" by deceitful men. In other words, the goals of wrongful seduction tort were not motivated by the desire to protect women or marriages, per se (though we note that the implicit assumptions that women "need protection," and that men are naturally deceitful and "sexually-crazed," are problematic for their own reasons). Rather, the motives were much more practical and less benign. Simply put, unmarried daughters were considered to be the property of fathers; thus, engagement in premarital sex by daughters marred fathers' chances of marrying off their daughters (Abrams, 2007). Therefore, within the larger American culture, wrongful seduction tort laws implicitly legitimized a model of womanhood more characteristic of property than personhood.

Today, 17 states retain wrongful seduction torts. Additionally, individuals residing in states that have abolished wrongful seduction laws can still pursue wrongful seduction-like claims under a different tort known as *fraud by intentional misrepresentation within a sexual context* (Larson, 1993). Thus, other legal avenues remain available for individuals who desire to file lawsuits involving wrongful seduction. In effect, fraud by intentional misrepresentation exemplifies how members within legal systems socially construct different legal means in order to preserve already-existing and historically-bounded cultural values. These laws also demonstrate that although the legitimacy of wrongful seduction tort may be waning, there remain other similar torts in play that are conducive for reproducing masculinism.

Alienation of Affections Tort

Similar to wrongful seduction tort, the alienation of affections tort portrays women as objects or pieces of property rather than as persons. Alienation of affections typically refers to a legal situation in which a third party diverts a married woman's feelings away from her husband and toward the third party (Everett, 2007). As a result, a husband in this scenario has cause to assert that the third party has taken his wife, who was viewed as personal property to which he has legal rights. This legal claim is grounded in historical common law which assumed that husbands possess property interests in their wives (Everett, 2007).

Currently, seven states (Hawaii, Illinois, Mississippi, New Mexico, North Carolina, South Dakota, and Utah) continue to endorse some form of alienation of affections tort (ABC News, 2007). For instance, the Supreme Court of North Carolina in *McCutchen v. McCutchen* (2006) expanded the period of time in which individuals can file an alienation of affections claim against their spouse or the third party (Everett, 2007). This state ruling reinforces masculinism in two ways: (a) by acknowledging that alienation of affections claims are permissible, and (b) by providing more legal freedom and flexibility for individuals to assert the claim within the American legal system. Interestingly, individuals living in states that have abolished this type of law can still pursue alienation of affections-like claims under a different tort known as *intentional infliction of emotional distress* (Corbett, 2001; Everett, 2007). As in the case of wrongful seduction tort, other legal avenues are available for individuals to file lawsuits when they have been "emotionally neglected." Altogether, these patterns demonstrate that certain heart balm torts are capable of culturally reproducing masculinism when those laws are grounded in specious assumptions about women's statuses and rights.

Wrongful Assumptions and the Alienation of Women in American Society

Considering the examples of wrongful seduction and alienation of affections torts, it can be argued that there exists a history that has implicitly and explicitly portrayed women, whether married or unmarried, as the property of men. Arguably, this perception may have contributed to the denial of women's rights during pre-contemporary America and to women's exclusion from the construction of laws (Kay, 2000). The denial of women's rights and women's civic participation continued up until the onset of the Women's Rights Movement and, in variant degrees, still persists today.

In both types of legislation, it appears as if heart balm torts served to reinforce outdated and inaccurate cultural beliefs about the nature of male and female sexuality; for instance, the belief that women are sexually submissive and males are sexually dominant by nature. These beliefs, in turn, also served to reproduce masculinism within the larger American culture. Interestingly, although women have made great strides within the legal sector, the construction of modern-day heart balm torts further implies that masculinism continues to prevail within America's legal system. Consequently, it can be expected that legislation in the 21st century will likely preserve masculinist remnants from the past, which in turn may hinder women's efforts to obtain equal rights within America's mainstream social institutions.

Discussion

The transmission of cultural norms and values is predicated on several factors that exist at the intersection of sociology, psychology, and history. The social psychological analysis presented here demonstrates that the cultural reproduction of masculinism proceeds successfully to the extent that effective legal institutions and social control systems are established and sustained. Put differently, legal systems successfully disseminate, socialize, and reproduce masculinism among the American populace when influential individuals endorse (psychologically) and institute (structurally) particular moral ideologies that foster the "normalization" of male-dominated social orders and conventional forms of sexual behavior.

When evaluated through the lens of a historical-social constructionist framework, it appears that the history of marriage restriction, anti-sodomy, and heart balm legislation is also a history of the perpetuation of masculinism. That is, the cultural reproduction of masculine ideology has been facilitated, in part, by a cultural process involving a network of individuals with shared moral agendas. Within this network, individuals tend to promote moral ideologies conducive to the maintenance of a male-dominated status quo.

The capacity to successfully disseminate, socialize, and reproduce masculinism among the American populace is not solely contingent on the moral development of individuals. Rather, systematic sociological contingencies also come into play. Accordingly, the cultural reproduction of masculinism also necessitates the establishment of legal institutions and other social control mechanisms (i.e., societal norms, roles, and expectations) that confer legitimacy onto male-oriented philosophies and perspectives. The historical-social constructionist account presented here suggests that certain marriage restriction laws, anti-sodomy laws, and heart balm torts have served in this capacity. If this is the case, it may be reasonable to suspect that the American legal system is administering laws in attempts to dispense principles other than justice.

References

ABC News. (2007). Lost love lawsuit may hit high court: Plumber won $750,000 under little used alienation of affection law. Retrieved July 18, 2008, from: http://abcnews.go.com/GMA/TurningPoints/story?id=3789033

Abrams, K. (2007). Immigration law and regulation of marriage. *Minnesota Law Review, 91*, 1625-1709.

Billig, M. (1995). *Banal nationalism*. London: Sage Publications.

Bowers v. Hardwick, 478 U.S. 186, 192 (1986).

Brewer, P. R., & Wilcox, C. (2005). Same-sex marriage and civil unions. *Public Opinion Quarterly, 69*, 599–616.

Chiu, C., & Hong, Y. (2006). *Social psychology of culture*. New York: Psychology Press.

Colb, S. F. (2002). The Supreme Court takes same-sex sodomy case: Why sexual orientation discrimination is also sex discrimination. Retrieved July 6, 2008, from: http://writ.lp.findlaw.com/colb/20021218.html

Colb, S. F. (2006). The essence of marriage and equality: The New Jersey Supreme Court considered same-sex marriage. Retrieved July 6, 2008, from: http://writ.news.findlaw.com/colb/20060222.html

Conrad, P., & Schneider, J. W. (1992). *Deviance and medicalization: From badness to sickness*. Philadelphia: Temple University Press.

Corbett, W. R. (2001). A somewhat modest proposal to prevent adultery and save families: Two old torts looking for a new career. *Arizona State Law Journal, 33*, 985-1055.

Duerst-Lahti, G. (2002). Governing institutions, ideologies, and gender: Toward the possibility of equal political representation. *Sex Roles, 47*, 371-388.

Eder, D., & Parker, S. (1987). The cultural production and reproduction of gender: The affect of extracurricular activities on peer-group culture. *Sociology of Education, 60*, 200-213.

Everett, S. H. (2007). The law of alienation of affections after *McCutchen v. McCutchen*: In North Carolina, breaking up just got harder to do. *North Carolina Law Review, 85*, 1761-1783.

Fradella, H. F. (2002). Legal, moral, and social reasons for decriminalizing sodomy. *Journal of Contemporary Criminal Justice, 18*, 279-301.

Graham, K. (2008). Why torts die. *Florida State University Law Review, 35*, 359-432.

Grenier, G., & Hogler, R. (1991). Labor law and managerial ideology: Employee participation as a social control system. *Work and Occupations, 18*, 313-333.

Grossman, J. (2003a). Is the tort of wrongful seduction still viable? A North Carolina court will get the chance to decide. Retrieved July 6, 2008, from http://writ.news.findlaw.com/grossman/20030211.html

Grossman, J. (2003b). Punishing adultery in Virginia: A cheating husband's guilty plea is a reminder of the continued relevance of adultery statutes. Retrieved July 6, 2008, from: http://writ.lp.findlaw.com/grossman/20031216.html

Grossman, J. (2005). New developments in the same-sex marriage wars: The fight over the issue in New York, and the growing international acceptance and American rejection of "genderless" marriage. Retrieved July 6, 2008, from: http://writ.news.findlaw.com/grossman/20051213.html

Hall, R. E. (2004). Entitlement disorder: The colonial traditions of power as white male resistance to affirmative action. *Journal of Black Studies, 34*, 562-579.

Johnson, C., Dowd, T. J., & Ridgeway, C. L. (2006). Legitimacy as a social process. *Annual Review of Sociology, 32*, 53-78.

Jost, J. T., & Burgess, D. (2000). Attitudinal ambivalence and the conflict between group and system justification motives in low status groups. *Personality and Social Psychology Bulletin, 26*, 293-305.

Jost, J., & Kay, A. (2005). Exposure to benevolent sexism and complementary gender stereotypes: Consequences for specific and diffuse forms of system justification. *Journal of Personality and Social Psychology, 88*, 498-509.

Jost, J. T., Pelham, B. W., Sheldon, O., & Sullivan, B. N. (2003). Social inequality and the reduction of ideological dissonance on behalf of the system: Evidence of enhanced system justification among the disadvantaged. *European Journal of Social Psychology, 33*, 13-36.

Kay, H. H. (2000). From the second sex to the joint venture: An overview of women's rights and family law in the United States during the twentieth century. *California Law Review, 88*, 2017-2093.

Khan, B. Z. (1996). Married women's property laws and female commercial activity: Evidence from United States patent records, 1790-1895. *The Journal of Economic History, 56*, 356-388.

Larson, J. E. (1993). Women understand so little, they call my good nature "deceit": A feminist rethinking of seduction. *Columbia Law Review, 93*, 374-472.

Lawrence v. Texas, 539 U.S. 558 (2003).

McCutchen v. McCutchen, 360 N.C. 280 (2006).

McIntyre, A., Lyons, A., Clark, A., & Kashima, Y. (2004). The microgenesis of culture: Serial reproduction as an experimental simulation of cultural dynamics. In M. Schaller & C. S. Crandall (Eds.), *The psychological foundations of culture* (pp. 227-258). Mahwah, NJ: Erlbaum.

Mueller, C., & Dimieri, T. (1982). The structure of belief systems among contending ERA activists. *Social Forces*, *60*, 657-675.

Murray, A. (2007). Marriage - The peculiar institution: An exploration of marriage and the women's rights movement in the 19th century. *UCLA Women's Law Journal*, *16*, 137-162.

O'Reilly, C. A., & Chatman, J. A. (1996). Culture as social control: Corporations, cults, and commitment. *Research in Organizational Behavior*, *18*, 157-200.

Perkinson, P. L. (2007). Eight annual review of gender and sexuality law: Constitutional law chapter: Sexual privacy after Lawrence v. Texas. *The Georgetown Journal of Gender and the Law, 8,* 203-233.

Ridgeway, C. L. (2006). Status construction theory. In P. J. Burke (Ed.), *Contemporary social psychological theories* (pp. 301-323). Stanford, CA: Stanford University Press.

Ridgeway, C. L., Boyle, E. H., Kuipers, K. J., & Robinson, D. T. (1998). How do status beliefs develop? The role of resources and interactional experience. *American Sociological Review*, *63*, 331-350.

Rudy, D., & Grusec, J. E. (2001). Correlates of authoritarian parenting in individualist and collectivist cultures and implications for understanding the transmission of values. *Journal of Cross-Cultural Psychology*, *32*, 202-212.

Schmitt, M. T., Lehmiller, J. J., & Walsh, A. L. (2007). The role of heterosexual identity threat in differential support for same-sex 'civil unions' versus 'marriages.' *Group Processes & Intergroup Relations*, *10*, 443–455.

Schooler, C. (2007). Culture and social structure: The relevance of social structure to cultural psychology. In S. Kitayama & D. Cohen (Eds.), *Handbook of cultural psychology* (pp. 370-388). New York: The Guildford Press.

PART III: PSYCHO-LEGAL BRIEFS

Part III of this book offers six short psycho-legal analyses. The briefs offer a variety of perspectives on underage sex, abortion rights, responses to offending, obscenity laws, and adultery laws. All articles bring a psychological perspective to the legal and social issues addressed.

In: Contemporary Perspectives on Legal Regulation...
Editor: Monica K. Miller
ISBN 978-1-60741-161-1

Chapter 9

THERAPEUTIC JURISPRUDENCE FOR TEEN SEX-RELATED ISSUES

Alayna Jehle
R&D Strategic Solutions, Lexington, Massachusetts 02421, USA

Therapeutic jurisprudence is based on the notion that legal decisions have social consequences, and therefore, legal actors should consider what effects these decisions have on the individuals involved (e.g., victims, offenders). The focus is on therapeutic effects that can help improve the situation rather than simply punishing the offender (Wexler & Winnick, 1996). The principles of therapeutic jurisprudence suggest approaches that can be useful in policy-making for a variety of social issues, including those that regulate sex, pregnancy, procreation, and parenting.

Policies regarding these issues sometimes focus on retributive goals, which often ignore the impact of those decisions on the parties involved. Mandatory reporting and statutory rape laws designed to address the issue of teen sex frequently have been treated with a punishment-focused approach (Oliveri, 2000; Olszewski, 2006; Scardina, 2007), but these legal outcomes can potentially create greater social problems than the ones that judges and policy-makers are attempting to solve. This article will examine some current legal attempts to address teen sex issues and explain how therapeutic jurisprudence can suggest a more beneficial approach in handling these issues.

MANDATORY REPORTING

One method of addressing the issue of teen sex involves mandatory reporting laws that require teachers and health care providers to report potential sexual abuse cases to the proper legal authorities (Olszewski, 2006). In an attempt to preserve the sanctity of American youths, some state officials (e.g., Kansas Attorney General) interpret sexual abuse legislation to include any sexual activity involving a minor, including consensual sex between two minors (Scardina, 2007). Therefore, mandatory reporting would be required for nearly all sexual encounters involving a minor. This would prevent health care providers and teachers from using their own judgment in determining whether or not the sexual encounter was abusive. Without mandatory reporting laws, these mentors would likely consider the facts on a case-by-case basis rather than labeling all sexual activity involving minors as abuse.

This punishment-focused approach for dealing with sexually active teenagers is intended to reduce the number of sexual encounters between minors; however, the legislation will probably fail in reaching that goal and instead will create larger problems (Scardina, 2007). If teenagers are aware that their health care provider or teacher must report their sexual activity, then they will likely stop seeking help from these mentors. Therefore, the original problem will not be solved through mandatory reporting, and the teenagers will be harmed much more (Scardina, 2007). Minors will continue to have sex and simply not see their doctors to obtain birth control, condoms, and STD tests if they cannot trust that their privacy will be respected. Such behaviors will likely result in increases in pregnancy and the spreading of STDs (BBC News, 2005).

Therapeutic jurisprudence principles would call for the health care providers and teachers to make a judgment about whether the sexual encounter is considered abuse and should be reported to authorities. These adults would remain trusted mentors that could give guidance to teens to help them make good decisions, resist peer pressure, and gain skills to reduce the chances they will be in a position in which they are pressured to have sex. Such an approach would focus on the social outcomes of the decision and would conclude that mandatory reporting of all teenage sexual activity would result in greater harm (BBC News, 2005; Scardina, 2007). Therefore, health care providers and teachers should remain as mentors that teenagers can trust to receive proper advice and medical attention.

Statutory Rape

Another legal method of dealing with the teen sex issue is statutory rape laws. Such laws make it illegal for someone over the legal age[1] to have a sexual encounter with a minor. Laws against statutory rape are intended to protect minors, who are believed to be too young to consent to sex (Oliveri 2000). Such legislation punishes adults who take advantage of minors by persuading the young partners to have sex with them (Scardina, 2007). Punishment is often a proper response in these cases in which adults are acting as predators and take advantage of minors. However, in some instances a therapeutic approach may be more beneficial than mere retribution because the victims in these cases are indirectly being harmed by the punishment given to their partners.

In some cases, the young woman involved with an older man gives birth to a child and the couple legally marries (Mason, 2006; see also Merz & Miller chapter "Recent judicial rulings in consensual underage sex cases: Analysis of legal case studies and policy implications," this volume). Although the victim and the offender wish to become a family and raise their child, the law may restrict their opportunities. In 2006, Matthew Koso received a prison sentence of 18 months for the statutory rape of his wife and mother of his child (Mason, 2006). As a result, the victim in the case must raise the child without help of the father for a year and a half. This outcome does not benefit any party or society as a whole and

1 Legal age varies by state. Some states add certain conditions, such as age disparity rules, that help define rape. Some laws can include sexual relations between two minors.

instead harms everyone involved. Both the young mother and the child will endure hardships without the father being present, and the father will suffer both from his prison sentence and his removal from his family.

Another case involved a 37-year-old mother who was prosecuted for the statutory rape of her 15-year-old husband and father of her child. The mother received a nine month jail term and was banned from contacting her husband until his 17th birthday (Los Angeles Times, 2006). In these types of cases, the husband and the child are harmed by the law because the child does not have her mother to care for her and the father is either left to raise the child alone or is forced to give up the child for someone else to raise. Thus, statutory rape cases involving a married couple that has a child together may be handled best through a therapeutic jurisprudence approach that focuses on helping the victim and the child rather than punishing the offender and harming all of the parties involved.

Conclusion

In sum, laws regarding teen sex issues often are handled using a punishment approach that focuses on retributive goals. However, this manner in dealing with teen sex appears to be flawed because the punishments fail to solve the problem and instead create more harm. Mandatory reporting laws that require health professionals and teachers to report consensual teenage sexual activity to authorities will likely result in more pregnancies and a greater spreading of STDs, rather than the intended goal of reducing teen sex (BBC News, 2005). Statutory rape cases that incarcerate a parent (e.g., Mason, 2006) cause negative outcomes for all parties because the victim and the child are left to struggle without a second parent to help raise the child. Therefore, a response based on the principles of therapeutic jurisprudence appears to be a more beneficial approach for handling these teen sex issues because the focus is more on healing the situation rather than creating more harms through punishment.

References

BBC News. (2005). Teen sex fears over advice plan. Retrieved July 10, 2008, at http://news.bbc.co.uk/1/hi/health/4353696.stm.

Los Angeles Times. (2006, Mar. 16). Wife pleads guilty to statutory rape of boy. Retrieved July 10, 2008, at http://articles.latimes.com/2006/mar/16/nation/na-briefs16.4.

Mason, C. E. (2006). Faith, harm, and neutrality: Some complexities of free exercise law. *Duquesne Law Review, 44*, 225-273.

Oliveri, R. (2000). Statutory rape law and enforcement in the wake of welfare reform. *Stanford Law Review, 52*, 463-508.

Olszewski, D. J. (2006). Statutory rape in Wisconsin: History, rationale, and the need for reform. *Marquette Law Review, 89*, 693-720.

Scardina, T. (2007). Aid for Women v. Foulston: The creation of a minor's right to privacy and a new preliminary injunction standard. *Denver University Law Review, 84*, 977-1000.

Wexler, D. & Winnick, B. (1996). *Law in a Therapeutic Key*. Durham, NC: Carolina Academic Press.

In: Contemporary Perspectives on Legal Regulation... ISBN 978-1-60741-161-1
Editor: Monica K. Miller

Chapter 10

ARE SOME ADOLESCENT SEXUALITY LAWS SELF-DEFEATING? A PROCEDURAL JUSTICE INTERPRETATION OF LEGALLY SANCTIONED SEXUAL REGULATION

Jose H. Vargas
University of Nevada, Reno, Nevada, USA

In the contemporary world, parental and societal concerns about adolescent sexuality are premised on specific and rational fears regarding the potential negative consequences that may arise when naïve youths engage in sexual intercourse. For the most part, these concerns and fears are understandable when evaluated against the daily circumstances faced by today's adolescents. Across several investigations, social scientists and scholars have identified trends in adolescent behavior and attitudes which suggest that adolescent sexuality is both highly prevalent and becoming more widely-accepted among today's youths (Denehy, 2007; Epstein & Ward, 2008). Unfortunately, naïve attitudes about sex leave adolescents vulnerable to a host of threats, many of which have the potential to endanger their physical and psychological well-being.

Due largely to the adverse consequences associated with premature sexuality, parents and influential social institutions have come to recognize differential interests in adolescents' general well-being. For instance, parents and legal guardians have vested interests in promoting and sustaining the well-being of loved-ones, and nations often have economic and social interests in maintaining healthy and productive citizenries. Thus, the enactment of sexual behaviors by young and psychosocially immature individuals presents a myriad of problems for several parties, including adolescents, families and society. In this psycho-legal brief, a social justice argument is outlined in which the concept of *fairness* takes precedence in contextualizing and explaining the enactment of adolescent sexual behavior within a "sexually regulated world." Generally, the argument stresses that although legally sanctioned sexual regulation may appear as an appropriate and efficacious recourse for addressing problems associated with adolescent sex, the legal practice may also hold inherent shortcomings worthy of scholarly attention. However, before this argument is discussed in greater detail, brief reviews of the social scientific literature on adolescent sexuality and legal responses to adolescent sex are first warranted.

"PROTECTING" SEXUALLY ACTIVE ADOLESCENTS: PARENTS, SOCIETY AND THE ROLE OF LAW

To date, the extant social scientific research has consistently found that sexually active adolescents are particularly vulnerable to numerous sexually-related problems, including teenage pregnancy (Garnier & Stein, 1998), early exposure to sexually transmitted diseases (STDs; Aspy et al., 2007), delinquency (Epstein & Ward, 2008; Zimmer-Gembeck & Helfand, 2008) and sexual exploitation (Zwane, Mngadi, & Nxumalo, 2004). From this standpoint, adolescents' lack of specific requisite sexual knowledge (e.g., knowledge about proper condom use), as well as limitations in their cognitive-affective facilities (e.g., inadequate problem-solving abilities, Talashek, Alba, & Patel, 2006), provide strong justifications for parents and youth-oriented organizations to opt for legislation aimed at regulating adolescent sexuality. The movement in support of the legal regulation of adolescent sexuality has resulted in the institutionalization of a variety of legal strategies. For example, some states have ratified *mandatory reporting laws*, in effect obligating youth educators and healthcare providers to report to state authorities—often under the pretext of suspected of sexual abuse—any cases in which a minor claims to be sexually active (Colb, 2006; see Jehle chapter entitled "Therapeutic Jurisprudence for Teen Sex-Related Issues" in this volume). Similarly, in the public school domain, some parents and legislators have rallied behind *abstinence-only sex education programs* (BBC News 2005; Denehy, 2007; Mariner, 2002), at times receiving federal funding that has been legally earmarked for these programs (Meier, 2007).

By legally regulating adolescents' sexual behaviors and sexual socialization (e.g., sex education), it appears that both parents and society have implicitly arrived at the same conclusion. Specifically, their consensus centers on the belief that legal systems possess the social influence necessary to achieve the dual-goal of precluding the occurrence of adolescent sexuality and averting the multitude of adverse consequences associated with premature sexual experience. The desires of parents and society to protect adolescents from the negative consequences of premature sex are laudable and worthy of serious consideration. However, if meting out the aims of adolescent sexuality laws hinges on the assumption that these legal maneuvers promote—whether through instruction or deterrence—adolescent behavior conducive to general physical and psychological well-being, then criticism of these laws ought to begin by evaluating the extent to which the logic underlying this assumption is valid.

Arguably, there may be reasons to suspect that legally sanctioned sexual regulation may entail inherent shortcomings that not only risk hindering efforts to reduce the prevalence of adolescent sexuality, but that also risk contributing to other unintended individual- and social-level consequences. Thus, even though the aims shared by concerned parents and youth-organizations are commendable, it may also be true that the implementation of legally sanctioned sexual regulation, as the "choice method" to achieve those aims, may itself be detrimental and self-defeating. In the next section, a procedural justice framework is offered in order to explain how the administration of particular adolescent sexuality laws may, under certain circumstances, contribute to the problems associated with premature sexuality.

WHY SOME ADOLESCENT SEXUALITY LAWS ARE SELF-DEFEATING: A PROCEDURAL JUSTICE INTERPRETATION

In order to fully appreciate the complexities inherent in the relationship between adolescent sexuality and sexual regulation, it is argued that matters of *fairness* must be understood to properly contextualize and explain the enactment of adolescent sexual behavior. This argument proposes that institutionalizing certain forms of regulation of adolescent sexuality within a legal context may be self-defeating, at least when viewed from the perspective of existing social scientific theory and research. That is, laws designed primarily to protect the general well-being of adolescents via the regulation of sexual information (e.g., sex education) and human sexuality may be inherently futile, given that such laws violate two important principles: *privacy* and *logic*. Specifically, the former principle is violated when the sexual privacy of adolescents is disregarded within influential and legitimate social institutions (e.g., legal systems, medical institutions; Jaruseviciene, Levasseur, & Liljestrand, 2006). The latter principle, logic, is violated when a discord emerges between the underlying assumptions of adolescent sexuality laws and actual human behavior.

Nevertheless, although the current research on social justice (e.g., Fagan & Tyler, 2005; Tyler, 2006a, 2006b; Tyler & Blader, 2003) may provide some plausible explanations with respect to the futility of certain adolescent sexuality laws, the same social justice literature may also provide some guidance towards proactive and fair solutions. Through the application of social justice theory and research, social scholars have the opportunity to coordinate the differential needs of adolescents, families and youth-oriented organizations. In turn, this perspective may allow scholars to construct policy that is truly capable of achieving, via procedurally fair practices, the commendable goals of adolescent sexuality laws.

On Social Justice: Linking Fairness, Legitimacy, Cooperation and Commitment

Within the social justice domain (Fagan & Tyler, 2005; Tyler, 2006a, 2006b; Tyler & Blader, 2003), the abstract concept of "fairness" is encapsulated in terms of the tenets and operations of *procedural justice*. Broadly, procedural justice refers to the extent to which individuals perceive that their treatment within a social system (e.g., legal system, medical system) adheres to fair practices and conduct (Tyler, 2006b). In this regard, the degree to which social systems treat their constituents fairly has direct social psychological and behavioral implications, not only in how individuals come to relate and identify with a social system (Tyler & Blader), but also in how they come to perceive a system's legitimacy and personal relevancy (Tyler, 2006a). Moreover, research on legal socialization (Fagan & Tyler) indicates that youths' early experiences with legitimate law-enforcing authorities (e.g., police officers) have noticeable effects on their attitudes and behavior. Specifically, this research reveals that children and adolescents who have negative experiences (e.g., unfair treatment) with law-enforcing authorities are less likely to perceive certain laws as "legitimate" compared to youths with more positive legal experiences. In turn, the perception of illegitimacy increases the likelihood that youths will fail to comply with those laws.

Thus, to a substantial degree, the existing social justice research lends credence to the notion that social systems are more likely to enhance their legitimacy when system-level practices and institutions reflect fairness and respect rather than inequity and disregard. More importantly, the same research also indicates that cooperation and commitment within a social system are likely to be encouraged when system members confer legitimacy onto that system. In this regard, the links between fairness, legitimacy, social cooperation and commitment are evident and worthy of attention, especially when constructing social policy pertaining to the regulation of adolescent sexuality. As the next section will articulate, these links carry serious implications for the efficacy of some adolescent sexuality laws.

Social Justice, Privacy and Logic: Implications for the Efficacy of Adolescent Sexuality Laws

Given that the links between fairness, legitimacy, cooperation and commitment are relatively strong and stable, the potential negative effects of adolescent sexuality laws on adolescent sexual behavior cannot be fully comprehended without first understanding how legally sanctioned sexual regulation relates to matters of procedural justice. From a procedural justice perspective (Tyler, 2006a, 2006b; Tyler & Blader, 2003), the institutionalization of adolescent sexuality laws, as a method by which to control adolescents' sexual behaviors, may be inherently futile. Arguably, this is because laws framed in terms of *sexual regulation*, where the primary aims are to control sexual information and human sexuality, violate the principles of privacy and logic.

In the case of privacy, the formulations of many adolescent sexuality laws, such as mandatory reporting laws, tend to be negligent of the sexual privacy rights of sexually active youths. In this regard, mandatory reporting laws and similar legislation are perceived as unfair and procedurally unjust by those directly affected—namely, adolescents. The perception that legal, educational and medical authorities are perpetuating procedural injustice, in turn, creates a social psychological context where adolescents are likely to mistrust and reject those authorities. In fact, research indicates that sexually active adolescents are likely to avoid medical consultations and prenatal care when they perceive that medical authorities may be unable to assure doctor-patient confidentiality (Jaruseviciene et al., 2006).

In the case of logic, a blatant violation of commonsense reasoning emerges given that the institutionalization of procedurally unjust adolescent sexuality laws appear to promote behaviors that are likely to lead to (rather than eliminate) the adverse consequences associated with premature adolescent sexuality. For example, many abstinence-only sex education programs tend to focus on the importance of sex after marriage and on the adverse psychological and physiological implications of premarital relations (Meier, 2007). Consequently, abstinence-only programs run the risk of unfairly denying adolescents access to pertinent sexual knowledge, such as information about proper condom use and reproductive health. In turn, inadequate sexual knowledge may translate into unpleasant and irreparable consequences for sexually active adolescents, which can include pregnancy, early exposure to STDs and sexual exploitation. When judged in terms of a procedural justice framework, it may stand to reason that violations of the principles of privacy and logic cast serious doubt on the assumptions underlying current adolescent sexuality laws. If this is the case, it is incumbent on social scholars to coordinate the differential needs of adolescents, families and youth-oriented organizations and, in turn, assist in constructing adolescent sexuality policy that is both efficacious and fair for all parties involved.

DISCUSSION

Based on the extant social justice literature, there is a strong indication that a procedural justice framework adequately explains the futility of certain adolescent sexuality laws. Specifically, procedural justice theory demonstrates that inextricable links exist between fairness, legitimacy, social cooperation and commitment to system-level norms (Fagan & Tyler, 2005; Tyler, 2006a, 2006b; Tyler & Blader, 2003). Because some adolescent sexuality laws blatantly violate the principles of privacy and logic, in effect by unfairly denying adolescents' sexual privacy and access to comprehensive sex education (Denehy, 2007), there is sufficient reason to suspect that such laws are more likely to do harm than good. Thus, although these laws are understandable societal and parental reactions laden with deep emotional structures, it may be that the more appropriate recourse for addressing the problems associated with adolescent sexuality requires a logical and social scientific foundation. Conceivably, a procedural justice framework may be able to highlight nuances about human behavior that both social scholars and policymakers should consider in their construction of fairer and more efficacious adolescent sexuality laws.

Final Comments: Implications for Adolescents, Families and the Legal System

In the contemporary world, perceptions toward minors and minors' rights stand in sharp contrast to those perceptions of just a few decades ago. Although it continues to stand true that the rights of children and adolescents are often overridden by the rights of parents and society, it is equally true that legal systems in the United States and abroad are routinely undergoing significant legal reforms that are contributing to a burgeoning of minor-oriented civil rights; a practice dating back to the 1960s and 1970s (Scheiwe, 2004). As a result, numerous questions and controversies will continue to manifest with respect to minors' rights to access comprehensive sexual information, as well as their rights to privately decide on matters of sexuality, reproduction and parenting (for more on adolescent sexuality, minors' rights and the law, refer to the chapter by DeArman & Miller, Jehle's "Therapeutic Jurisprudence for Teen Sex-Related Issues," Merz & Miller's "Recent Judicial Rulings in Consensual Underage Sex Cases: Analysis of Legal Case Studies and Policy Implications," and Summers & Miller's "The Law and the Psychology of Parental Notification: Implications for Policy and Future Research," this volume). Arguably, through a social justice framework, social scholars can take an active role in identifying the requisite criteria needed to construct procedurally just and efficacious adolescent sexuality policy, in turn improving the likelihood that adolescents will be able to make well-informed and autonomous decisions regarding their own sexuality.

For parents and families, active participation in the sexual socialization of their children may be the most practical recourse for obviating the adverse outcomes of premature adolescent sexuality. Social researchers have observed that although a tradition exists in which it is socially expected that parents or guardians will act as the primary raconteurs of sexually-related information, very few adolescents report receiving sexual knowledge from their primary caregivers (Epstein & Ward, 2008). However, this finding is qualified by other data, which have determined that the nature of parent-adolescent communication about sex often varies as a function of adolescent gender and culture (DiIorio, McCarty, Denzmore, & Landis, 2007; Schouten, van den Putte, Pasmans, & Meeuwesen, 2007). Still, the existing literature suggests that the majority of adolescents receive most of their sexual socialization through other environmental sources, including peers (Whitbeck, Conger, & Kao, 1993) and the media (Epstein & Ward). Indeed, this is problematic, mainly because social peers and the media fail to portray human sexuality within more realistic contexts. Thus, it is the main responsibility of parents and families to mitigate potential distortions in sexual knowledge by providing their adolescents with better access to comprehensive sex education.

Finally, with respect to the role of the legal system in the regulation of adolescent sexuality, the social justice literature presented here reveals that social systems and system authorities play major parts in establishing institutional legitimacy (Tyler, 2006a, 2006b; Tyler & Blader, 2003) and in the legal socialization of children and adolescents (Fagan & Tyler, 2005). Accordingly, legal systems are vested with the power to shape human behavior in ways that will be either resistant or acquiescent to system-level norms and laws. The social justice argument offered here stresses that the construction of fair and efficacious policy requires consideration of four issues: 1) the extent to which a policy is perceived as "fair" by those directly affected, 2) the extent to which perceived fairness comes to influence the legitimacy of the authority behind the policy, 3) the extent to which the assumptions of a policy adhere to the principles of privacy and logic, and 4) the extent to which a policy successfully promotes and maintains its legitimacy, given its treatment of those directly affected. Policies that consider each of these factors will be more likely to successfully address concerns related to adolescent sexuality. Viewed in these terms, it is evident that what is *fair* for adolescents, and what is in their *best interest*, are not mutually exclusive ideals.

REFERENCES

Aspy, C. B., Vesely, S. K., Oman, R. F., Rodine, S., Marshall, L., & McLeroy, K. (2007). Parental communication and youth sexual behaviour. *Journal of Adolescence*, *30*, 449-466.

BBC News (2005). Teen sex fears over advice plan. Retrieved July 16, 2008, http://news.bbc.co.uk/1/hi/health/4353696.stm

Colb, S. F. (2006). Should sexually active minors have a right to privacy? A Kansas case reveals that dark side of mandatory reporting. Retrieved July 16, 2008, http://writ.news.findlaw.com/colb/20060208.html

Denehy, J. (2007). Education about sexuality: Are we preparing our youth for today's realities? *The Journal of School Nursing, 23*, 245-246.

DiIorio, C., McCarty, F., Denzmore, P., & Landis, A. (2007). The moderating influence of mother-adolescent discussion on early and middle African-American adolescent sexual behavior. *Research in Nursing & Health, 30*, 193-202.

Epstein, M., & Ward, L. M. (2008). "Always use protection": Communication boys receive about sex from parents, peers, and the media. *Journal of Youth and Adolescence, 37*, 113-126.

Fagan, J., & Tyler, T. R. (2005). Legal socialization of children and adolescents. *Social Justice Research, 18*, 217-242.

Garnier, H. E., & Stein, J. A. (1998). Values and the family: Risk and protective factors for adolescent problem behaviors. *Youth & Society, 30*, 89-120.

Jaruseviciene, L., Levasseur, G., & Liljestrand, J. (2006). Confidentiality for adolescents seeking reproductive health care in Lithuania: The perceptions of general practitioners. *Reproductive Health Matters, 14*, 129-137.

Mariner, J. (2002), Just say "not until we're married": Legislating morality and undermining HIV/AIDS prevention. Retrieved July 16, 2008, http://writ.news.findlaw.com/mariner/20021014.html

Meier, A. M. (2007). Adolescent first sex and subsequent mental health. *American Journal of Sociology, 112*, 1811-1847.

Scheiwe, K. (2004). Between autonomy and dependency: Minors' rights to decide on matters of sexuality, reproduction, marriage, and parenthood. Problems and the state of debate—an introduction. *International Journal of Law, Policy and the Family, 18*, 262-282.

Schouten, B. C., van den Putte, B., Pasmans, M., & Meeuwesen, L. (2007). Parent-adolescent communication about sexuality: The role of adolescents' beliefs, subjective norm and perceived behavioral control. *Patient Education and Counseling, 66*, 75-83.

Talashek, M. L., Alba, M. L., & Patel, A. (2006). Untangling the health disparities of teen pregnancy. *Journal for Specialists in Pediatric Nursing, 11*, 14-27.

Tyler, T. R. (2006a). Psychological perspectives on legitimacy and legitimation. *Annual Review of Psychology, 57*, 375-400.

Tyler, T. R. (2006b). Restorative justice and procedural justice: Dealing with rule breaking. *Journal of Social Issues, 62*, 307-326.

Tyler, T. R., & Blader, S. L. (2003). The group engagement model: Procedural justice, social identity, and cooperative behavior. *Personality and Social Psychology Review, 7*, 349-361.

Whitbeck, L. B., Conger, R. D., & Kao, M.-Y. (1993). The influence of parental support, depressed affect, and peers on the sexual behaviors of adolescent girls. *Journal of Family Issues, 14*, 261-278.

Zimmer-Gembeck, M. J., & Helfand, M. (2008). Ten years of longitudinal research on U.S. adolescent sexual behavior: Developmental correlates of sexual intercourse, and the importance of age, gender and ethnic background. *Developmental Review, 28*, 153-224.

Zwane, I. T., Mngadi, P. T., & Nxumalo, M. P. (2004). Adolescents' views on decision-making regarding risky sexual behaviour. *International Nursing Review, 51*, 15-22.

In: Contemporary Perspectives on Legal Regulation...
Editor: Monica K. Miller

ISBN 978-1-60741-161-1

Chapter 11

ABORTIONS FOR MEN? A FEMINIST PERSPECTIVE

Jennifer A. Reisig
University of Nevada, Reno, Nevada, USA

The issue of reproductive rights has been fiercely debated for many years. The reproductive rights of women have generally been at the center of the issue, focusing on topics such as adoption, abortion, and the right to choose. In the wake of the reproductive rights debate, some men are now expressing concern over their perceived *lack* of reproductive rights in comparison to women. In the courts, some men and national organizations are advocating for equal rights between men and women when it comes to choosing to be a parent (*Dubay v. Wells,* 2007; The National Center for Men, 2008). Rather than advocating for authority in a women's abortion or adoption decision, they are advocating for the right to obtain a "financial abortion" from an unwanted child. A financial abortion would consist of the relinquishment of all legal ties between father and child, severing all financial and parental responsibilities, as well as visitation rights.

Generally, after conception, there is no way for a man to opt out of fatherhood unless the mother makes the decision to abort the fetus or place the baby in adoptive care; in neither decision does the man legally have any influence. The legal rights of men and women in the decision to enter parenthood are asymmetrical (Brake, 2005). Given this, it is easy to see that some men feel denied equal rights in terms of entering parenthood, but the question remains: would granting financial abortions be the solution that brings equality? This chapter will examine the issue of financial abortions through the lens of feminist theory. Feminist theory, rooted in social activism, provides insightful perspectives on gender related issues. After reviewing the current controversy surrounding financial abortions, this chapter will review feminist theory and discuss how its main concepts (sex and gender, family, and sexism) apply to this issue. Finally, legal opinions of financial abortions and possible alternatives will be discussed.

The Controversy Of Financial Abortions

The issue of financial abortions has recently made its way into the court system. A 2007 court case, *Dubay v. Wells*, exemplifies this struggle over reproductive rights. Matthew Dubay and Lauren Wells were in a consensual sexual relationship, with the understanding that Wells was infertile. As an additional measure of protection, contraception was also used. Throughout the couple's relationship, Dubay made it clear that he was not interested in becoming a father. After the couple's relationship ended, Wells announced that she was pregnant with Dubay's child. Dubay continued to express his unwillingness to be a father throughout the pregnancy and claimed that he did not want to be involved in the child's life. After Wells gave birth, she sought child support payments from Dubay, which he challenged in the Michigan court. The court denied his claim, and the case was appealed in federal court.

Dubay's claim was based on the premise that forcing a man to pay child support for an unwanted baby is a violation of his right to "disclaim parenthood." In the event of an unwanted pregnancy, women have the right to disclaim parenthood via abortion, abandonment at a safe haven location, or adoptive care; each of which may take place without the consent of the father.[1] Under Dubay's logic, men should also have the right to disclaim parenthood by obtaining a financial abortion from an unwanted child, without the consent of the mother. On the surface, Dubay's case does not sound entirely unreasonable. As Hiester (2004) states, "In the same way that forcing a woman to bear a child...against her will burdens her procreational autonomy, forcing a man to bear parental responsibility against his will burdens his right of procreational autonomy" (p. 233). Under the current legal system, however, women can force men to bear parental responsibility legally and financially. Nevertheless, while financial abortions may sound like a reasonable compromise to avoid "forced parenthood," looking at the issue through the lens of feminist theory highlights some potential social implications.

Feminist Theory

In order to analyze financial abortions from a feminist perspective, it is first necessary to understand the underlying tenets of the theory. Feminist theory is unique in comparison to traditional theoretical frameworks used to analyze social issues. White and Klein's (2002) review of feminist theory highlights the distinctinve "evaluative and ideological" (p. 171) nature of feminist thought, mainly due to the theory's roots in social activism. Although feminist theory is sometimes criticized as lacking scientifically testable assumptions, it has been incredibly influential in critically examining issues centering around the historical oppression of women (as well as children and minority groups) and other gender related topics (Osmond & Throne, 1993).

One major assumption of feminist theory is that the experiences women have are real, valid, and historically different than the experiences of men (Osmond & Throne, 1993). Feminist theory is comprised of multiple schools of thought, each viewing relationships

1 Because fathers lack consent in these areas, various states have begun to implement provisions to protect fathers from losing their rights. For example, many states have adoption laws that require a woman to attempt to notify the father of her child before giving the child up for adoption, even if she is unsure of who the father is.

between men and women from a slightly different perspective (White & Klein, 2002). Radical feminist thought tends to take a more fundamentalist approach, advocating for strict equality between the sexes, sometimes ignoring biological differences. Other branches, such as cultural feminism, acknowledge the biological and social differences between men and women, advocating for awareness and understanding of these differences. Despite these different viewpoints, all branches of feminist theory emphasize the concepts sex and gender, family, and sexism (White & Klein).

From a feminist perspective, sex (defined biologically) and gender (defined socially) structure life experiences (White & Klein, 2002). Physical and social experiences individuals face are often framed by their sex and gender. For example, the physical experiences of childbirth and breastfeeding are unique to the female sex. Physical experiences each sex are capable of experiencing contribute to the conceptualization of each gender (i.e., what it means to be male or female). For example, if a woman is a mother, part of the definition of femininity is the concept of motherhood, which is partially defined by biological experiences (experiences that can never be associated with the concept of fatherhood). Countless other life experiences are similarly shaped by perceptions and definitions of sex and gender. A feminist perspective seeks to recognize the effect of sex and gender on the life experiences of women, making their experiences considerably different to those of men (White & Klein).

Feminist theory examines experiences that take place at the individual level, as well as at the family level. Traditionally, conceptualization of the "family" has been treated as an ideology; the family has been portrayed as a system with certain divisions of labor and specific patterns of co-residence that are considered normal and desired (i.e., the traditional nuclear family) (Osmond & Throne, 1993). A feminist perspective challenges this outdated viewpoint, wargning that a false ideology only perpetuates stereotypes about females' abilities, such as assumptions that women are better suited for domestic duties and nurturing children, while men are better suited to be financial supporters.

Based on its roots in social activism, a large portion of feminist theory is devoted to the concept of sexism. Historically, men have controlled many aspects of women's lives (Osmond & Throne, 1993). Feminist theory is especially concerned with the social forces that highlight unwarranted inequalities between the sexes (White & Klein, 2002). The promotion of sexist values has unnecessary and hindering effects on female life experiences. As previously discussed, social forces such as the false ideology of the family, assume that men and women can only take on particular roles within the household. For example, a workplace may be accepting of female employees taking leave to care for a new child, but disapprove of male employees taking leave for the same purpose. Defining women as "natural" caretakers of children (and other sexist labels) reduces women to victims of their biology, stunting women socially. Feminist theory seeks to identify these forces and find strategies to bring equality between the genders (either culturally or more radically).

A feminist perspective of the topics sex and gender, family, and sexism can be applied to the financial abortion debate. Examining financial abortions through a feminist lens can provide some interesting insights to this controversial issue.

Financial Abortions and Feminist Theory

If men were allowed to obtain financial abortions from an unwanted child, what impact would this have on men, women, children and families? Using what has been previously discussed about feminist theory, two main social consequences arise. Firstly, granting financial abortions would create unfair and unbalanced choices between the sexes. Specifically, men and women have different choices regarding parenthood, and financial abortions amplify this disparity. Secondly, granting financial abortions would reinforce sexist stereotypes concerning gender and the family, a result that would harm women, men, and children.

Unbalanced Choices

Despite the claim that financial abortions would bring equality, granting men this option would actually further divide the choices between the sexes. Currently, women's options in disclaiming parenthood are abortion, adoption, or abandonment of the child. Men's options would be the withdrawal financial support and the forfeiting of parental rights. Ethically, these are not equal choices. The biological experience of carrying a fetus makes a woman's decision to terminate parental rights more intrusive, both physically and mentally. In the event of adoption or abandonment, a woman must carry the fetus for nine months, then experience childbirth and postpartum effects; in the event of abortion, a woman undergoes an extremely invasive procedure to remove the fetus.

It is not appropriate to equate these choices with the withholding of financial support. A father who wishes to exercise a financial abortion would not have to first carry a fetus inside his body, potentially becoming attached to the child. Nor would he have to experience and abortion and the emotional toll that the procedure potentially brings. It is recognized, however, that, for some men, forfeiting their parental rights may be a difficult personal decision. Even so, the emotional and physical toll women face arguably is a more complicated and taxing decision than the decision men would face if financial abortions were available.

Reinforcement of Gender and Family Stereotypes

Granting financial abortions would reinforce traditional gender and family stereotypes. The symbolic or cultural gender of a society contributes to how masculinity and femininity are defined (Osmond & Throne, 1993). Traditionally, masculinity defines the parental role as breadwinner and femininity defines the parental role as nurturer. Financial abortions would reinforce the idea that the only way men can *not* be a parent is if they revoke their breadwinning role from the child's life. Reducing the presence of fatherhood to either financially supporting or not finically supporting a child reinforces outdated stereotypes. With the rise in dual-earner households and single fathers, it is clear that the divide between parental roles is closing, and fatherhood is much more complex than the breadwinning stereotype portrays (Murphy, 2005). Downplaying fatherhood is a hindrance to those fathers who are actively involved in their children's lives.

Reinforcing the idea of a breadwinner role for fathers simultaneously reinforces the assumption that women are better suited for the nurturer role. Making assumptions that women are naturally suited for certain roles is generally associated with the perpetuation of patriarchal structures, which has been a source of oppression for women for centuries (White & Klein, 2002). Granting financial abortions would contribute to the reinforcement of these traditional gender stereotypes, indirectly placing women, and involved fathers, at a social disadvantage.

Children Lose

Granting financial abortions to men wishing to disclaim parenthood would have social implications as discussed above, but unfortunately the issue is even more complex, with effects that would trickle down to the potential children involved. Many U.S. family laws are based on the traditional idea of family; relationships are determined biologically (Murphy, 2005). Traditional child support laws are based on the biological connection between parent and child. Granting financial abortions to men that wish to avoid paying child support would place the children involved at a severe disadvantage. Children would lose a portion of their financial support structure. Generally, children benefit from having access to as many financial resources possible (Bradley & Corwyn, 2002), which may require contributions from both parents. Forcing an uninvolved father to pay child support negatively impacts the image of fatherhood, but at least children are receiving monetary support. Children would not receive any financial benefits from one parent if financial abortions were granted.

A feminist perspective seeks to highlight the experiences of all groups that lack power, including children (Osmond & Throne, 1993). The children that are born in the midst of "disclaiming parenthood" disputes possess no power in the situation, yet their lives are directly affected. Ultimately children benefit from economic support from both parents and would be disadvantaged by financial abortions.

Sexism?

As previously discussed, granting financial abortions would create unbalanced choices, disadvantaging women and children; however, the current choices are already unbalanced, disadvantaging men. Is it sexist to "force" men into parenthood, or is it sexist to grant financial abortions? The answer is probably both. Nevertheless, because men and women differ biologically (i.e., women carry the fetus, men cannot), this debate must favor women. In a world of ultimate equality, men and women would each have equal authority in decisions concerning pregnancy; however, this would ultimately force some women to have abortions against their will, violating their right to bodily autonomy. Additionally, some women would be forced to have children against their will, in violation of the right not to share their bodies for the benefit of another individual (Manninen, 2007). There may not be a solution that is balanced equally for both sexes; thus, the women who bear a larger biological and emotional cost should prevail.

Granting financial abortions to men who wish to disclaim parenthood clearly has complex social consequences affecting sex, gender, the family, and even the potential children involved. Matthew Dubay's request to disclaim parenthood was initially denied by the Michigan court and was appealed in federal court (*Dubay v. Wells,* 2007). Fortunately, the complex social consequences surrounding this issue are somewhat appeased by previous pregnancy-related judicial interpretations of the Fourteenth Amendment. Previous court rulings have made it difficult for men to make a compelling legal case in favor of financial abortions.

THE FOURTEENTH AMENDMENT AND PREGNANCY

Dubay's argument (and other similar financial abortion claims) is based on the violation of one's rights under the Equal Protection Clause of the Fourteenth Amendment of the United States Constitution. The Fourteenth Amendment guarantees that no citizen of the United States shall be deprived of "life, liberty, or property" nor "equal protection of the law." Simply put, as long as individuals are similarly situated, they must be treated equally. However, in the case of pregnancy, previous court rulings have determined that men and women are not subject to equal treatment (e.g., *Geduldig v. Aiello*, 1974). Pregnant women are not similarly situated to non-pregnant women and men.

Men and women are similarly situated as potential parents up until the point of conception and then again after childbirth. During pregnancy however, because of the physical and emotional toll involved on women's bodies and lives, men and pregnant women are not similarly situated (Poland, 2006). Nine months later, after the child is born, both the mother and father are again similarly situated and equally responsible as parents.

The most profound consequence of this interpretation of the Fourteenth Amendment is that there is no constitutional guarantee that men and pregnant women must be treated equally (*Geduldig v. Aiello*, 1974). Therefore, potential fathers may not use the Equal Protection Clause of the Fourteenth Amendment as an argument for terminating their potential parental rights (Poland, 2006). The federal court denied Dubay's appeal. For now, such court decisions make it clear that the decision to have sexual intercourse is the only control a man has over the possibility of being held legally and financially responsibility for a child.

DISCUSSION

Unfortunately, for men, their decision to become a parent ends with the decision to have sexual intercourse. Financial abortions are a complex idea, rooted in many social issues. While those in favor of financial abortions make a compelling case, legally they fall short. From a feminist perspective of gender and the family, granting financial abortions would create unfair reproductive choices between men and women, reinforce traditional gender and family stereotypes, and disadvantage children.

While some men may see their lack of options in choosing to be a parent as unfair, the consequences of creating equality among reproduction would have unfortunate consequences for women and children. The current position men are in legally is for the best, but that does not mean it is particularly fair. Strict equality in this area is something that may never be achieved. Exploring this topic in more depth from a cultural feminist approach, one that acknowledges the biological limitations of both sexes, will be most helpful in bringing men and women to some sort of compromise (Brunner, 1996). Brunner has suggested that under certain circumstances (e.g., non-abusive relationships and marriages), fathers should be afforded a moral right in the decision to enter parenthood. This could perhaps be achieved through counseling and communication designed to merge differing interests between the potential mother and father (Brunner).

The issue of morality and virtue should not be ignored when discussing men and women's rights in entering parenthood (Manninen, 2007). Women and men need to acknowledge their legal roles in this debate, and acknowledge what can and cannot be changed. Rather than pitting one sex against the other and treating unborn children as legal disputes, emphasis needs to be placed on communication and joint decision-making in the choice to enter parenthood. While the unequal legal position may at face value seem unfair, a bigger ethical dilemma arises when children and families are unsupported and stereotypes are reinforced. As such, men must bear the financial responsibility for the children they produce; this is the position of the current legal system, which is supported by the analysis above.

Conclusion

Ultimately, both men and women can avoid parenthood by abstaining from sexual intercourse. Nevertheless, women have a choice in bearing parental responsibility after conception occurs. Perhaps, as Matthew Dubay suggests, men should also have a choice in bearing parental responsibility after conception occurs. Granting financial abortions to men who wish to disclaim parenthood is an accepted viewpoint of some organizations. The National Center for Men (2008) supported Dubay's position stating, "A man's life can be held hostage to an unplanned pregnancy, but his female partner will have complete control over her reproductive life and future...Only women have the extraordinary freedom to enjoy sexual intimacy free from the fear of forced parenthood." Such organizations suggest that allowing men to similarly avoid forced parenthood would bring equality. On the other hand, the feminist theory perspective discussed above indicates that a variety of negative outcomes might arise if this plan is carried out. Inequality between the sexes is typically an unfortunate outcome, but in such cases, it is necessary in order to best protect children and families.

References

Bradley, R. H., & Corwyn, R. F. (2002). Socioeconomic status and child development. *Annual Review of Psychology, 53,* 371-399.

Brake, E. (2005). Fatherhood and child support: Do men have a right to choose? *Journal of Applied Philosophy, 22,* 55-73.

Dubay v. Wells, 506 F. Supp. 3d 422 (6th Cir. Mich. 2007).

Hiester, E. M. (2004). Child support statutes and the father's right not to procreate. *Ave Maria Law Review, 2,* 213-241.

Geduldig v. Aiello, 417 U.S. 484 (1974).

Manninen, B. A. (2007). Pleading men and virtuous women: Considering the role of the father in the abortion debate. *The International Journal of Applied Philosophy, 21,* 1-24.

Murphy, J. C. (2005). Legal images of fatherhood: Welfare reform, child support enforcement, and fatherless children. *Notre Dame Law Review, 81,* 325-386.

Osmond, M. W., & Thorne, B. (1993). Feminist theories: The social construction of gender in families and society. In P. Boss, W. J. Doherty, R. LaRossa, W. R. Schumm, & S. K. Steinmetz (Eds.), *Sourcebook of family theories and methods* (pp. 591-623). NY: Plenum.

Poland, B. A. (2006). He said, she said: Diverging views in the emerging field of fathers' rights. *Washburn Law Journal, 46,* 163-187.

The National Center for Men (2008). Our issues. Retrieved on June 4, 2008, from http://www.nationalcenterformen.org/page3.shtml.

White, J. M., & Klein, D.M. (2002). *Family theories*. Thousand Oaks, CA: Sage Publications.

In: Contemporary Perspectives on Legal Regulation...
Editor: Monica K. Miller

ISBN 978-1-60741-161-1

Chapter 12

MORAL OUTRAGE TOWARD SOCIAL VIOLATIONS REGARDING SEX AND PROCREATION

Alayna Jehle
R&D Strategic Solutions, Lexington, Massachusetts 02421, USA

When people commit a wrongdoing that harms another person, the victim and third party decision-makers can respond in numerous ways. First, they can seek compensation from the offender to restore the victim's losses (Darley & Pittman, 2003). They can also seek retribution toward the offender through punishment. Negligent acts generally elicit the compensatory reaction and low moral outrage, whereas intentional acts elicit the retribution reaction and high moral outrage (Darley & Pittman, 2003). Some behaviors that are seen as morally wrong and are committed intentionally also have the potential for creating moral outrage, even if the individual did not intend harm to occur as a result of the action. Morality is often inherent in judgments regarding sex and procreation. As such, related acts that violate social morality often elicit retributive reactions, especially when proper compensation is not feasible. In such cases, the need for retribution strengthens and the offender is punished severely. This article will examine moral outrage toward social violations regarding sex and procreation, focusing on how these morality objections produce a desire for retributive justice.

MORAL OUTRAGE TOWARD SEXUAL NORM VIOLATIONS

There are many norm violations regarding sexual activities that create moral outrage. First, a person who commits adultery violates social norms by seeking sexual pleasure from a person who is not one's spouse. This produces moral outrage because it breaks the sacred vows of marriage. In nearly half the states, adultery is considered a crime (Herold, 2005). Military law also considers adultery a crime and there have been recent cases of officers getting fired to punish them for this violation of social norms (Moniz, 2005). Offenders in these cases probably do not intend for their spouses to find out about the adulterous behavior, and therefore, they are not intentionally trying to hurt someone. However, their actions to commit adultery are intentional and it could be argued that they should be aware of the harmful consequences if the immoral behavior is discovered. When the spouse and the third party decision-makers hear of the adulterous act, they usually begin feeling moral emotions, such as anger and disgust (Darley & Pittman, 2003). These moral emotions are associated with the moral outrage they are experiencing because the act itself is intentional and violates the social values inherent in marriage. Therefore, the spouse often seeks punishment for the offender, which can range from emotional punishment (e.g., guilt trips) to divorce and custody battles. They can also seek compensation, which can range from gifts to alimony and property settlements. The court can also seek retribution on behalf of the spouse and society by punishing the offender with a jail sentence or monetary fine (Haggard, 1998-1999).

Similarly, prostitution also is viewed as a violation of social norms and morality because it involves a sexual act between two people who are not married to each other. Additional norms are violated if the john is married and committing adultery. Although prostitution is considered a victimless crime, especially when the john is not married, both the prostitutes and johns are viewed with moral outrage because they are intentionally violating the social values related to sex. Societal norms dictate that sexual activities should be between two people who are seeking a relationship; therefore, the sexual acts are viewed as "sinful" when they are performed simply for monetary gain (for the prostitute) and pleasure (for the john; Thompson, 2000). Although some people might view marriage as a similar exchange of money and pleasure, marriage is a valued institution in society, whereas prostitution is judged as immoral because it is a more blatant form of this reciprocity without a stable relationship. Therefore, prostitution evokes moral outrage because the parties are viewed as intentionally violating social morality. Thus, society seeks to punish the johns and prostitutes through legal sanctions, such as incarceration or fines. Society also experiences moral emotions, especially disgust toward the two parties. This allows for another sanction to punish johns, which involves posting photographs of convicted johns on billboards and television to elicit shame from the johns (Huschka, 2006). For instance, in 2005, Oakland officials started a "shaming campaign" that involved posting convicted johns' photos on billboards to punish them for their social norm violations (Associated Press, 2005). The johns are punished using this shaming technique because society is disgusted by their actions and this form of retribution forces the johns to experience negative emotions (e.g., loss of dignity; Darley & Pittman, 2003) that are similar to the negative moral emotions that society feels due to their moral outrage.

Finally, moral outrage exists when people knowingly spread HIV through sexual activities (Kromm, 1999; Turner, 2003). Although the offender may not have intentionally meant to harm the victims, they knowingly and intentionally had unprotected sex with numerous partners and failed to inform them of their illness. One man did not disclose to his victims that he had HIV and subsequently infected at least ten women with the disease (Kromm, 1999; Turner 2003). Such behaviors produce extreme moral outrage because the victims cannot be properly compensated when their injury is life-threatening. Therefore, retributive justice must be achieved through extreme punishment to account for the lack of appropriate compensation. Judges have punished these HIV-spreading offenders with lengthy prison sentences (e.g., Kromm, 1999) to address the moral outrage. Society feels moral emotions, such as anger and disgust (Darley & Pittman, 2003) toward the offender for intentionally engaging in behaviors that they know will possibly result in the death of their sexual partners.

Moral Outrage toward Norm Violations Regarding Pregnancy Termination

In addition to sex-related norm violations, moral outrage is also produced from violations regarding the proper way to terminate a pregnancy. Sometimes pregnant females decide that they do not wish to have their babies and attempt to abort the fetuses through physical force (Back, 2007). This violates social norms, which dictate that abortions should be conducted surgically by doctors rather than forcefully by untrained professionals. These women generally cannot be charged with murder, however, because they have a legal right to abortion. However, if a woman asks her boyfriend to help terminate the pregnancy, then the boyfriend can be prosecuted for murder (Back, 2007). In 2005, this was the case for a 19-year old male who continually stepped on his girlfriend's stomach because she wanted to terminate the pregnancy and her own attempts had failed. He received two life sentences carrying a minimum of 40 years in prison to punish him for his social norm violation (Back, 2007). The extreme sentence is because the act of intentionally assaulting a pregnant female to abort her fetus, even if the female is an accomplice, evokes moral outrage in society. Community members begin to feel moral emotions, such as anger and disgust, toward the offender because the fetus is deprived of autonomy and dignity (Darley & Pittman, 2003). The legal system responds with retributive goals intended to punish the offender, and because the victim in the case (e.g., the dead fetus) cannot be compensated, the offender is punished more severely. If these males are convicted of murder, they face lengthy prison sentences, which may be as punitive as life imprisonment (Back, 2007).

Conclusion

In sum, social norm violations regarding sex and pregnancy termination can evoke moral emotions, such as anger and disgust, and result in moral outrage. Victims and society react to these wrongdoings with retributive goals in mind, which cause third party decision-makers to punish these offenders and compensate the victim. For example, adultery and prostitution produce moral outrage because they violate social values inherent in marriage, and therefore, these offenders are punished by fines (Herold, 2005) and shaming (Huschka, 2006). However, when the victim cannot be compensated, retributive justice becomes the sole goal and the offender is punished more severely. Offenders who spread HIV and terminate pregnancies cannot adequately compensate their victims because the victims either will die or are already dead, respectively, as a result of the wrongdoing. Thus, society responds with greater moral outrage and treats these offenders more punitively than offenders who can properly compensate and restore their victims.

References

Associated Press. (2005, June 5). Billboards aim to shame 'johns'. *Washington Times*. Retrieved July 10, 2008, at http://www.washtimes.com/news/2005/jun/05/20050605-120636-7950r.

Back, L. E. (2007). Improperly performed abortion as fetal homicide: An uneasy coexistence becomes more difficult. *Hastings Women's Law Journal, 18*, 117-134.

Darley, J. M., & Pittman, T. S. (2003). The psychology of compensatory and retributive justice. *Personality and Social Psychology Review, 7*, 324-336.

Haggard, M. A. (1998-1999). Adultery: A comparison of military law and state law and the controversy this causes under our Constitution and criminal justice system. *Brandeis Law Journal, 37*, 469-483.

Herold, J. A. (2005). Breach of vows but not criminal: Does *Lawrence v. Texas* invalidate Utah's statute criminalizing adultery? *Journal of Law and Family Studies, 7*, 253-261.

Huschka, R. J. (2006). Sorry for the jackass sentence: A critical analysis of the constitutionality of contemporary shaming punishments. *University of Kansas Law Review, 54*, 803-835.

Moniz, D. (2005, Aug. 10). General lost job over romance, his lawyer says. *USA Today.com.*Retrieved July 10, 2008, at http://www.usatoday.com/news/washington/2005-08-10-general-romance_x.htm.

Kromm, D. (1999). HIV-specific knowing transmission statutes: A proposal to help fight an epidemic. *St. John's Journal of Legal Commentary, 14*, 253-277.

Thompson, S. E. (2000). Prostitution- A choice ignored. *Women's Rights Law Reporter, 21*, 217-247.

Turner, D. C. (2003). Safer laws?: Problematic civil/criminal liability and curbing New York's HIV/AIDS epidemic. *Quinnipiac Health Law Journal, 6*, 173-192.

In: Contemporary Perspectives on Legal Regulation...
Editor: Monica K. Miller
ISBN 978-1-60741-161-1

Chapter 13

Concerns with the Obscenity Law

Alicia Summers
University of Nevada, Reno, Nevada, USA

In the United States, laws must evolve with the changing times. Those that do not evolve become static laws on the books, ever present but rarely (if ever) enforced and are often seen as a humorous remnant of times past. Consider the cohabitation and fornication laws, rarely are either upheld or enforced in modern society. With today's new and emerging laws and precedents, as well as advances in technology, the obscenity law, established by the *Miller* (1973) case, is soon to be one of the outdated laws on the books. This article seeks to explain why the 1973 obscenity standards have already become problematic in the legal arena and make recommendations for the evolution of obscenity in the twenty-first century.

The standard by which obscenity cases are measured was set forth in the now infamous *Miller v. California* (1973) case. According to the standards set forth by *Miller,* whether something is obscene or not depends largely on three factors. First, whether an average person, applying community standards, would find that the work appeals to a prurient interest (an unhealthy, morbid or degrading interest in sex). Second, whether the work depicts sexual conduct specifically defined by the state in a patently offensive manner. Finally, obscenity is determined by whether the work, taken as a whole, lacks any artistic, literary, political or scientific value (*Miller v. California*). As may be obvious, this definition is somewhat problematic. The first concern with the *Miller* standard is its vagueness.

The obscenity law is vague on three important accounts. First, the standard does not clearly define what is meant by 'community.' Second, the standard does not delineate who will be determining community standards. Finally, the standard does not express who is responsible for determining the lack of artistic, literary, political, or scientific value. Points two and three shall be addressed herein, while point one will be addressed in detail in the following paragraph. The subject of who determines community standards is fraught with ambiguity. One might rationally assume that jury members are made up of community members and are thus more than capable of determining standards of the community, as many judges have assumed (Scott, 1991). However, researchers have also argued that jurors are not capable of determining community sentiment, only their own biases, and thus would benefit from expert testimony based on empirical evidence of public opinion or community standards

(Holley, 1996). The standard of artistic, scientific, literary or political value has the same weaknesses. If beauty is in the eye of the beholder, then artistic value should be a matter of opinion. Opinion in this area is also varied. In a review of three recent obscenity cases, Greene (2005) brings attention to the fact that expert testimony of artistic value may or may not be persuasive to a jury. In all three cases, experts testified to the artistic value of the object in question. However, results of the case varied. That is, sometimes the jury believed the expert and sometimes they applied their own standards, with dramatically differing results. Both decisions of who determines community standards and who decides value are vague and open to much interpretation, causing the potential for a legal nightmare.

The third objection is the vagueness of 'community.' Community could be considered the town or state of which an individual resides. Research has demonstrated that the size of the community in question impacts ratings of obscenity, with more urban areas having less restrictive standards of obscenity than more rural areas (Glassman, 1978). One might assume from the research that community has clearly been defined, as the town, city, or state of residence. The rise of the internet and the computer age has changed all that. Consider the virtual child pornography law struck down by the Supreme Court (Aronson, 2002). The Supreme Court ruled that virtual child pornography (that does not include real children) is not susceptible to the child pornography laws (Aronson). However, it still is susceptible to obscenity laws which represent community sentiments of what is obscene. Hear comes the problem. What if a woman in a small conservative town sees the virtual porn on the internet and finds it obscene. She can file suit against the purveyor of the virtual porn site. Now, what if the man that runs the site lives in a very liberal urban city where virtual child porn is not really considered that obscene. In his 'community,' it would not be a problem, but in hers, it is a big deal. Legally, what action can be taken? Well, if recent cases are any indication, individuals can still press charges against others even if they live in different communities all the way across the country (Walters & DeWittt, 2005). The use of the internet and proliferation of potentially obscene materials on the web thus totally changes the meaning of community. This means that presently, community can be considered anywhere the internet is accessible, so basically anywhere in the world.

Another major concern with the obscenity law is the inevitable clash between the *Miller* (1973) decision and the *Lawrence* (2003) decision. Thirty years after the establishment of the obscenity decision, the Supreme Court has ruled in a key legal case that individuals have a fundamental right to conduct their private lives in matters pertaining to sex (*Lawrence v. Texas*). When obscenity and privacy are both a concern, this might be problematic. Consider two recent cases concerning sex toys. In one, a federal court upheld an Alabama law making it illegal to sell or advertise sex toys (Dorf, 2004). In a similar vein, a Texas mother of three was arrested for the promotion of sex toys (i.e., explaining how they work; Grossman, 2004). While the former concern might be legitimate, at least in terms of advertising materials inappropriate for children, both might be considered in violation of the *Lawrence* decision. For example, a young couple talks to their friend in the privacy of her home concerning their sex life and asks for advice on something to spice it up. Should not the *Lawrence* decision protect both their right to privacy and their right to do whatever they want (within limits) concerning sex? Also, by prohibiting selling of sex toys, the state is exercising control over the residents and trying to limit their sexual options. Thus, the obscenity laws are directly conflicting with the privacy rights.

When considering the value of the obscenity laws, researchers must consider the many problems that have evolved over the years with defining obscenity and interaction of new legal standards (such as the *Lawrence* decision). With so many problems, it is far past time for an update. In order to update the obscenity standard, the law will need to address four important factors. First, the law will need to specify what is meant by community. A clear cut operational definition would be best. Second, the law will need to specify who will determine (and how they will determine) community standards of obscenity. The conflict of opinions between judges concerning the use of expert testimony and the jury's ability to determine community standards needs to be resolved with empirical evidence and the final ruling should determine which is valid and best to use. Third, the law needs to address who will determine (and how it shall be determined) the value (artistic, scientific, political, or literary) of the material in question. Among other things, the law should specify when experts are needed and what qualifications the expert must have in order to determine value. Finally, the obscenity laws should address the emerging complexities that the widespread use of the internet has brought to light in recent years. There should be a determination of what constitutes "online" community and how to avoid shutting down sites that many do not find obscene, but are considered obscene by the few. Until changes are made, the obscenity laws will continue to be vague and problematic in the courts. Times have changed dramatically since the 70's and laws must keep up with the changing times to be effective.

REFERENCES

Aronson, B. (2002). The Supreme Court strikes down a "virtual" child porn law, but other legal constraints on child porn and obscenity remain strict. Available online at http://writ.news.findlaw.com/aronson/20020418.html.

Dorf, M. C. (2004). Is there a constitutional right to sexual privacy? Available online at http://writ.news.findlaw.com/dorf/20040804.html.

Glassman, M. B. (1978). Community standards of patent offensiveness: public opinion data and obscenity law. *Public Opinion Quarterly, 42*(2), 161-170.

Greene, D. (2005). The need for expert testimony to prove lack of artistic value in obscenity cases. *Nexus: A Journal of Opinion.*

Grossman, J. (2004). Is there a constitutional right to promote the use of sex toys? Available online at http://writ.news.findlaw.com/grossman/20040127.html.

Holley, P. (1996). Obscenity and child pornography: sociology in defense of sexually oriented materials. In P. J. Jenkins & S. Kroll-Smith *Witnessing for Sociology: Sociology in Court.* Westport, Connecticut: Praeger.

Lawrence v. Texas, 539 U.S. 558, 123 S. Ct. 2472 (2003).

Miller v. California, 413 U.S. 15, 93 S. Ct. 2607 (1973).

Scott, J. E. (1991). What is obscene? Social science and the contemporary community standard test of obscenity. *International Journal of Law and Psychiatry, 14*(1-2), 29-45.

Walters, L. G., & DeWittt, C. (2005). Obscenity in the digital age: The Re-evaluation of community standards. *Nexus: A Journal of Opinion, 10,* 59-70.

In: Contemporary Perspectives on Legal Regulation... ISBN 978-1-60741-161-1
Editor: Monica K. Miller

Chapter 14

THE SOCIAL SIGNIFICANCE OF THE MARITAL CONTRACT: WHY CIVIL TORT LAW IS NEEDED TO REGULATE ADULTERY

Jennifer L. Lowman
University of Nevada, Reno, Nevada, USA

Marriage[1] has traditionally organized social and economic relations between families, defined roles and obligations within families, and signified a commitment to monogamous sexual activity between two people. Since the 20th century, marriage has also come to symbolize the monogamous *emotional* commitment two people make to each other (Attridge & Berscheid, 1994; Coontz, 1996). As a social institution, marriage both structures and defines a person's social position relative to others and provides a normative framework of socially appropriate emotional states (e.g., love, happiness, satisfaction) and affective expectations (e.g., support, rapport, romantic excitement) (Attridge & Berscheid, 1994). Simply, married couples are expected to both act and feel a certain way. Marital partners are expected to behave in a manner that furthers their combined social, emotional, and economic interests and support one another's emotional growth and fulfillment. Marriage is an exchange relationship in which two people negotiate, compromise, and exchange resources to further their individual and combined goals.

The relatively new expectation of emotional monogamy and fulfillment in marriage is often a topic in popular media and the subject of research in academia (Kitson, Babri, & Roach, 1985; Glenn & Weaver, 1988). Academic journals and popular magazines alike contain surveys, scales, and reports which promote continual appraisals of close relationships, especially regarding compatibility and relationship quality. This increased focus on individual fulfillment in relationships has raised the question as to whether or not such a focus has influenced the nature of marriage in society (Kitson et al., 1985; Glenn & Weaver, 1988). For

1 This chapter focuses on marriage in the United States for which monogamy is the marital norm; though there are notable exceptions such as the polygamy practiced by the Fundamentalist Latter Day Saints. Monogamy, however, is currently the only form of marriage legally permitted in the U.S.

example, researchers have noted a relationship between the social emphasis on individual fulfillment/satisfaction and an increased incidence of marital dissolution in the United States (Attridge & Baerscheid, 1994; Thorton & Young-DeMarco, 2001). Basically, an increased societal preoccupation with fulfillment/satisfaction has increased the amount of time people spend evaluating and ruminating over the negative aspects of their relationship and this may be a factor in increased rates of divorce. The question remains, however, whether or not there is actually a fundamental change in marital expectations or simply a change in access to and acceptance of divorce (Attridge & Berscheid, 1994; Thorton & Young-DeMarco, 2001).

This article employs a social psychological perspective to examine extramarital sex as a breach of the marital exchange relationship; that is, a violation of the behavioral and emotional interests of a married couple. The issue in question is why in a social environment that accepts "no fault" divorce would a person engage in extramarital sex before dissolving an unsatisfactory or unfulfilling marriage? Social psychology contributes to our understanding of the legal significance of individual choices and actions by elevating the informational relevance of contextual influences (e.g., marital norms) on behavior. By developing our understanding of marital norms and expectations (i.e., context), the mechanisms through which individual actions come to have social and legal consequences may be revealed. Moreover, understanding the relationship between social structures and individual behaviors serves this investigation into whether or not legal intervention and regulation of marital and extra-marital behaviors is necessary and in fact legitimate.

Social contexts emerge at the intersection of interpersonal interaction and social convention. Context refers to those situational features which shape individual thoughts and behaviors. Lewin (1935) referred to context as the situational "background" against which everything is perceived and understood – he also noted that the background itself is often not directly perceived. Marital expectations serve as the background against which behavior and emotion in intimate relationships are perceived and interpreted by both married and unmarried people. Essentially, a social context frames what information interacting individuals find relevant and salient to interpret ongoing communication and evaluate the state of a relationship – something people in close relationships spend more time doing than ever before (Attridge & Berscheid, 1994). Although individual perceptions and judgments often differ according to personal experiences, motivations, and biases, identifying contextual features focuses attention on what constitutes normative behavior within marriages.

The marital exchange relationship or marital contract is a significant exemplar of a relational social context. As the reified objectification of intimate relationships, the marital contract reveals social roles, values, and beliefs shared between two people in an intimate relationship and to a lesser degree, among people in other types of interpersonal relationships. By examining patterned interpersonal behavior, the mechanisms through which the social order emerges may also be revealed (Berger & Luckman, 1966). It is through an understanding of the basis of the social order that a breach of the marital contract may be viewed as having both relational and social consequences. The relational consequences are obvious as affairs often contribute to (or speed up) the dissolution of close relationships (Previti & Amato, 2004). However, the social consequences of extramarital sex are not as apparent. The argument made in this chapter is that extramarital sex (EMS) challenges the relevance and meaningfulness of the relational context through which the marital exchange relationship is understood and protected. EMS challenges the legitimacy of marriage as a meaningful social institution for individual fulfillment - emotional or otherwise – most importantly, it threatens the integrity of the exchange relationships upon which social contracts are based.

The purpose of this chapter is to demonstrate how the marital contract has great social significance, and thus, why civil tort intervention is relevant and necessary to maintain this fundamental institution. The following review begins with a discussion of the nature and significance of social contracts followed by a discussion regarding marriage as a specific instance of a social contract. Second, the incidence of extramarital sex is discussed as a specific case of a contractual violation and the use of civil tort law to regulate EMS is reviewed. Finally, a discussion of legal protections as a significant source of contextual information is offered as support for "heart balm" civil tort law enforcement in an effort to ensure that marriage remains a legitimate social institution.

The Social "Marital" Contract

People enter into voluntary contracts to receive some benefit or attain some privilege; however, every agreement has some cost and obligation associated with it (Locke, 1689/1993). The fundamental cost associated with a social contract is freedom – specifically, the freedom to act solely in one's self-interest either generally or in a specific domain of life. According to Locke (1689/1993), the natural pursuit of life, liberty, and property compels individuals to come together to form social contracts, and eventually governing bodies, to protect and manage their rights, pursuits, and obligations to each other. In the creation of a social contract, a fundamental tension between self-interested action and collaborative action develops. Conceptually, this tension is one between contradictory drives for independence and interdependence, autonomy and belonging, predictability and novelty (Baxter, 1996).

In the traditional Western marriage ceremony that accompanies the formation of a marital contract, the dialog and symbols used in the ceremony represent the transition from independent self to an interdependent couple, from self-interested action to collaborative self-sacrificing action. The idea of joining together of two individuals into one permeates the traditional wedding ceremony. The lighting of a "unity" candle by the couple, the exchange of vows to "love, honor, cherish, through sickness and health" and "forsake all others" symbolizes the formation of a partnership that supersedes individual identities and rights. Each person promises to give up the right for self-interested action and agrees to act for mutual goals (or at least not against the interest of the significant other) until death parts.

The marital contract is a legally sanctioned agreement between two people to pursue and protect each other's interests. Those interests may be emotional, physical, financial, or social (e.g., family interests, religious interests). Interests may be mutual as with the attainment of marital status, access to economic resources, or a plan to raise children. In contrast, interests may remain individual, as with the pursuit of personal career or leisure goals. Of course, any combination of interests is possible; a couple may have mutual emotional and physical interests while at the same time have more individualized financial or social interests. Similarly, one person's interests may attain dominance in one domain or across domains or the couple may achieve a more egalitarian balance between interests. The negotiation of the pursuit and protection of interests may be communicated prior to entering the martial contract or worked out over time. One certainty couple's face is that their interests and priorities will change and they will have to renegotiate their arrangements. Consequently, how couples handle change predicts the continuation or dissolution of their marriage (Clements, Cordova, Markman, & Laurenceau, 1997).

Research shows that the division of labor, physical, emotional, or otherwise, often changes with social transitions that occur within the marriage, such as the transition to parenthood (Belsky, Lang, & Huston, 1986). For example, role arrangements in the transition to parenthood often become more traditional for both men and women; however, the emotional role arrangements do not necessarily change in accordance and this may become a source of conflict and strain between the marital partners (Belsky et al., 1986). Such a change in terms of the balance of interests or a failure to maintain arrangements may lead to the dissolution of the marital relationship and the marital contract may terminate with divorce (Clements et al., 1997; Gager & Sanchez, 2003; Sanchez & Gager, 2000). Simply, the arrangement of interests within a marriage is less important than each person's satisfaction with the arrangement (Berscheid & Lopes, 1997; Buunk & Dijkstra, 2006). Satisfaction is an individual's perceptual evaluation of their condition once positive and negative interactions (i.e., benefits and costs) are taken into account (Berscheid & Lopes, 1997). People monitor their degree of satisfaction in their relationships closely (Buunk & Dijkstra, 2006) and assess available alternatives and opportunities for improving their level of satisfaction regularly (Attridge & Berschied, 1994).

A common theme to emerge from research on the effect and balance of marital interests on satisfaction is the importance of spousal support. Brunstein and colleagues (1996) found that support for marital goals and support for the personal goals of one's spouse contribute independently to marital satisfaction, just as does one's perception of the spouses support for marital and personal goals. The important point being that marital satisfaction is influenced by both support received in shared and personal domains, as well as support given. Similarly, marital or collective efficacy also contributes to marital satisfaction; that is, a couple's belief that they can actually achieve their shared goals is positively related to their satisfaction with their relationship (Kaplan & Maddux, 2002).

In sum, research has found that support given is as important as support received for marital satisfaction. In addition, the belief that marital goals can be fulfilled (i.e., collective efficacy) is influenced by a couple's satisfaction with their arrangements and relationship. The marital contract is one people enter into to pursue particular interests, whatever they may be (e.g., support, sex, happiness, security). No matter the individual motives that compel people to marry, the benefits and costs associated with entering into a marriage have been protected by social governing bodies for most, if not all, of human social history (Fox, 1967/1998). Marriage is a protected institution because two people enter into an exchange relationship. As Locke suggested when he described social contracts, by entering into a marital contract people give up their natural freedom to pursue personal interests over and above collective, marital interests. This is not to say that personal interests cannot be pursued, but only that the couple must come to an arrangement that satisfies both individual's shared and personal goals.

Extramarital Sex and Civil Regulation

In most Western countries, the marital contract includes an expectation of sexual monogamy between marital partners. Monogamy, from an evolutionary psychology perspective, is often viewed as a cost for men and a benefit for women (Buss & Schmitt, 1993; Davis & Daly, 1997). It has been theorized that men are more promiscuous in order to increase their chances of passing on their genetic material while women are less promiscuous in order to foster a relationship with one man who will be a good father and support her children (Buss & Schmitt, 1993; Davis & Daly, 1997). Research has found that men tend to have more EMS than women, roughly 25% of men and 15% of women are estimated to engage in EMS (Treas & Giesen, 2000). However, the occurrence of EMS among younger cohorts is on the rise – a trend especially evident among younger women (Treas & Giesen, 2000). This suggests that that it may not be the gender of the individual that drives EMS but some aspect of the martial institution or societal regulation. For example, it may be that differential rates between genders in the past were due to the severe consequences women who engaged in EMS faced rather than a natural proclivity to be sexually monogamous.

Attridge and Berscheid (1994) suggest that EMS is the result of partner availability, accessibility, and opportunity. In a social environment in which married men and women work closely with others and spend as much or more time with others who are not their spouses, the opportunity to seek gratification and fulfillment through one's spouse may be increasingly frustrated at the same time as the opportunity to do the same through another (e.g., coworker, nanny) becomes increasingly available (Attridge & Berscheid, 1994). Exposure to and the accessibility of alternative partners coupled with an increased societal preoccupation with fulfillment and satisfaction has effectively fostered an environment in which marital expectations cannot be reasonably fulfilled – either as a matter of lack of opportunity or because expectations for fulfillment during quality time spent with one's marital partner are too high (Gager & Sanchez, 2003).

This raises the question as to whether availability, opportunity, and the need for fulfillment and satisfaction are enough to fuel the increase in EMS noted by Treas and Giesen (2000). The social psychological investigation of justice in relationships has revealed that people voluntarily follow rules and norms when they perceive those rules and norms to be legitimate (Tyler, 2006). Because legitimacy is an important factor for the survival of social institutions (Tyler, 2006), it may be that the boundaries of the marital contract are not considered legitimate, especially by younger Americans. Research by Thorton and Young-DeMarco (2001), which covers four decades of trends in attitudes on family issues including marriage and EMS, revealed that the desire to have a monogamous marriage remains a very strong attitude within the United States across generational cohorts. Thus, perceived legitimacy of institutional boundaries does not appear to explain the rise in EMS at the individual level.

Legitimacy, however, is not only a person level perception but also a system-level attribute (Tyler, 2006). According to Tyler (2006), the acceptance of rules and norms must exist within the climates and cultures of social and legal institutions, as well as among the people. The American public continues to believe in monogamous marriages, however, the legal system appears to have failed to maintain a climate and culture of support for marital obligations. Nearly half of the states have a variety of laws that contain harsh penalties to punish married men and women who have sex with another person yet these laws are rarely enforced (Grossman, 2003; Siegel, 1992). Laws exist, for instance, that could remove the right of a person who has EMS to vote, raise their children, practice law, or even serve alcohol (Siegel, 1992). Although these are unquestionably harsh punishments, it may be that no enforcement is more detrimental to the legitimacy of the institution of marriage than the enforcement of such penalties.

In the past, "heart-balm" tort laws imposed fines and penalties against those who violated the contract of marriage by having sex with another person. "Criminal conversation" or sex with another married person, "alienation of affections" or sex with an unmarried person, and "enticement" or persuading a woman to leave her husband were heart-balm tort categorizations for acts of EMS (Grossman, 2003). However, these civil tort penalties were not used consistently and without bias. Women, for instance, were more likely to be the target of fines or penalties than men (Siegel, 1992). Moreover, in the age of *Lawrence v. Texas* (2003), the decision by the United States Supreme Court that asserted privacy over state regulation of the behavior of consenting adults, it is likely that no court would uphold a law, tort, or penalty against an adult engaging in EMS. However, there is no need to legislate against the sexual act itself but only against the harm done to the martial contract.

Lawrence asserts that consenting sexual activity between adults is protected under the Due Process Clause of the Fourteenth Amendment to the Constitution. Specifically, no state has the right to deprive any person of life, liberty, or property, without due process of law. Consensual sex between adults is a matter of individual liberty; it is a protected privilege. Nevertheless, the marital contract between two people is considered a substantive contract with obligations other than sexual fidelity. For instance, the New Jersey Supreme Court ruled that a man who engaged in EMS before the dissolution of his marriage still deserved alimony from his wife (Grossman, 2005). The message from the New Jersey Supreme Court affirmed the primacy of contractual arrangements between married couples even over sexual misconduct. In other words, a married person who has sex with someone other than their partner breaks a specific contractual obligation in a particular domain of the relationship but this act does not negate the significance of obligations in other domains (e.g., economic support). Therefore, the contract in its entirety must be considered in the design and enforcement of civil torts.

Legal regulation and intervention on behalf of the well-known expectation of monogamy legitimates more than the marital contract, it legitimates the social context against which interpersonal agreements and arrangements are developed and maintained. Reinstating "heart-balm" torts reasonably and without bias would help to both justify and legitimate marital contracts, as well as social contracts more generally. System-level action or inaction influences the social context (e.g., expectations, norms) against which people interpret not only their arrangements but the potential consequences of their actions. The legal system needs to consistently and objectively protect every contract to ensure that actions against the collective interests of the relationship have real consequences.

DISCUSSION

EMS is a serious breach of marital investments and interests negotiated between two people. Marriage today is foremost a choice – at least currently for heterosexual couples. Cohabitation and living single are socially accepted, viable alternatives to marriage (Thorton & Young-DeMarco, 2001). Except for religious and socio-cultural pressures to marry, no person should feel exceptionally compelled to enter into a contract of marriage with another person. Furthermore, divorce allows someone to leave a marriage from which satisfaction is no longer attained. No-fault divorce allows two people to amicably end their marriage without codifying what went wrong in the relationship. These freedoms, to enter into or to leave a marriage, make extramarital sex an especially negligent act. Even when a marriage is likely to end in divorce, EMS ensures the marriage will end and in an emotionally injurious manner (De Stefano & Oala, 2008).

Civil tort law should be used to assign and enforce penalties against those who engage in EMS. Adultery should continue to be considered a breach of a social contract and a waste of the spouse's accrued investments. Research shows that for people in the United States, marriage continues to be an important social institution and EMS continues to be considered an objectionable and selfish act (Thorton & Young-DeMarco, 2001). In addition, divorce has become an accepted form of marital dissolution in the eyes of Americans (Thorton & Young-DeMarco, 2001). Therefore, people who break the marital contract before they seek to dissolve their responsibilities in a civil manner through divorce should face a reasonable fine or punishment.

Formulation of civil tort law should be mindful of the history of discrimination against women and care should be taken to expect evidence of EMS before punishments and fines are leveled. Both men and women engage in EMS, thus both men and women should be fined or penalized equally and objectively. Even if the spouse is not willing to pursue civil reprisal, the state should impose penalties in order to deter others from committing EMS. Furthermore, the state should regulate the tort for EMS independent of divorce proceedings, though as Grossman (2005) suggests marital misconduct should remain a consideration in determinations of fault though it should not prevail over the marital contract. A fine should be designed to protect the legitimacy of the exchange relationship of the marital contract. It should protect the dignity and privacy of individuals, especially the person who commits EMS. For as *Lawrence v. Texas* asserts, people have a right to engage in sexual consenting relations with others.

EMS violates the history of compromise and accommodation two people invest in the pursuit of shared and personal interests. Such an accumulated investment, however, is not easily quantified because the compromises people make are investments in their relational satisfaction and emotional fulfillment. Marriage has long been recognized and characterized for the compromises people make in order to make their marriage "work." The state should protect this history of investment in an effort to legitimate marriage as a viable social institution. The legitimacy of the marital contract may be dependent on the climate and culture of its' governing institutions. Only through consistent and reasonable punishments can states shore up the legitimacy of marriage as a fundamental institution through which meaningful exchange takes place between two people.

The social contract of marriage may be the most basic civil contract in social life. It may also likely be one of the oldest contracts in the history of human social affairs (no pun intended). It should be maintained and enforced as a valued social contract and social institution. Though it is not the responsibility of the state to make its' citizens act responsibly, the fact that the investments and interests of a person are squandered when EMS is committed should be the concern of the state. As the basic human contract, the health of society may be contingent on how married people choose to enter and leave a marriage. Furthermore, promoting accountability in this domain of dyadic relations may serve to promote conscientious decisions in other contractual associations. People barter with their natural rights and freedoms when they enter into a social contract to receive some benefit. Defending the social contract by making people accountable for their contractual responsibilities is a fundamental matter of protecting individual freedom.

REFERENCES

Attridge, M., & Berscheid, E. (1994). Entitlement in romantic relationships in the United States: A social-exchange perspective. In M.J. Lerner & G. Mikula (Eds.), *Entitlement and the affectional bond: Justice in close relationships*. New York: Plenum.

Baxter, L. A., (1996). Dialectical contradictions in relationship development. In L.A. Baxter & B.M. Montgomery (Eds.) *Relating: Dialogues and dialectics*. New York: Guilford Press.

Belsky, J., Lang, M., & Huston, T. L. (1986). Sex typing and division of labor as determinants of marital change across the transition to parenthood. *Journal of Personality and Social Psychology, 50*, 517-522.

Berger, P. L., & Luckman, T. (1966). *The social construction of reality*. New York: Doubleday.

Berscheid, E., & Lopes, J. (1997). A temporal model of relationship satisfaction and stability. In R.J. Sternberg & Hojjat, M., *Satisfaction in Close Relationships, pp. 129-159*. New York: Guilford Press.

Brunstein, J. C., Dangelmeyer, G., & Schultheiss, O. C. (1996). Personal goals and social support in close relationships: Effects on relationship mood and marital satisfaction. *Journal of Personality and Social Psychology, 71*, 1006-1019.

Buss, D. M., & Schmitt, D. P. (1993). Sexual strategies theory: An evolutionary perspective on human mating. *Psychological Review, 100*, 204-232.

Buunk, A. P., & Dijkstra, P. (2006). The ultimate betrayal? Infidelity and solidarity in close relationships. In D. Fetchenhauer, A. Flache, A.P. Buunk, & S. Lindenberg, *Solidarity and Prosocial Behavior*. New York: Springer.

Clements, M. L., Cordova, A. D., Markman, H. J., & Laurenceau, J-P. (1997). The Erosion of Marital Satisfaction over Time and how to Prevent It. In R.J. Sternberg & Hojjat, M., *Satisfaction in Close Relationships, pp. 335-355*. New York: Guilford Press.

Coontz, S. (1996). Where are the good old days? In M. Hutter (ed.), *The Family Experience*, pp. 15 – 21. Boston: Pearson Education Inc.

Davis, J., & Daly, M. (1997). Evolutionary theory and the human family. *The Quarterly Review of Biology, 72*, 407-435.

De Stefano, J., & Oala, M. (2008). Extramarital affairs: Basic considerations and essential tasks in clinical work. *The Family Journal: Counseling and therapy for couples and families, 16*, 13-19.

Fox, R. (1967/1998). *Kinship and marriage: An anthropological perspective*. Cambridge: Cambridge University Press.

Gager, C. T., & Sanchez, L. (2003). Two as One? Couples' perceptions of time spent together marital quality, and the risk of divorce. *Journal of Family Issues, 24*, 21-50.

Glenn, N. D., & Weaver, C. N. (1988). The changing relationship of marital status to reported happiness. *Journal of Marriage and the Family, 50*, 317-324.

Grossman, J. (2003, December 16). *Punishing Adultery in Virginia*. Find Law. Retrieved September 16, 2008 from http://writ.news.findlaw.com/grossman/20031216.html

Grossman, J. (2005, May 3). The New Hersey Supreme Court says yes, but marital misconduct can lower the award in egregious circumstances. Find Law. Retrieved September 16, 2008 from http://writ.news.findlaw.com/grossman/20050503.html

Kaplan, M., & Maddux, J. E. (2002). Goals and marital satisfaction: Perceived support for personal goals and collective efficacy for collective goals. *Journal of Social and Clinical Psychology, 21*, 157-164.

Kitson, G. C., Babri, K. B., & Roach, M. J. (1985). Who divorces and why: A review. *Journal of Family Issues, 6,* 255-293.

Lawrence v. Texas, 539 U.S. 558 (2003).

Lewin, K. (1935). *A dynamic theory of personality: Selected papers.* (D.K. Adams & K.E. Zener, Trans.). New York: McGraw-Hill.

Locke, J. (1993). *Two treatises of government.* (M. Goldie Trans.). London: Orion Publishing Group. (Original work published 1689)

Previti, D., & Amato, P. R. (2004). Is infidelity a cause or a consequence of poor marital quality? *Journal of Social and Personal Relationships, 21*, 217-230.

Sanchez, L., & Gager, C. T. (2000). Hard living, perceived entitlement to a great marriage, and marital dissolution. *Journal of Marriage and the Family, 62*, 708-722.

Siegel, M. J. (1992). For better or worse: Adultery, crime and the constitution. *Journal of Family Law, 30,* 45-95.

Thorton, A., & Young-DeMarco, L. (2001). Four decades of trends in attitudes toward family issues in the United States: The 1960s through the 1990s. *Journal of Marriage and Family, 63,* 1009-1037.

Treas, J., & Giesen, D. (2000). Sexual infidelity among married and cohabitating Americans. *Journal of Marriage and the Family, 62,* 48-60.

Tyler, T. R. (2006). Psychological perspectives on legitimacy and legitimation. *Annual Review of Psychology, 57*, 375-400.

CONTRIBUTORS

Sarah DeArman, M.A. (expected 2009) University of Nevada, Reno

Sarah R. DeArman is a master's student in the Criminal Justice program at the University of Nevada, Reno. She received her B.A. in Criminal Justice in 2006 from the University of Nevada, Reno and expects to graduate with her M.A. in 2009. Sarah is interested in policy and issues pertaining to family, gender and the law.

Alayna Jehle, Ph.D. R&D Strategic Solutions

Alayna Jehle is a trial consultant at R&D Strategic Solutions in Massachusetts. She received her Ph.D. in Social Psychology at the University of Nevada, Reno in 2007.

Sarah D. Merz, M.A. University of Nevada, Reno

Sarah D. Merz received her B.A. in Human Development from the University of California, San Diego in 2004 and her M.A. in Social Psychology from the University of Nevada, Reno in 2007. Her interests include psychology, law and policy analysis.

Monica K. Miller, J.D., Ph.D. University of Nevada, Reno

Monica K. Miller is an Assistant Professor with a joint appointment between the Criminal Justice Department and the Interdisciplinary Ph.D. Program in Social Psychology at the University of Nevada, Reno. She received her J.D. from the University of Nebraska College of Law in 2002 and her Ph.D. in Social Psychology from the University of Nebraska-Lincoln in 2004. Her interests lie in the intersection of psychology, law and policy.

Jennifer Lowman, M.A. University of Nevada, Reno

Jennifer L. Lowman earned an M.A. in sociology from the University of Nevada, Reno in 2005. She is currently a doctoral student in the Interdisciplinary PhD Program in Social Psychology at the University of Nevada, Reno. Her research interests focus on the manner in which social institutions, especially the family and educational systems, influence child outcomes such as perceived opportunities, motivation, and perceptions of self and others.

Jennifer A. Reisig, M.S. (expected 2009) University of Nevada, Reno

Jennifer A. Reisig is a graduate student in human development and family studies with an emphasis in early childhood development at the University of Nevada, Reno. She is expected to receive her M.S. in May 2009. Jennifer received her B.S. in early childhood education from the University of Nevada, Reno in 2007.

Lorie L. Sicafuse University of Nevada, Reno

Lorie L. Sicafuse is a doctoral student in the Interdisciplinary Ph.D. Program in Social Psychology at the University of Nevada, Reno. Her interests include jury decision-making, social norms and deviance, and the effects of media exposure and emotion on attitudes toward legal and health-related issues.

Alexandra E. Sigillo, B.S. University of Nevada, Reno

Alexandra E. Sigillo graduated from the University of California, Davis, with a B.S. in psychology. She is currently pursuing her doctoral degree in the Interdisciplinary PhD Program in Social Psychology at the University of Nevada, Reno. Her research interests include social psychology and law, with emphases in the areas of families, reproduction and infertility, and policy development.

Misty H. Sanchez, M.A. University of Nevada, Reno

Misty H. Sanchez, M.A. is a Specialty Court's Pretrial Services Officer with the Second Judicial District Court in Reno, Nevada. Within this occupation she supervises and provides case management for specialized populations within the juvenile drug court, mental health court, felony DUI court, and family drug court. Currently she is working on her doctoral degree in counseling and educational psychology with an emphasis in human development. She received her master's degree in criminal justice from the University of Nevada, Reno in 2007 studying crime mapping and specialized law enforcement response teams. She received a bachelor's degree in criminal justice, a bachelor's degree in psychology, and a certificate in substance abuse prevention and counseling in 2005 also from the University of Nevada, Reno. Misty is interested in moral development, crime as a societal issue, and how to better the judicial system through alternative methods.

Alicia Summers, M.S., Ph.D. (expected 2009) University of Nevada, Reno

Alicia Summers received her PhD from the Interdisciplinary PhD. Program in Social Psychology at the University of Nevada, Reno in 2009. She has a Masters Degree in Psychology from Radford University. Her research interests are in the area of social psychology and law, specifically in legal decision-making and policy analysis.

Jose H. Vargas, M.A. University of Nevada, Reno

Jose H. Vargas is a doctoral student in the Interdisciplinary PhD Program in Social Psychology at the University of Nevada, Reno. His general research foci are in social psychology and the law, social philosophy and culture. Specific interests include the role of media and children in the law, decision-making, social justice, cultural reproduction and ethics. Jose obtained his M.A. in social psychology from the University of Nevada, Reno in the spring of 2008.

INDEX

A

D

E

F

G

H

K

L

M

N

Q

R

S

W

Y

Z